Ninja Attack!

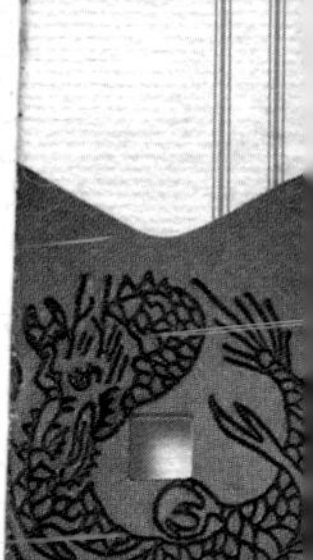

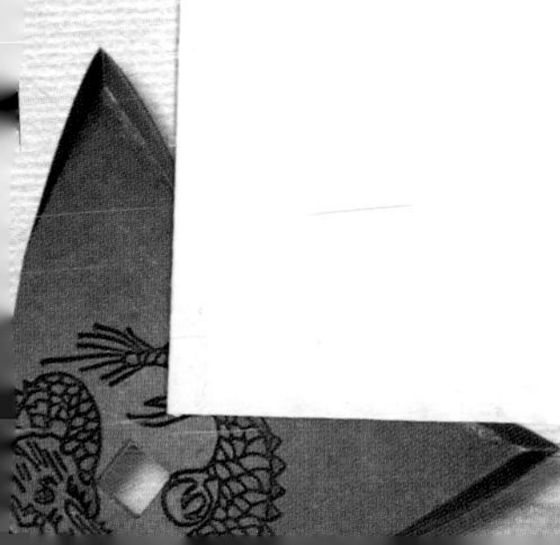

REVISED EDITION WITH 16 NEW PAGES
ALL IN FULL-COLOR FOR THE FIRST TIME!

Ninja Attack!

True Tales of Assassins, Samurai, and Outlaws

Hiroko Yoda and **Matt Alt**
Illustrations by **Yutaka Kondo**

TUTTLE Publishing

Tokyo | Rutland, Vermont | Singapore

Published by Tuttle Publishing, an imprint of Periplus Editions (HK) Ltd.

www.tuttlepublishing.com

Copyright © 2010, 2012 Hiroko Yoda and Matt Alt
Illustrations © 2010, 2012 Yutaka Kondo

Library of Congress Cataloging-in-Publication Data

Yoda, Hiroko.
  Ninja attack! : true tales of assassins, samurai, and outlaws / Hiroko Yoda and Matt Alt ; illustrations by Yutaka Kondo
     p. cm.
  Includes bibliographical references and index.
  ISBN 978-4-8053-1218-6 (pbk.)
 1. Ninjutsu. 2. Ninja. 3. Espionage--Japan--History. I. Alt, Matt. II. Title.
  UB271.J3Y63 2012
  355.5'48--dc23

                                        2012009837

ISBN 978-4-8053-1218-6

Distributed by

North America, Latin America & Europe
Tuttle Publishing
364 Innovation Drive
North Clarendon,
VT 05759-9436 U.S.A.
Tel: 1 (802) 773-8930
Fax: 1 (802) 773-6993
info@tuttlepublishing.com
www.tuttlepublishing.com

Asia Pacific
Berkeley Books Pte. Ltd.
61 Tai Seng Avenue #02-12
Singapore 534167
Tel: (65) 6280-1330
Fax: (65) 6280-6290
inquiries@periplus.com.sg
www.periplus.com

Japan
Tuttle Publishing
Yaekari Building, 3rd Floor
5-4-12 Osaki
Shinagawa-ku
Tokyo 141 0032
Tel: (81) 3 5437-0171
Fax: (81) 3 5437-0755
sales@tuttle.co.jp
www.tuttle.co.jp

15 14 13 12   5 4 3 2 1
1205CP

Printed in Singapore

TUTTLE PUBLISHING® is a registered trademark of Tuttle Publishing, a division of Periplus Editions (HK) Ltd.

TABLE OF CONTENTS

contents continued next page

This book is dedicated
to those ninja so good
at their jobs we'll never
even know their names.

FOREWORD

You know your ninja. You've seen every movie—from the 1967 James Bond film, *You Only Live Twice* (the first ninja screen appearance abroad) to Eighties classics like *Enter the Ninja* and the more recent *Ninja Assassin*. Your collection of ninja comic books is embarrassingly large, spanning the "Teenage Mutant Ninja Turtles" and "Usagi Yojimbo," Frank Miller's 1980s ninja-inflected reboots of "Wolverine" and "Daredevil," to every appearance of Storm Shadow and Snake Eyes in "G.I. Joe." You've followed ninja through anime—"Ninja Scroll" to "Naruto." And it goes without saying you've vanquished the video games: "Shinobi," "Mortal Combat," "Ninja Gaiden." The list goes on. And on.

You may notice, however, that your favorite characters do not appear within the pages of this book, or that their profiles do not match what you have read or seen onscreen. This is deliberate. Actual, historical ninja are fascinating enough subjects without needing to muddy the waters with fantasy. We gathered intelligence from a wide variety of academic and historical sources, mainly Japanese-language, in an attempt to piece together the most likely descriptions of people and events.

Ninja Attack! contains more than a thousand years' worth of true stories of Japan's most famous masters of espionage. Their successes and failures. Their allies and rivals. Their dedication to their families, their masters, and their craft of unconventional warfare. A lot of their stories are wilder than the plot of any ninja action flick, but here's the twist. None of it is fiction. It's historical fact.

That said, this book certainly doesn't represent the alpha and omega of ninja exploits. For all the tales we've chronicled here, more than a few ninja have undoubtedly taken equally awesome feats to the grave. There's actually an old ninja saying that goes, "if you've got a reputation, you're still a *chunin*"—just a mid-level practitioner of the craft.

The concept of *ninjutsu*, the term for the martial art of espionage, is maddeningly difficult to pin down. Perhaps none has expressed the quantum nature of it as well as Masaaki Hatsumi, the last living descendent of the Togakushi school, who explained, "If one can even know the truth about ninjutsu, it isn't really ninjutsu." This is one reason why we chose to focus on the stories of the

"If one can know the truth about ninjutsu, it isn't really ninjutsu."

ninja themselves, rather than their martial art. The other is that martial arts are only part of the story. The trappings so intimately associated with ninja both in Japan and abroad—the outfits, the death-defying leaps and jumps, the exotic weapons and accoutrements—are, in the end, secondary to the men and women behind the masks.

Which brings us to another point. Those masks are largely a work of fiction, as are the infamous all-black outfits. As for the question of what ninja actually did wear, ask yourself this: what does the average spy wear? The answer, of course, is whatever it takes to blend in and get the job done, whether that means shorts and a T-shirt, military fatigues, or a suit and tie. The same was true of the ninja. Hiding in plain sight was their entire modus operandi. Most dressed like farmers, both because it worked well as camouflage in a nation of farmers, and because most of them really were farmers. A real ninja would laugh at the portrayal of an intruder tiptoeing across a rooftop wearing black pajamas in broad daylight.

But if that's the case, why is that particular image so enduring, both in Japan and abroad? It's safe to say that the Japanese didn't invent the concept of assassins or spies, yet the ninja have pretty much become the world's poster children for espionage, mayhem, and generally sneaky behavior. One possible answer lies in Japan's proven ability to create internationally compelling pop-cultural characters, from ferocious monsters like Godzilla all the way down to cute and cuddly kittens like Hello Kitty. The key points of what constitute a ninja in the public mind—the masks, the *shuriken* stars, the black outfits—have been honed into a visual shorthand that happens to appeal to people around the world. Ninja may have been some scary customers in real life, but they have been tamed and distilled down to an instantly recognizable essence over generations of books, comics, films, and television shows.

Another conflicting point with what appears in fiction: ninja didn't harbor a blind allegiance to traditional weaponry. They were, in fact, at the forefront of the military technology of their day. Already innovators in explosives,

A ninja as seen by woodblock print master, Katsushika Hokusai. This 1814 sketch is thought to be the first depiction of the classic black ninja suit.

innovators in explosives, firearms, and communication systems, a sixteenth-century ninja would undoubtedly have been overjoyed with a modern pair of night-vision goggles or a high-powered sniper rifle. They devised cunning new techniques through direct observation and experimentation, making them something akin to field scientists as well. As you will dis-

> "Ninja are inseparable from the historical context in which they evolved."

cover in the pages of this book, they certainly didn't let tradition get in the way if they discovered a better tool for doing a job. The image of a traditional ninja stalking the streets of a modern city is undeniably seductive, but even if one did somehow find his or her way to the modern era, it's hard to imagine them sticking with a vintage sword and chainmail instead of, say, an assault rifle and a bulletproof vest.

Let us cut right to the next point. Ninja don't exist anymore. Or more precisely, they don't exist in the form in which they appear in the pages of this book. This isn't to say that there aren't intrepid martial arts students out there who study and even practice ninjutsu. But the era in which ninja represented the cutting edge of espionage, in which great rulers turned to them for assistance on and off the battlefield, in which clans kept their traditions secret in hidden villages far from the prying eyes of the authorities, is long over. The ninja are inseparable from the historical context in which they evolved.

But this doesn't mean that there is nothing for the ninja of old to teach us.

Ninja History in a Nutshell
Legend has it that the first ninja in Japan, called the *shinobi*, were employed in the seventh century. This isn't really saying much, as leaders have relied on spies since time immemorial. (There is something quintessentially ninja about Ulysses dressing as a beggar to sneak within the walls of Troy in the *Odyssey*. And there is even a ninja-like episode in the Bible, in which Joshua dispatches a pair of secret agents to infiltrate the city of Jericho.)

But there is no question that the Japanese took the general idea and ran with it. The fifteenth century marked the rise of the ninja as we generally portray them today. As regional warlords jockeyed for power and position, the weakening of central authority prompted villages in certain areas to fortify themselves into independent entities. Perhaps nowhere was this trend more evident than in the isolated mountain provinces of Iga and Koga, where heavily forested terrain offered tremendous advantages to local fighters inclined toward guerilla tactics. In 1487, a tiny number of Koga ninja did the unthinkable by slicing an expeditionary force of the shogun's heavily armed troops to ribbons. (You can read more about the battle on page 47.)

Word of the Koga's success in repelling the shogun's forces—and according to some accounts, actually killing the shogun—spread like wildfire among the other warlords, and thrust the ninja into the spotlight of legend. The ninja "arms race" was officially on.

Realizing that their home-grown skills were suddenly in high demand served to strengthen the various ninja clan organizations, and the Iga and Koga in particular. They abandoned their farming work on the infertile local soil for the more lucrative field of military consulting, and continued to hone their unique suite of abilities for various "clients." Some clans, such as the Koga, or the Rappa of the Kanto region, went on to associate themselves with specific warlords. Others chose to remain fiercely independent,

"Ninja proved so good that they became a direct threat to the warlords."

selling their skills to the highest bidder. Sometimes allies, sometimes rivals to the point of finding themselves on opposite sides of the battlefield, it was always business and never personal with these guys.

Over the next century, the ninja proved so good at their work that they grew into a direct threat to the warlords themselves. In 1579, "ninja destroyer" Oda Nobunaga flooded the Iga region with troops in an ultimately successful campaign to rid himself of the threat that the ninja there posed to his authority. He countered their guerilla tactics with an indiscriminate swath of destruction through the countryside, killing many thousands of civilians in the process. And by co-opting or destroying rival warlords, he deprived many of the other ninja clans of their main benefactors. By the last decade of the 1500s, the era of unrestrained ninja warfare was rapidly drawing to a close.

But it can be tough to keep masters of tactics and subterfuge down, especially when they are still a useful commodity. Tokugawa Ieyasu, the warlord who became Japan's most powerful Shogun, relied heavily on remnants of ninja forces to lead a personal army that vanquished his enemies on the battlefield and defended his capital city of Edo. And, in fact, a ninja can be said to run through the city even today. One of Tokyo's major subway lines, the Hanzomon, is named after the most famous ninja of all: Tokugawa's lead military advisor, Hattori Hanzo.

So put aside your preconceptions. Put aside, for the moment, the ninja movies you've seen, the games you've played, the comic books you've read over the years. You're about to spend some time with Japan's—and the world's—most fearsome shadow warriors, as well as other rogues, thieves, warlords, and samurai. When you run with company like this, you'll need to keep your wits about you and keep an open mind. This book may not teach you how to sprint along a rooftop in your pajamas, pluck arrows out of air in midflight, or walk on water, but then again, true power comes in the form of knowledge. Use it wisely . . . because the ninja are about to attack!

Hiroko Yoda and Matt Alt
Tokyo
2012

ABOUT THIS BOOK

We have arranged this new edition of the book chronologically, the better to see the ebb and flow of ninja history. Each profile is also tagged with a heading to help you understand just who you're dealing with.

"Ninja's Ninja" are the shadow warriors other shadow warriors looked up to. They are among the very few names known from the hundreds and even thousands of ninja that operated over the last millennium.

"Ninja Gone Bad" are exactly what the name implies: ninja who used their skills for personal gain rather than in the service of a client or master. As you will learn, however, quite often the distinction was a hazy one.

"Ninja Magic" covers so-called mystical ninja, masters of magic and illusion who harnessed sleight of hand and other tricks to confuse or dazzle their opponents.

"Ninja Rivals" weren't ninja at all, but many operated in and around the same times as the ninja did, and very likely crossed paths with them. More than a few had a direct influence on the ninja themselves.

"Ninja Masters" are military leaders who relied on the skills of the ninja, in one way or another, for you can't understand the ninja unless you understand the individuals who employed them. Which brings us to . . .

"The Ninja Destroyer." A category of one, the savage Oda Nobunaga, who crushed the ninja clans in the late sixteenth century.

Last but certainly not least, **The Illustrated Ninja** sections are a handy guide to the tools and tactics that made a ninja a ninja. Intended as a counterpoint to the portraits painted by the individual dossiers, these pages provide a "macro" view of the ninja life: maps; timelines; details about ninja dress, weapons, and techniques; a walk through a stereotypical ninja house; and even a ninja-related tour of modern-day Tokyo. Stay alert—you'll encounter these entries lying in wait here and there as you proceed through the book.

The Illustrated Ninja

FOR ASSASSINS OF ALL AGES!

TOP SECRET

A guide to the weapons, tools, tricks, techniques, and more . . . of Japan's legendary warriors.

MILESTONES
A rough guide to Ninja history

BC 500-400?
Sun Tzu pens *The Art of War*

AD 600?
Prince Shotoku Taishi establishes the first ninja, the *shinobi*

919
First use of gunpowder in combat, China

1183
Togakushi Daisuke lets the cows out during the Battle of Kurikara Pass

1192
Minamoto no Yoritomo appointed first shogun of Japan

1332
Hino Kumawaka-maru avenges his father's death at the age of 13

1487
First "official" clandestine ninja operation, the battle of Magari, led by Mochizuki Izumo no Kami

1536
Infant Oda Nobunaga gleefully chews nipples off of hapless wet-nurses

1542
First Portuguese traders and Jesuit missionaries arrive in Kyushu; matchlock rifle introduced to Japan

1558
Hattori Hanzo makes his ninja debut at age 16

1560
Takeda Shingen orders creation of manually operated flush toilet, Japan's first

1560s?
Mochizuki Chiyojo teaches ninja skills to Takeda Shingen's "walking maidens"

1570
Sugitani Zenjubo attracts Oda Nobunaga's attention by trying to blow his head off with a matchlock rifle

1561
Kumawaka sets a land speed record of 128 kilometers per hour . . . on foot

1574
Mystical ninja Kashin Koji attracts Oda Nobunaga's attention with a magical scroll

1582
Hattori Hanzo's ninja help Tokugawa Ieyasu to safety during the chaos following the Honnoji incident

1590
Ishikawa Goemon and his posse are livin' large in Kyoto

1597
At the age of 13, Miyamoto Musashi kills his first opponent

1599
376 years hence, James Clavell
will set his novel *Shogun* in this year

1600
Battle of Sekigahara seals
Tokugawa Ieyasu's claim as Japan's
first shogun. Edo period begins. Ninja
role decreases steadily thereafter

1603
Kosaka Jinnai snitches on Fuma
Kotaro. Fuma Kotaro executed

1612
Miyamoto Musashi clobbers
Sasaki Kojiro on Ganryu Island

1615
Sanada Yukimura's
doppelgangers terrorize
Tokugawa Ieyasu's forces during the
summer siege of Osaka

1618
Eleven year old prodigy Yagyu Jubei
begins tutoring Shogun Tokugawa
Iemitsu in swordsmanship

1645
Miyamoto Musashi completes the *Book
of Five Rings* just before he dies

1689
Matsuo Basho launches his
journey (and some say spy mission)
chronicled in *The Narrow Road
to the Interior*

1701
Chushingura, a.k.a.
the "Tale of the 47 Ronin,"
takes place

1716
Tokugawa Yoshimune, the eighth
shogun, establishes his secret service:
"Oniwa-ban" (The Gardeners)

1746
"Police sketch" of
Nippon Zaemon becomes
Japan's first wanted poster

1806
The Story of Jiraiya debuts

1853
Commodore Matthew Perry's
crew unwittingly meets the
"last ninja," Jinzaburo Sawamura,
while docked in Edo Bay

1860
Japan's first official delegation to
the United States includes an
Oniwa-ban by the name of
Muragaki Norimasa

1865
Tom Cruise joins
The Last Samurai. . . in a 2003 film

1868
Tokugawa Shogunate collapses,
ushering in the Meiji Restoration
and Japan's modernization

1912
The novel *Sarutobi Sasuke* debuts

2010
Ninja Attack! debuts!

The Ninja Nation

This map portrays many of the events described in the pages of this book, from En no Ozunu's travels in times of antiquity all the way through American warships arriving in Edo harbor in 1853. This covers a massive swath of history, and therefore it is intended as a stylized composite rather than to represent any one moment in time. It is not only out of proportion to what we know to be Japan today, but sharp-eyed readers will notice that the illustration omits the island of Hokkaido and the archipelago of Okinawa. This is because it is based on a centuries-old chart created in an era before these territories were officially incorporated into the nation.

PATH OF "IGA-GOE"
(Tokugawa Ieyasu's Escape)

TOKAIDO ROAD
(Connects Edo and Kyoto)

MATSUO BASHO'S ROUTE THROUGH JAPAN
(Narrow Road to the Interior)

GANRYU ISLAND
(Miyamoto Musashi defeats Sasaki Kojiro)

DAN-NO-URA
(Yoshitsune's defeat of the Taira clan)

SATSUMA
(Mamiya Rin
secret infiltra

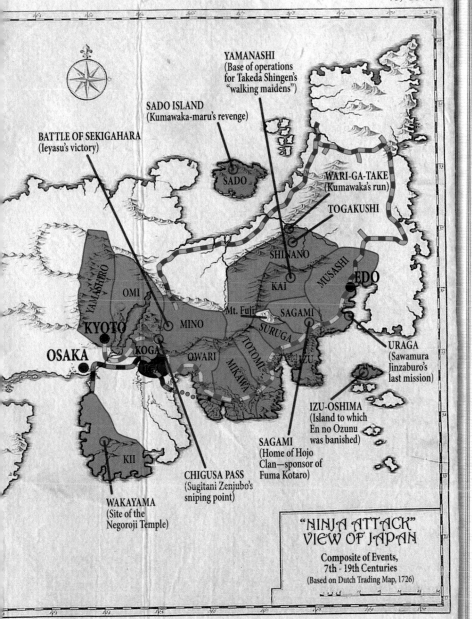

YAMANASHI
(Base of operations
for Takeda Shingen's
"walking maidens")

SADO ISLAND
(Kumawaka-maru's revenge)

BATTLE OF SEKIGAHARA
(Ieyasu's victory)

SADO

WARI-GA-TAKE
(Kumawaka's run)

TOGAKUSHI

SHINANO

KAI

MUSASHI

EDO

YAMASHIRO

OMI

Mt. Fuji

SAGAMI

KYOTO

MINO

SURUGA

OSAKA

KOGA

OWARI

TOTOMI

IZU

URAGA
(Sawamura
Jinzaburo's
last mission)

MIKAWA

IZU-OSHIMA
(Island to which
En no Ozunu
was banished)

SAGAMI
(Home of Hojo
Clan—sponsor of
Fuma Kotaro)

KII

CHIGUSA PASS
(Sugitani Zenjubo's
sniping point)

WAKAYAMA
(Site of the
Negoroji Temple)

"NINJA ATTACK"
VIEW OF JAPAN

Composite of Events,
7th - 19th Centuries
(Based on Dutch Trading Map, 1726)

NINJA
nĭn'jə
(Plural: "ninja." No "s," please.)

The colloquial name for groups and individuals who carried out intelligence-gathering, assassinations, and other espionage-related work for Japanese warlords, mainly between the twelfth and nineteenth centuries, with their peak being in the mid-to-late sixteenth century. In Japanese, the word is written with the kanji characters *nin* 忍, meaning "clandestine," and *ja* 者, meaning "person." The use of the term "ninja" to refer to these individuals is relatively recent; historically, they were more commonly called by a wide variety of regional colloquialisms including (but by no means limited to):

Hayamichi no mono (The Short-cutters)
Iga-mono (One from Iga)
Kamari (Those Who Hide)
Koga-mono (One from Koga)
Kusa (The Grasses)
Ninjutsu-tsukai (A practitioner of ninjutsu)
Nokizaru (Roof-monkeys)
Onmitsu (The secret service)
Rappa (in the Kanto region)
Shinobi
Shinobi no mono
Suppa (in the Kai region)
Ukami (The Silent Watchers)
Yama-kuguri ("Mountain-runners")

NOTE: Although the kanji characters are identical, the name of the region that the Koga ninja hail from is actually pronounced "Koka." For ease of understanding, we use Koga to refer to both throughout the book.

NINJA ANCESTORS
(~1500)

The Ninja "Family tree" begins here.

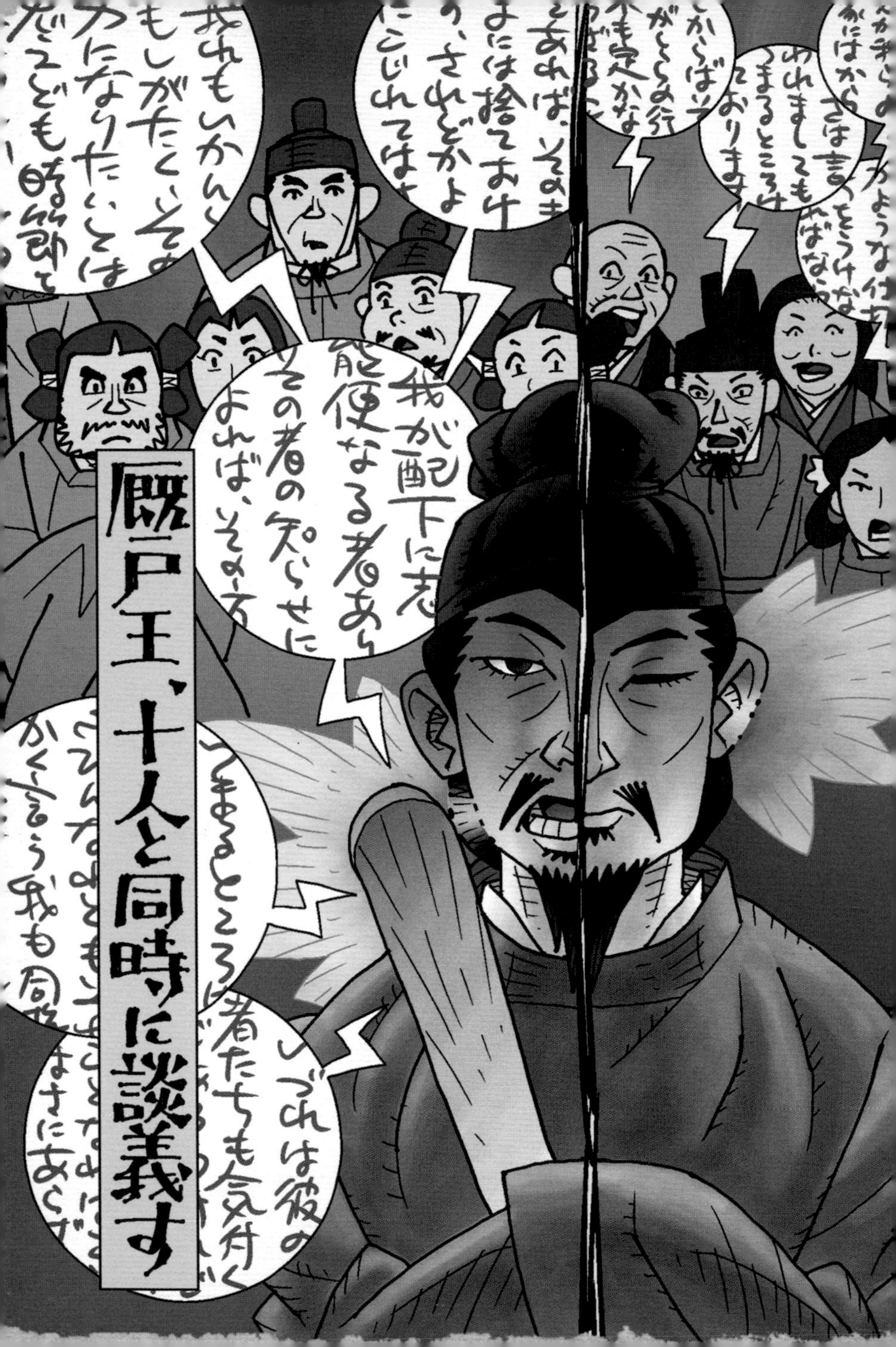

我が配下に志
能便なる者あら
その者の知らせに
よれば、その方
厩戸王、十人と同時に談義す

593 A.D.

Name: **PRINCE SHOTOKU**
聖徳太子

Birth/Death: 574–622

Occupation: Regent

Duration of Reign: 593–622

Cause of Death: Unknown

A.K.A.: Shotoku Taishi
Prince Umayato
Umayato-no-oh
Umayato-no-mikoto
Toyoto-mimi
Toyoto-mimi-no-nori-no-ohokimi
Uetsumiya-no-umayato-no-oyotomimi-no-mikoto

Known Associates: Otomo-no-sabito (see below)

Hobbies: Multi-tasking

Preferred Weapon: Shinobi

Existence: Confirmed

The Man

Prince Shotoku was a precocious young politician with a literal gift of gab, said to be capable of holding discreet conversations with ten people simultaneously (quite a trick, close to a millenium and a half before the Internet chat room was invented). Never actually taking the throne, the prince served as the regent to Empress Suiko, his aunt. In title, he was a humble advisor. It is believed, however, that he ruled the entire country in her name.

Having lived so long ago, he occupies the crossroads between Japanese history and mythology, and over the centuries all sorts of incredible achievements have been ascribed to him. Some are down-to-earth (establishing the nation's first constitution and promoting the spread of Buddhism), while others are obvious flights of fancy (inventing sushi and giving Japan its now-official name of "Nihon").

Insightful and talented though he may have been, the path to the empress' side was anything but smooth for the prince. Perhaps this is why he was among the first proponents of Sun Tzu's *Art of War* in Japan. Its teachings—particularly good old chapter 13, "The Use of Spies"—played a key role in his rise to power at the age

This well is undoubtedly a metaphor for just how informed he was kept by his spies.

Ten conversations simultaneously: Prince Umayato

23

of eighteen, particularly in his befriending of a brilliant tactician named (perhaps a little too fittingly) Otomo-no-saibito, or "Otomo the Clandestine." Like the prince, Otomo posessed a few special comunication skills. In the *Nihon Shoki*, Japan's oldest historical text (written in 720 AD), Otomo's family line was said to be able to communicate in words only intelligible to other clan members and allies— or to put it more precisely, secret code.

The two men's relationship changed the course of Japanese history in more ways than one. For Otomo is now known as the very first ninja—or more precisely, *shinobi*, as the young prince dubbed both him and his operatives. The word has remained a synonym for ninja ever since.

The Moment of Glory

The 587 death of Emperor Yomei, Prince Shotoku's father, touched off a bloody power struggle between his clan and that of the rival Moriya. Being just thirteen, the young prince knew he needed expert advice if he was to triumph in the confrontation—after all, his troops were hugely outnumbered by the enemy. (By some accounts, he led just two hundred men against some thirty thousand Moriya soldiers.)

The enemy onslaught had already forced the prince into retreat three times; now there would be no avoiding a decisive battle. It should have been a clear rout. But as dawn broke, something strange hap-

← Until the mid-1980s, prince Shotoku appeared on several Japanese bank notes.

pened. The Moriya men began panicking, loosing arrows wildly, swinging swords blindly, running around like chickens with their heads cut off. Legend ascribes the once-mighty army's subsequent defeat at the prince's hands to divine intervention. But reading between the lines, it is highly likely that the prince's clandestine friend Otomo played a role in the affair, for throwing terror into the hearts of a superior-sized force is one of the founding principles of *ninjutsu*. And in an era before ninja were widely known or employed, his feat could well have looked like the hand of god intervening to smite the enemy troops.

It isn't known exactly how he pulled this off, but history offers a tantalizing clue: in the fourteenth century, a warrior named Kusunoki Masashige

pulled off a similar trick by preparing dozens of extra battle-pennants and hiring hundreds of civilians to pose as warriors, fooling his overconfident enemy into thinking that they had sorely underestimated the size of the forces they were facing.

The End
The victory sealed Prince Shotoku's clan's claim to the throne, and one of his first official acts was recognizing Japan's clandestine operatives with the title of "Shinobi." A millenium later in the sixteenth century, the *Ninjutsu-Ogiden*, annals of the Koga ninja, would explicitly describe Otomo-no-sabito as an honored ancestor—of themselves, and of all ninja.

Somewhat strangely for someone otherwise quite well documented, there is absolutely no record of what caused Prince Shotoku's death at the age of 48, some three decades after he assumed power. Given the lack of any reports to the contrary, not to mention the limited medical technology available at the time, it is entirely likely that natural causes were to blame. ✳

701 A.D.

Name: **EN NO OZUNU**
役小角

Birth-Death: 634?.-701?

Literal Translation: "En of the Horn"

Occupation: Shaman/Mystic

Cause of Death: Unknown

A.K.A.: En no Gyoja (En the pilgrim)
Kamo-no-e-no-kimi (Birth name)
Ubasoku (The Unordained Devout)
Jinben Daibosatsu (After death:
"Great Bodhisattva of Heavenly
Change")

Known Associates: Zenki (red, male oni)
Goki (green, female oni)

Hobbies: Collecting medicinal herbs
Housebreaking ogres

Preferred Technique: The Kujaku-o
(peacock King) mantra

Clan Affiliation: His own bad-ass self

Existence: Confirmed

The Man

A mountain man who was more of a mystic than a fighter, En no Ozunu would have scratched his head in confusion if asked if he was a ninja. (Not least of all because it would be many centuries before the word was actually used.) Yet a deep connection exists nonetheless. He is the legendary founder of the religion of Shugendo—a fusion of native Japanese mountain worship and Buddhism, inflected with Taoist and cosmological teachings from China. The *yamabushi*, as its practitioners are known, were a tough crew of self-reliant alpine survivalists and martial artists. They treated mountains as sacred ground, and first taught the ninja many of their tricks. In turn the ninja venerated En no Ozunu as an honored ancestor, akin to their patron saint.

He was born with a horn growing from his skull, a flower clutched in his hand, and the ability to hold conversations even as a newborn. Long years spent meditating deep in the mountains earned him the nickname En no Gyoja, or "En the Ascetic."

The charismatic holy man eschewed formal ordination, choosing instead to practice and espouse his new brand of

He who commands Oni: Gyoja

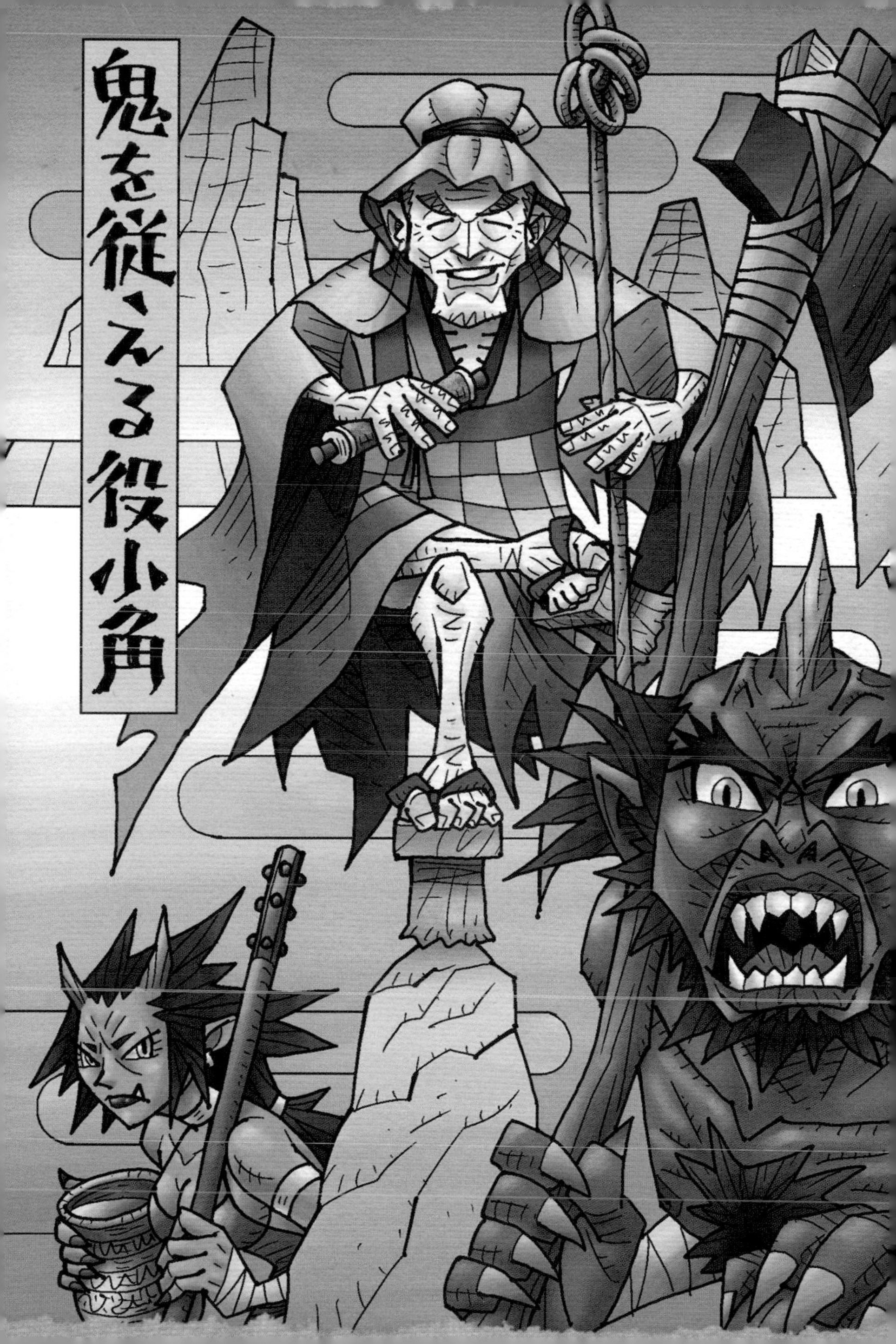
鬼を従える役小角

Schooling ogres is all in a day's work for this holy man

religion on Mount Katsuragi in Nara. His iconoclastic example and growing number of followers represented a direct threat to the emperor's authority. Before long, he was falsely accused of treason and exiled to a distant island for three years.

In exile, En no Ozunu took to climbing and meditating atop Mt. Fuji, a trek considered so arduous that it is often said "he who climbs Mount Fuji once is a wise man; he who climbs it twice is a fool." Apparently climbing it more than a thousand times grants one supernatural powers, for his perfection of a magical mantra called "The Peacock King" on its slopes turned the already talented En no Ozunu into something more than human. (Did we mention that he accomplished this feat while officially confined to the remote island of Oshima, many miles removed from the foot of the mountain?)

Packed with peacock power and blessed with the ability to flit about the skies on clouds, Ozunu now began split-

En no Ozunu makes a brief appearance in Koji Suzuki's best-selling J-Horror novel The Ring, in which it is suggested that he is the spiritual father of Sadako.

"Ascetic," by the way, is the term applied to those who isolate themselves from humanity, utilizing severe physical training, such as fasting or praying beneath the hammering onslaught of a freezing mountain waterfall, to enhance their spiritual focus.

ting his time between heaven and Earth. Not a bad gig if you can swing it, but man, what a commute!

The Moment of Glory

It's hard to pick a single shining moment from the life of a super-shaman. Was it the first time he walked on water? When he realized he could subsist on nothing but mist and air? The time he transformed himself into a tiger? Certainly his most famous triumph involves a pair of *oni*, or ogres, known as Zenki and Goki.

Like a monster Bonnie and Clyde, Zenki and Goki were a couple that terrorized the residents of a mountain range near Nara. Until En no Ozunu showed up, that is, invoking the power of a Buddhist deity to stun them into submission. He then captured their five infant offspring and hid them in a large cauldron to convince the demon couple their children were dead. Recognizing their sense of loss as the exact same sort of distress felt by their victims, Zenki and Goki pledged to renounce their evil ways and assist En no Ozunu in his future endeavors. He took them up on their offer, reunited the family, and the oni couple remained loyal associates for many years.

The End

When you're talking about a man with connections to some literal "higher-ups," life's end is just another beginning. Some say En no Ozunu achieved enlightenment and walked across the ocean to China in 701. Others say he took to the skies, accompanied by his mother, in a Buddhist alms bowl. Whatever the case, he is now considered a *Sennin*, or Great Immortal, who is still out there, somewhere, watching over the yamabushi for as long as they walk the earth. ✳

DOJO OF THE GODS

In the centuries after his death, the yamabushi established an elaborate training facility on a Koga mountain called Hando-san, where En no Ozunu is believed to have once dwelled. Ninja visited the area to learn the use of herbs and minerals, weather patterns, and camouflage strategies from the warrior monks.

HARD-HEADED IMMORTAL

Legend has it that a series of attempts were made to assassinate En no Ozunu, but the blades of the axes inevitably shattered harmlessly upon coming into contact with his head.

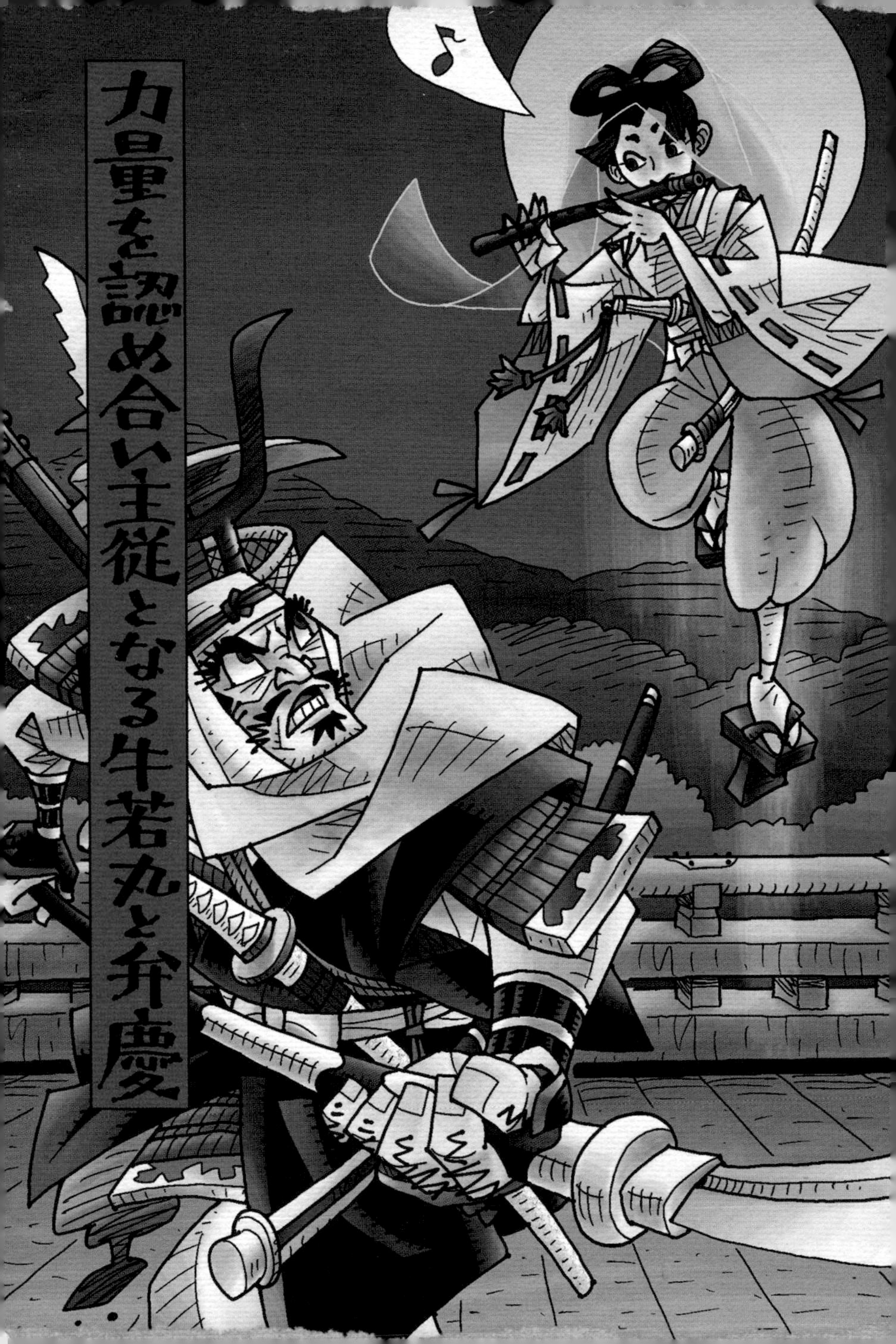
力量を認め合い主従となる牛若丸と弁慶

1185 A.D.

Name: **MINAMOTO NO YOSHITSUNE**
源義経

Birth/Death: 1159–1189

Occupation: General

Cause of Death: Seppuku

A.K.A.: Ushiwakamaru
Just "Yoshitsune"
Hougan (Title bestowed by Emperor)

Known Associates: Benkei (see below).

Preferred Technique: Swordplay

Clan Affiliation: Minamoto

Existence: Confirmed

planting the seeds of mutual respect: Ushiwakamaru and Benkei

The Man

The quintessential *bishonen* ("beautiful boy") of Japanese literature, Yoshitsune's exquisite balance of looks, valor, and skill made him a prototype for generations of androgynous Japanese heroes. Dying young and leaving a good-looking corpse didn't hurt, either.*

Yoshitsune—then known as Ushiwakamaru—was born during a civil war called the Heiji Rebellion. His father was slain on the battlefield, his older brother sentenced to death, and his mother captured as a concubine by the leader of the victorious Taira clan, all while he was still an infant. At the age of seven (eleven according to some sources) Yoshitsune was banished to Kurama-dera Temple, deep in the mountains of Kyoto, with the idea that he would spend the rest of his life as a cloistered monk.

Things didn't exactly play out that way. Quickly tiring of religious study, Yoshitsune spent the next decade training body and soul in the martial arts. Popular legend has it he learned swordsmanship from the Tengu, fearsome yokai famed for their superhuman strength, agility, and prowess with all manner of human weaponry. He also studied the basics of guerilla warfare under warrior monks in the area; the techniques he mastered—including *kasumi*, "The Mist," for blinding opponents with dirt or other found objects; *hien sandangiri*, "The Flying Swallow Triple Slice," an aerial sword technique for killing opponents left, right, and front simultaneously; and his legendary ability to leap great distances—even-

* Notwithstanding the fact that his legendary beauty isn't borne out by any actual historical evidence.

tually formed the basis for what came to be called "Yoshi-tsune-style *ninjutsu*" centuries later.

Yokai or not, whoever taught Yoshitsune must have been good. By his late teens, he was second to none with a blade in his hand. And once he learned the truth about his lineage, he dedicated the remainder of his short life to making the Taira clan pay for what they had done to his family.

Yoshitsune and Benkei

The tale of how Yoshitsune met his best friend and constant companion, Musashibo Benkei, is as much a part of myth and legend as the men themselves. A bear of a man, Benkei supposedly spent a full eighteen months in the womb before finally emerging at the size of a normal three-year-old. By the time he completed training as a warrior monk at the age of seventeen, he towered some two meters tall and was near invincible with a *naginata* polearm in his hands.

Determined to prove the superiority of his abilities, Benkei stationed himself at Gojo Tenjin Shrine in Kyoto, challenging any and every swordsman who happened to pass to a duel. He had successfully deprived some 999 of them of their weapons when the diminutive, effeminate young Yoshitsune appeared,

nonchalantly playing a flute. Understandably quite confident by this point, Benkei rushed his thousandth opponent without hesitation. But Yoshitsune leapt over the sweep of the blade, using Benkei's own chest as a springboard to reach a perch atop a three-meter wall, where he continued to evade the giant's increasingly furious attacks. It wasn't until a second match on the veranda of Kiyomizu Temple that Yoshitsune even gave Benkei a taste of his sword. He inflicted so many nicks that the huge warrior called the bout, pledging allegiance to the mysterious young David who taught a Goliath never to judge a book by its cover.

The Moment of Glory

The battle of Dan-no-Ura, 1185. When it came to the Taira clan, Yoshitsune was a human Terminator. For years he had pursued his vendetta. Joining forces with his brother Yoritomo, long since given a reprieve from death and now head of the Taira's archrivals, the Minamoto clan, Yoshitsune harried the Taira from the mountains to the plains to what must have seemed like the ends of the earth: a naval engagement off of Dan-no-Ura, the southern tip of the island of Honshu. The battle represented a desperate last stand for the outnumbered Taira, who had

Yoshitsune gets an education, yokai-style, as a Tengu instructs him in the ways of the sword.

hidden the child-emperor Antoku aboard one of the ships. Using both intelligence gleaned from a turncoat Taira general and the tides to his advantage, Yoshitsune discovered the location of the prize. His archers pounded it with salvo after salvo, sending the emperor's skiff out of control and throwing the enemy forces into chaos. Knowing their time was up, the emperor's regents took their lives along with that of their charge, ending the Taira clan's claim on the throne once and for all—and setting the stage for Yoshitsune's brother Yoritomo to become first shogun of Japan by the end of the decade.

The end

Alas, a great warrior doesn't necessarily make a great politician.

With the Taira clan eliminated, Yoshitsune found himself adrift. A lone wolf far more fond of leaping right into the fray than in the subtleties of administration, he unwittingly became caught up in a political intrigue between his brother and Emperor Go-Shirakawa. Accused of treason and cornered by forces loyal to his brother, he chose suicide rather than capture. Benkei singlehandedly held off the incoming troops to give his master time to commit *seppuku* and preserve his honor; legend has it that he remained standing even after perforated by innumerable arrows, steadfastly protecting Yoshitsune even in death. ✳

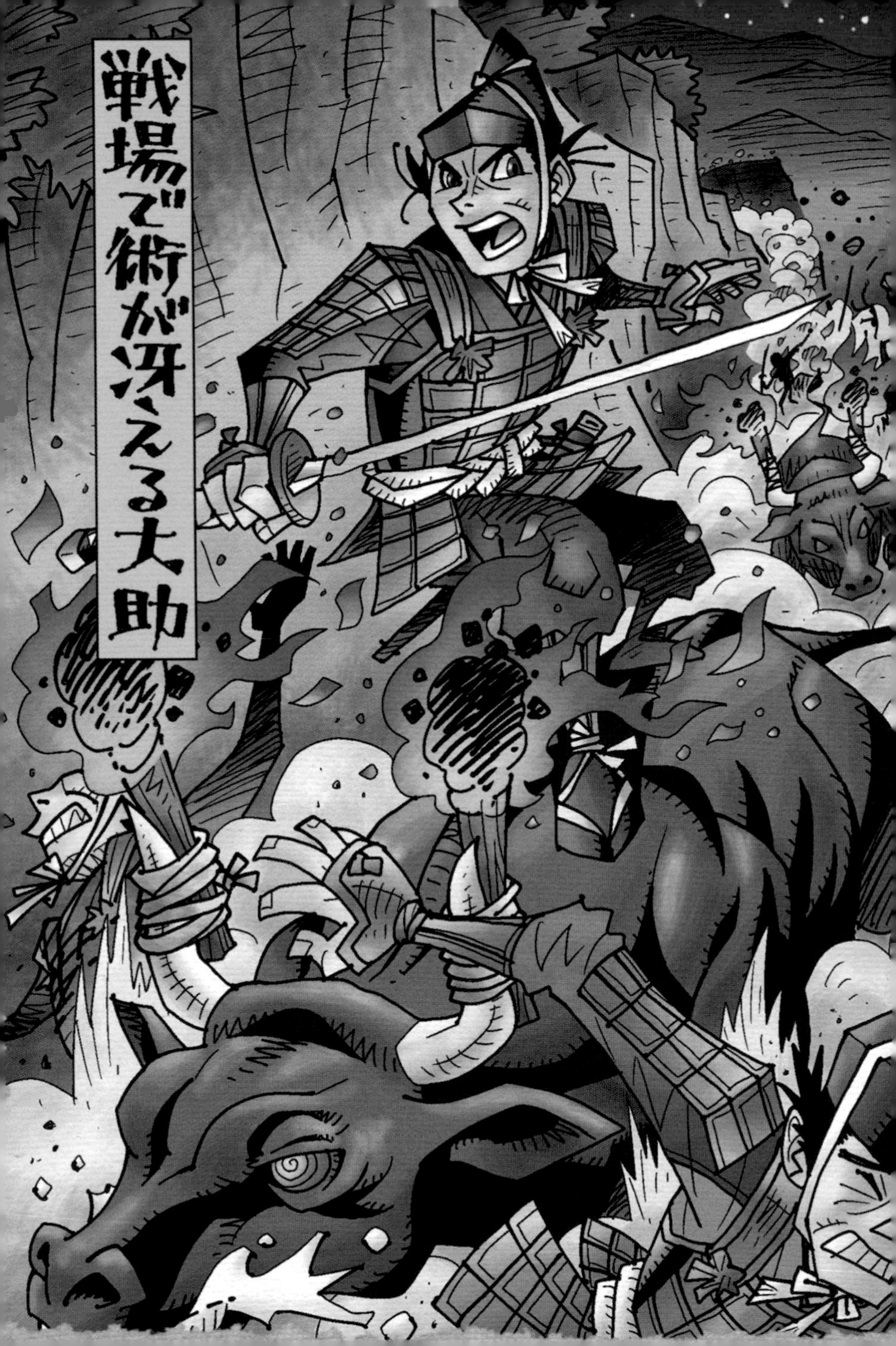
戦場で術が冴える大助

1183 A.D.

Name: **TOGAKUSHI DAISUKE**
戸隠大助

Birth–Death: 1161?–Unknown

Occupation: Ninja Innovator

Cause of Death: Unknown

Gender: Male

A.K.A.: Nishina Daisuke (birth name)
Togakure Daisuke (alternate pronunciation)

Hobbies: Training

Preferred Technique: The Flaming Cow

Clan Affiliation: Togakure

Existence: Confirmed

The Man

Nothing is known of Togakushi Daisuke's physical appearance, which shouldn't be particularly surprising for someone born close to eight-and-a-half centuries ago. Originally known as Nishina Daisuke, he was born in the village of Togakushi in present-day Nagano prefecture's Northern Alps, whose soaring peaks were long used as sacred training grounds by the *yamabushi* warrior-monks of the Shugendo religion.

It's safe to say Daisuke's upbringing was far from the pampered standards of today's youth. Under the yamabushi, he learned secret techniques such as bladed weapon throwing and the "flying bird," an Olympic-worthy method of jumping extreme heights and distances.

At some point, Daisuke set out from his hometown to serve as a warrior under Minamoto no Yoshinaka, an early shogun of Japan. When his master was felled on the battlefield in 1184 by an arrow to the eye, Daisuke hacked his way through some three thousand enemy troops to escape. Terribly wounded, he managed to make his way to the mountains of Iga, where he was nursed back to health by the local martial artists.

It was there that he would fuse the Shugendo techniques he studied as a boy with guerilla warfare tactics he gleaned from the Iga inhabitants. His all-new system of deception, survival, and combat is widely considered to be the direct precursor of "modern" ninjutsu. In fact the teachings he left behind, refined by his descendents into a school called

Sharpening his skills on the battlefield: Daisuke

the Togakure-Ryu, represent the only ninja arts that are still openly taught today.

The Moment of Glory

Daisuke's early interest in unorthodox tactics likely forecast his future as a ninja.

According to the local history of the Togakushi area, he led a special forces team called the Nishina-to (Team Nishina) during the battle of Kurikara Pass in June of 1183. The pass, part of a major alpine throughway, represented prime strategic ground in a battle playing out between the Heike and Yoshinaka clans for dominance in the region.

Late one evening, as the Heike forces bivouacked in preparation for another day of battle, Team Nishina launched a surprise assault. Raising a din loud enough to wake the dead, they startled the Heike soldiers into an immediate retreat—and then Daisuke cowed them into submission. Literally. He had hit upon the novel tactic of strapping flaming torches to the horns of a herd of cattle, which he

TOOLS OF THE TRADE

As eventually refined, the Togakure-ryu school of ninjutsu employed a variety of then unique weapons: *senban shuriken*, distinctive diamond-shaped throwing stars; *shuko*, spiked bands slipped over palms or feet for climbing like a cat; *oni-bi*, the use of fireworks and monster masks to terrify opponents before they have a chance to attack; the use of hollow bamboo tubes that doubled as blowgun and snorkel; and a distinctive knife called the *kyoketsu shoge*: a forked dagger attached to a metal ring via a length of rope originally made of braided horsehair. And the best part? Designed from commonly found materials, all could be carried without arousing the suspicion of the authorities.

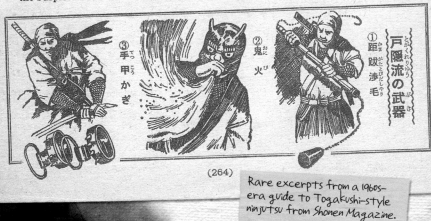

(264)

Rare excerpts from a 1960s-era guide to Togakushi-style ninjutsu from Shonen Magazine.

①高げたで氷の上を走る

②水をこぼさないように走る

③とびあがって木の幹を切る

戸隠流の
三つの修業

TOGAKURE TRAINING

In contrast to other martial arts, the Togakure-ryu is a largely defensive style of ninjutsu, focusing on avoiding detection and incapacitating opponents rather than direct assaults. While it utilizes a wide variety of tools and weapons, the heart and soul of the art is the ability to defeat enemies even while totally unarmed. To this effect, it includes a wide variety of physical training such as *kosshi-jutsu*, strengthening one's fingers to the point where they can be used to "defeat a raging beast."

All of this requires serious endurance. Basic training involves walking some 120 to 160 kilometers a day (80 to 100 miles) at a speed fast enough to keep a straw rain-hat pressed to one's chest, wind-sprints in high wooden geta clogs across frozen lakes, and long jogs with buckets of water slung over one's shoulders.

stampeded directly into the terrified mass of Heike soldiers. In their haste to escape the flaming beasts, some ten thousand men tumbled from the narrow confines of the Kurihara Pass to their deaths. Some speculate that he may have gotten the idea from a Chinese story in which cattle with daggers tied to their horns were sent careening across a battlefield. (History is silent as to whether Team Nishina celebrated their victory with hamburgers afterwards.) ✳

1184 A.D.

Name: **TOMOE GOZEN**
巴御前

Birth/Death: 1157?–1247?

Occupation: Taisho (Military Commander)

Cause of Death: Unknown

Gender: Female

A.K.A.: Lady Tomoe
伴絵 (alternate kanji for "Tomoe")
鞆絵 (alternate kanji for "Tomoe")

Known Associates: Minamoto no Yoshinaka

Preferred Technique: Decapitation

Hobbies: Horseback riding

Clan Affiliation: Minamoto

Existence: Confirmed

Tomoe was especially beautiful, with white skin, long hair, and charming features. She was also a remarkably strong archer, and as a swordswoman she was a warrior worth a thousand, ready to confront a demon or a god, mounted or on foot.

Tomoe wasn't a ninja in any sense of the word. She was, if anything, a samurai. But her bravery on the battlefield undoubtedly served as an inspiration to generations of women who found themselves having to engage in battle, including female ninja. In fact, she may well have crossed paths with at least one proto-ninja of sorts: Togakushi Daisuke. Tomoe was one of the commanders of the legendary battle of Kurikara Pass in 1183, in which Daisuke secured victory for the Minamoto by stampeding flaming cattle directly into the midst of enemy Heike forces. While it is unlikely that he was under her direct command, word of Daisuke's innovative strategy undoubtedly spread through the ranks back to her.

The Woman

A lone female face amid a millennium of testosterone-fueled warriors, it is tempting to compare Tomoe Gozen to another fighting femme from times of old: Joan of Arc. But the comparison ends with the swords and armor, for unlike Joan, Tomoe wasn't a warrior of God. She was a warrior of love.

The thousand-year-old *Tale of the Heike* describes her thus:

The Moment of Glory

The battle of Awazu, January 21, 1184. Tomoe is twenty-seven. Sheathed in samurai armor, she

A match for any man on the battlefield: Tomoe Gozen

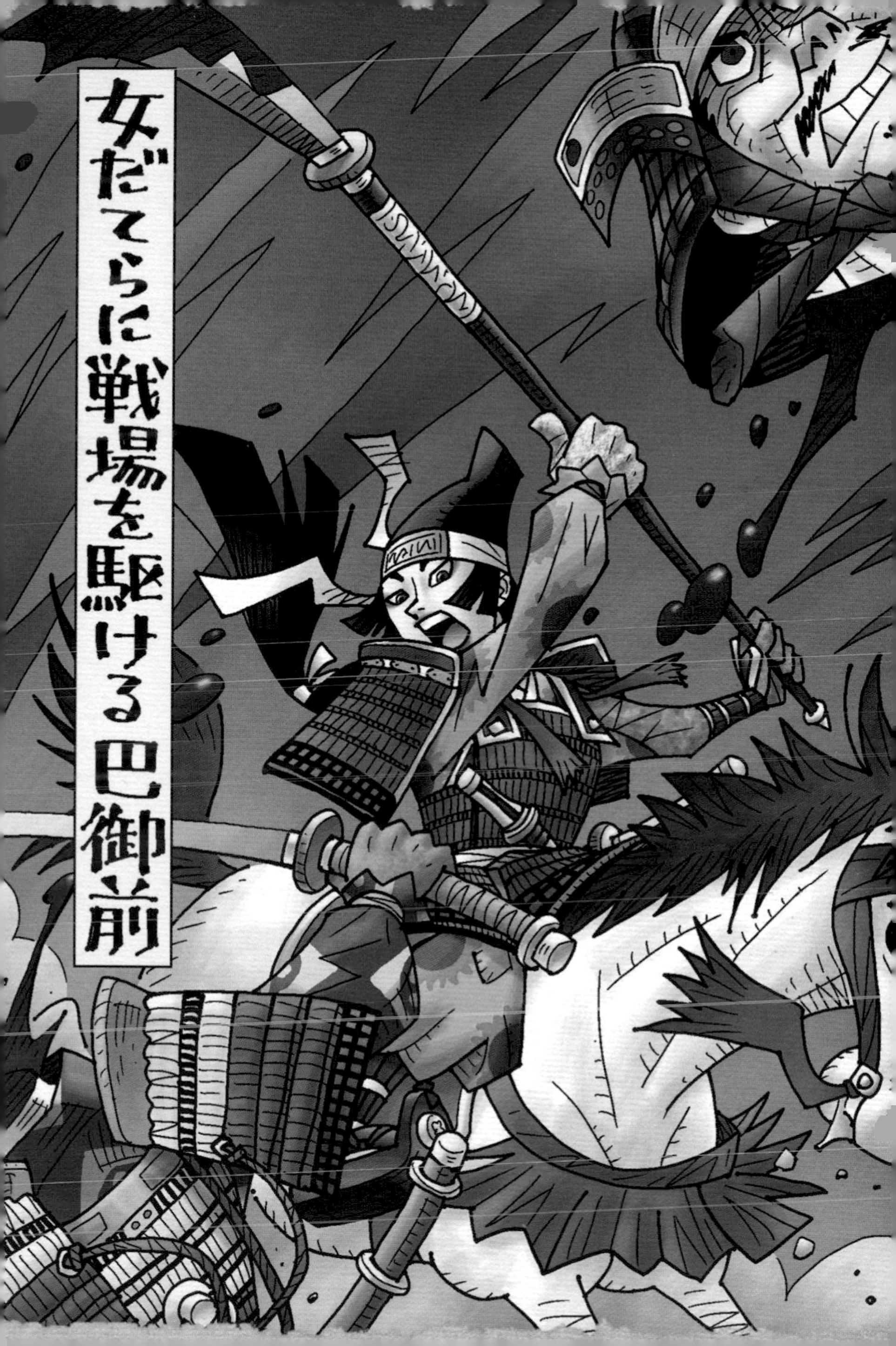
女だてらに戦場を駆ける巴御前

FACT OR FABLE?
The Tale of the Heike is more saga than history book, and there is no physical or even circumstantial evidence proving that Tomoe actually fought on the battlefield. On the other hand, neither is there any evidence conclusively proving that she did not. The topic remains controversial among historians.

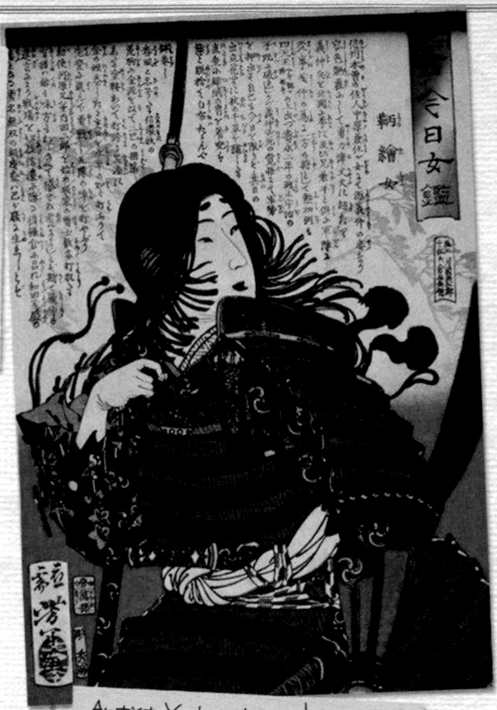

Artist Yoshitoshi's take on Tomoe, from his 1875 "Mirror of Ladies past and present" series.

sits astride her steed surveying the carnage of the just-concluded battle. Does a rivulet of the blood of fallen enemies mingling on her *tachi* blade drop upon the trampled grass below?

She turns to face her lover, her confidant, her superior officer: General Minamoto no Yoshinaka. Officially, she was but another of his (ahem) "consorts." But she was no stay-at-home concubine. Tomoe was an ass-kicker to rival any Amazon out of ancient Greece. That this manly man in an age of manly men deigned to ride into battle alongside someone with two X chromosomes is a testament to the respect in which she was held. A beast on the battlefield, her beauty was equally legendary; even in crimson-spattered armor, with an elaborate helm hiding her silken tresses, Tomoe must have been a sight to behold.

But her fellow warriors proved no match for those of the enemy, Yoshinaka's cousin and rival, the legendary Minamoto no Yoshitsune (see p. 30). The once-proud army of Yoshinaka, a thousand men and one woman strong, now numbers just five survivors.

Yoshinaka is no fool. He knows he and his men will not be returning from this battle. But as a woman, Tomoe Gozen is exempt from the normal code of conduct for a samurai. So he tells her to run.

Of course she refuses. It is unthinkable. But the general stands fast. Precious moments remain before his inevitable last stand, and there is no time to argue. In desperation he orders Tomoe off the battlefield, forcing her hand with the only currency he now possesses: he declares that her continued presence is an embarrassment to his honor. It must sting Tomoe to the quick—not out of humiliation but rather because it means her Yoshinaka will really and truly never return.

Tomoe grudgingly acquiesces —but follows with a flourish only she could pull off. Spurring her horse directly into the midst of the enemy forces, she clotheslines the biggest soldier she can find, physically dragging the utterly surprised man from his steed onto her saddle.

Viciously twisting her opponent's neck while drawing her blade, she severs his head from his body with a fluid motion driven in equal parts by skill and fury. Does she turn and raise the gruesome trophy in a final salute to her master? We'll never know, but legend has it she rode through the stunned forces unscathed.

The End

Legend also has it that she never took up the sword again, marrying and spending her remaining years first as a devoted wife and later, after her husband's death, as a Buddhist nun. She eventually passed away at the age of ninety-one, some six decades after cheating death alongside General Yoshinaka. ✳

Tomoe standing guard over Kiso Yoshinaka, at Nagano's Yoshinaka Yakata museum.

41

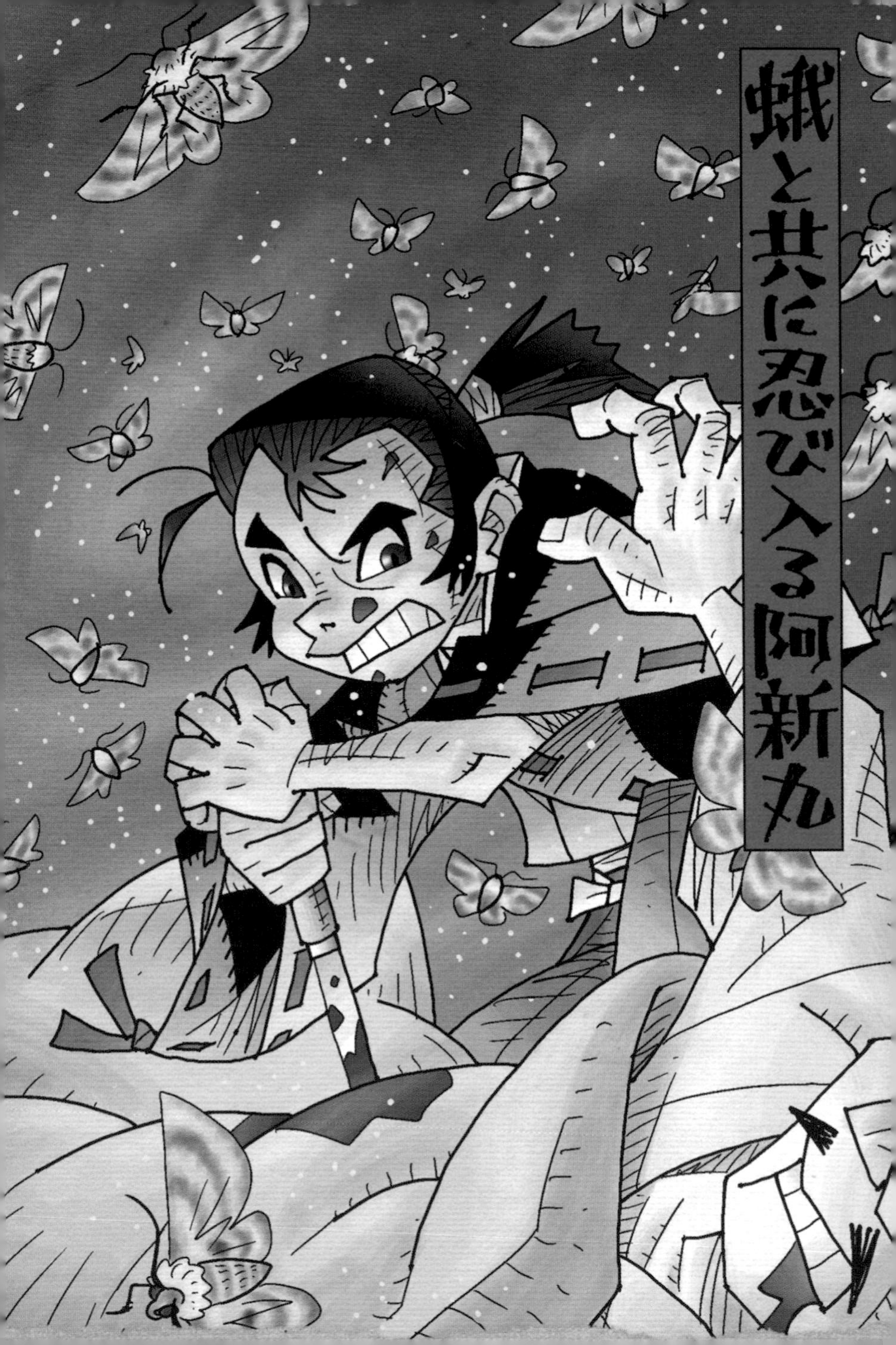
蛾と共に忍び入る阿新丸

1332 A.D.

Name: **HINO KUMAWAKA-MARU**

日野阿新丸

Birth–Death: 1320?–Unknown

Occupation: Faithful son

Cause of Death: Unknown

Gender: Male

A.K.A.: Kumawaka
Master Kumawaka

Known Associates: A certain unnamed monk

Hobbies: Watching and waiting

Preferred Weapon: A sharp sword

Clan Affiliation: None

Existence: Unconfirmed, but believed to be fact

The Man

The very first official account of a ninja-like assassination concerns not an actual ninja but rather an enterprising thirteen-year-old by the name of Kumawaka-maru. Think of it as the sort of tale ninja fathers tell their children as a bedtime story.

Kumawaka-maru was the son of a man named Hino Suketomo, a talented imperial counselor. After it came to light that the emperor was plotting to undermine the shogun's authority in a coup d'etat of sorts, the ever-loyal Suketomo took the fall for his master, accepting banishment to await a death sentence.

Kumawaka-maru knew that his father had been sent to the distant realm of Sado, a desolate island located in the Sea of Japan. Ignoring his mother's pleas, he resolved to see his father one last time. Donning a sedge hat to keep off the sun and rain, his feet shod in nothing but a pair of straw sandals, he set off on a ten-day journey to reach the coastline. He paid a local merchant to take him across the strait in a boat, and made a beeline for the mansion of a certain Lord Honma, protector of the island, in whose home Suketomo was incarcerated.

Although Honma greeted Kumawaka-maru politely, he declined to allow to the boy to see his father, explaining that it would only make death harder to bear for the man. But that said, explained Honma magnanimously, Kumawaka-maru was welcome to remain as a guest and accept his father's remains once the sentence was carried out.

The execution took place several days later. Whether Honma really felt as though he was doing Suketomo and his son a

Killing with moths: Kumawaka-Maru

Kumawaka-maru's big escape. Woodblock print by Utagawa Kuniyoshi.

silently prowling the dark corridors of Lord Honma's residence, memorizing every corner and staircase, and eventually discovering the room where the master himself slept.

One night a violent storm descended upon the island. Kumawaka-maru knew his chance had come, and made his way to Honma's room, only to find it empty (like many samurai, Honma often slept in different rooms as a safety precaution). Frustrated, the boy began making his way back, only to spot the light of a lamp burning in a small room along the way. He peered inside to find— what luck!—a sleeping Honma. Even better, he was alone, protected by nothing save the lamplight.

Kumawaka-maru spied the traditional pair of swords lying at the ready next to the samurai's bed. He knew he would have precious little time to get his hands on the weapons, so he devised an ingenious plan. This being summer, he knew the outside-facing doors would be covered with hundreds of moths of all sizes, attracted both by the light and the chance to shelter from the storm. Creeping outside, he quietly slid the outer screen open. The insects silently

favor, or whether he actually intended to snub the lad as a final insult to his prisoner, we'll never know. But the news of his father's demise sent Kumawaka-maru into a slow burn.

The Moment of Glory

Presented with his father's cremated remains, Kumawaka-maru collapsed, apparently stricken by a combination of grief, exhaustion, and sickness. Carried back to his room, he lay abed for days, accepting the ministrations of Honma's servants.

But the illness was a ruse. Kumawaka-maru spent his nights

swarmed the lamp, extinguishing it—and giving Kumawaka-maru his chance.

He unsheathed Honma's *tachi* blade, the same one used to kill his father. Taking position with his feet planted on either side of the sleeping man and the tip of the sword grazing his bedclothes, he kicked the pillow to awaken his prey. And struck. Steadily he drove the sword's razor-sharp tip into Honma's navel, leaning into it with all his weight, driving it through the man's torso, through the mattress, even to the tatami mats underneath; and then he swiftly withdrew it and sunk it again into his throat to silence the terrible death-screams. Leaving the longsword behind, he retreated to a bamboo grove outside to evade Honma's guards.

LEGEND OR HISTORY?

Kumawaka's story is chronicled in a fourteenth-century text called the *Taiheiki*, a forty-chapter epic about then-emperor Go-Daigo and his various domestic military campaigns. Like many texts of the era, it freely mixes the historic and the supernatural, making it difficult in many cases to separate fact from fiction. Given that the actual people chronicled in the book are historical personages, Kumawaka's assassination of Honma seems well within the realm of possibility.

The Escape

The series of small, bloody footprints leading away from the scene left no doubt as to its perpetrator, and Honma's men set up a perimeter to search for the boy. The Honma residence was surrounded by a deep moat some eighteen feet wide to prevent unauthorized entry or escape, but Kumawaka-maru bided his time. When he noticed a break in the search pattern, he scampered to the top of a bamboo stalk and used his weight to ride it downwards, like a pole-vaulter in reverse, to safety on the other bank.

Of Kumawaka-maru's life after his successful escape from the "crocodile's mouth" there is no record; but this one exploit was easily enough to make him a legend. While it is unlikely he ever worked as such ever again, many consider him to be one of the very first true ninja—in soul if not in terminology. ✳

悪天候を味方にする出雲守

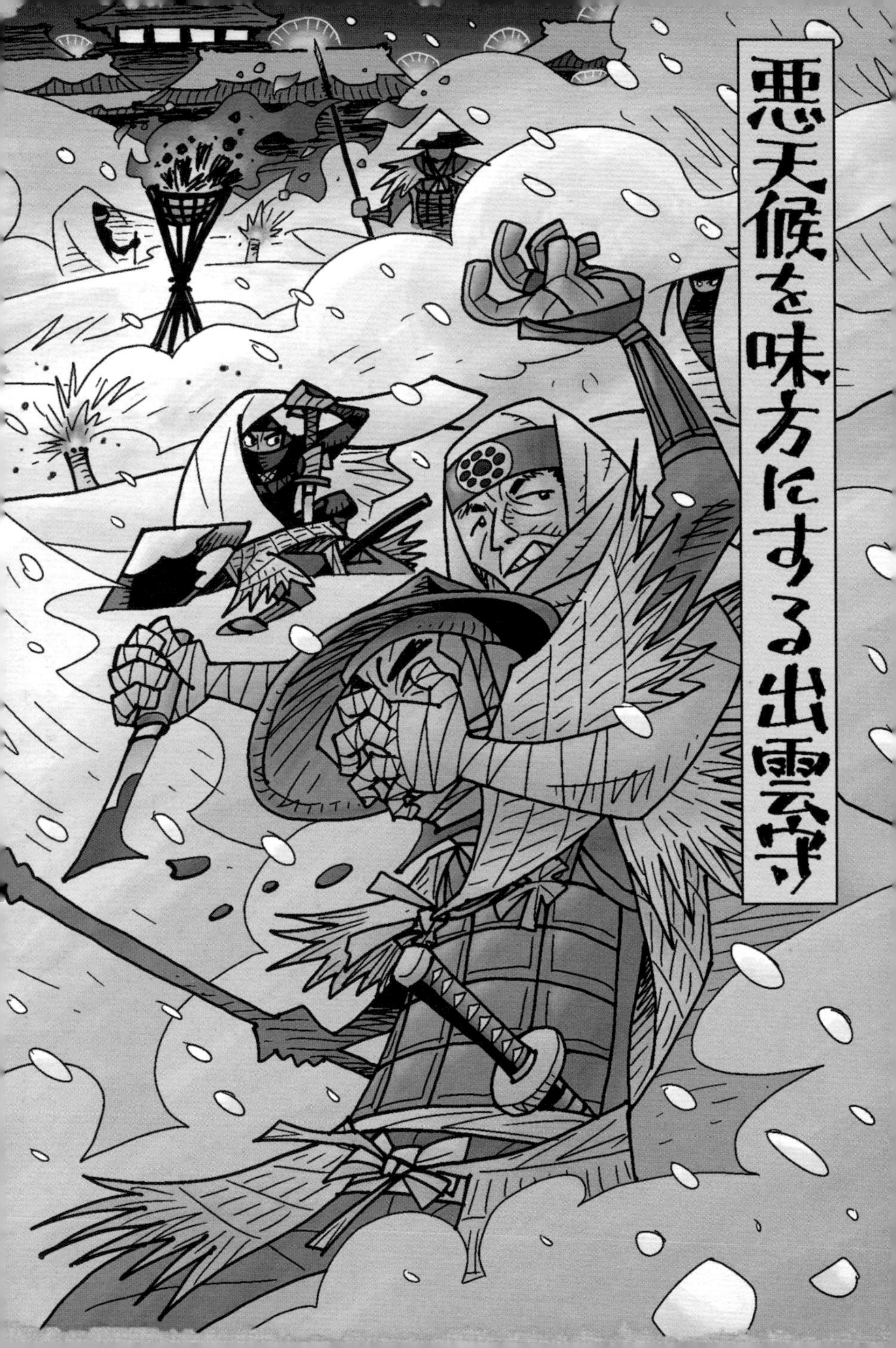

1487 A.D.

Name: **MOCHIZUKI IZUMO NO KAMI**

望月出雲守

Birth-Death: Unknown-1490s?

Occupation: Chunin (Ninja Commander)

Cause of Death: Unknown

Gender: Male

Known Associates: Rokkaku Takayori

Preferred Techniques: Kameroku-no-ho ("Turtling")

Kasumi-no-ho (Smoke attacks)

Clan Affiliation: Koga

Existence: Confirmed

> **"THE IGA CLAN HAS HATTORI; THE KOGA CLAN HAS MOCHIZUKI."**
> —Old Ninja Saying

The Man

A master strategist with the soul of a magician, Mochizuki Izumo no Kami (literally, "Mochizuki Izumo the Protector") ruled the Koga ninja clan at a crucial moment in its history. And while he may not have been teenaged or mutant, he most definitely was a ninja turtle.

Mochizuki, who claimed to be a descendant of the mythical founder of the clan, Koga Saburo, was born and raised in Koga, one of two major birthplaces of ninja tactics. Located in hilly, rugged terrain adjacent to Japan's then-capital of Kyoto, the valleys of the Koga region were home to dozens and dozens of "hidden villages" whose isolated inhabitants had long developed their own brand of guerilla tactics. By the time of Mochizuki's command, the Koga clan had distinguished themselves as a formal ninja collective similar to their sometime partners, sometime rivals in neighboring Iga.

They were unlike the fiercely independent people of Iga, however, in one regard: they had a treaty with another neighboring clan, the warlord-led Rokkaku. The agreement guaranteed that as long as Koga regional affairs were left to the Koga clan, they would provide shelter and manpower should the Rokkaku ever come under attack.

History's first major ninja-led guerilla warfare campaign involves Mochizuki honoring his clan's hereditary promise.

The Moment of Glory

The story begins in 1487, with the Rokkaku castle in ruins and its fleeing forces taking their agreed refuge in the hills of Koga. Hot in pursuit is the

Home Court Advantage

Mochizuki Izumo no Kami's personal residence was outfitted, James Bond style, with a variety of ingenious systems intended to tilt the odds against potential intruders. Residences of this sort are called *karakuri yashiki* (literally, "gimmicked mansions"), and include concealed floor spaces, retracting ladders, a double wall structure allowing movement around rooms without passing through them, and more. Beautifully restored, it stands in its original location in Shiga prefecture, and is actually open to visitors. For more information, visit: http://www.kouka-ninjya.com/

Shogun Ashikaga, at the head of some twenty-five thousand troops on a campaign to wipe the Rokkaku clan off the map. Things were heating up for a serious battle royale. But as Ashikaga crossed the border into Koga territory, he met only with a deafening silence.

Centuries before a band of rag-tag colonials dissed the Redcoats of the mighty British army with hit-and-run tactics, Mochizuki's ninja were about to wreak havoc on Ashikaga's troops from camouflaged positions, communicating troop strengths and positions with hoots and calls based on those of monkeys, deer, and other local animals.

Holding the Rokkaku regular forces in reserve, Mochizuki carefully dispatched his ninja throughout the area's hills and forests so they could quickly strike when the opportunity warranted. Ashikaga patrols often failed to return to camp, or limped back, slashed to ribbons, with stories of terror in the trees. On occasion entire contingents were wiped out. This wasn't how samurai battles were supposed to work, undoubtedly fumed Lord Ashikaga. His disciplined but conventionally trained forces were completely unable to cope with the ferocious appearances and sudden withdrawals of what Mochizuki called his *kameroku-no-ho*—the "six-turtle strategy" of using the mountains to shield his ninja like the impenetrable carapace of the reptile.

Mochizuki proved that a small contingent of well-trained ninja could keep huge numbers of troops at bay. But he wasn't through. When Ashikaga moved into a fortified compound in the northeastern part of Koga territory, Mochizuki licked his lips at the bigger challenge.

One snowy December evening, the ninja leader personally led a daring nighttime raid into the fortress. Night offensives were a risky business, and this night's weather made it even harder to distinguish friend from foe. Yet Mochizuki and his ninja led sixteen hundred of Rokkaku's men into the compound and out again without losing a single man to "friendly fire."

To determine the best day to launch his final assault, Mochizuki had used a contraption involving a feather placed atop an upended teacup as a makeshift barometer. When the device predicted that a snowstorm would soon descend upon the area, he knew the night had come to attack. To further conceal their approach, he utilized a smokescreen concocted of gunpowder and other chemicals to reduce the already low visibility to the absolute minimum.

NAME THAT NINJA
The hierarchy of ninja clans is usually divided into *genin* (literally "lower ninja": footsoldiers), *chunin* ("middle ninja": commanders), and finally *jonin* ("top ninja": absolute leaders.) Koga leaders were not given the jonin title due to their clan's relationship to the Rokkaku warlords. (A simple sign of respect, it in no way implies that their chunin were any less skilled than Iga's jonin, or that the Rokkaku actually commanded any of the ninja themselves.)

His men also used a secret system of code words to identify each other without visual contact, allowing Mochizuki to up the terror level inside the fortress with his personal forte: firecrackers, explosives, and *noroshi* smoke bombs. When the sun rose on the handful of stunned survivors the next day, the fortress lay in smoking ruins, and Ashikaga lay mortally wounded by a ninja spear. He succumbed shortly thereafter at the age of 25.

News of Ashikaga's failure to rout Rokkaku's forces in spite of his superior numbers and tactical position rocked the country and firmly established the Koga reputation as total badasses. Japanese warfare would never be the same. ✳

DEMOCRATIC NINJA
The fifty-three families of Koga ruled their clan by democratic consensus—a rarity in Japan (or anywhere else, for that matter) at the time.

The Illustrated Ninja

Ninja style*

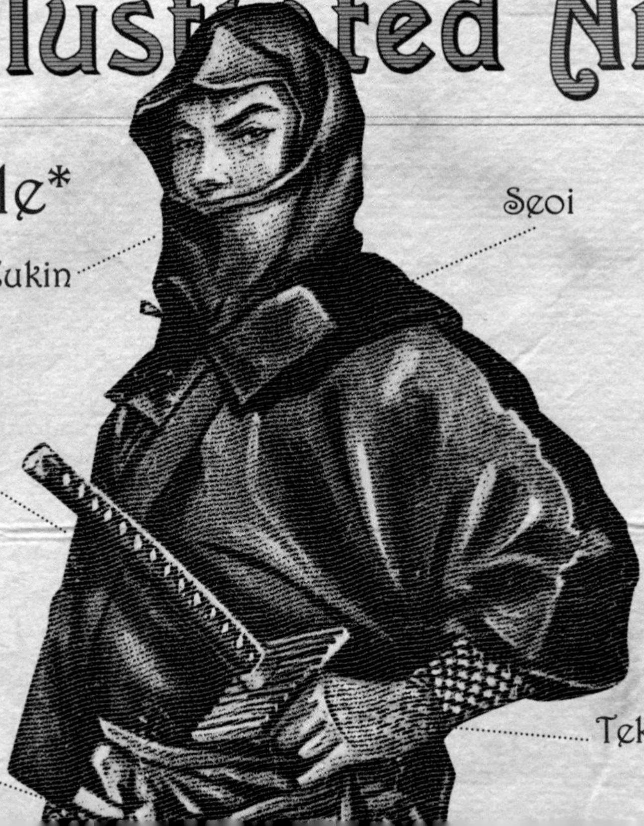
Zukin
Seoi
Uwagi
Fundoshi
Teko

Tabi

Hakama

Waraji

*see next page for definitions

Ninja style (continued)

The jet-black ninja outfit—seductive as it may be—is more myth than reality. The truth is that ninja wore whatever it took to unobtrusively blend in—think "plainclothes." And though records do exist of dark outfits being employed in cases that required stealth, they were usually shades of blue, gray, or brown rather than black. Perhaps most common was indigo, similar to blue jeans, for it was believed that the dye helped repel insects and venomous snakes. Occasionally, reversible clothing was used, with a darker color on one side and a lighter on the other, allowing for on-the-spot adjustments to ambient light conditions, or a quick color-change to help mask one's appearance—helpful for getaways.

Zukin: A single sheet of cloth thirty centimeters wide and two meters long, wrapped around the head to cover the face and mask the human silhouette.

Uwagi: Based on a farmer's shirt, the ninja version featured extra pockets for secreting away various implements of mayhem.

Fundoshi: The loincloth was the typical underwear of the period, a version of which is still seen on sumo wrestlers. It consisted of a long cloth folded and wrapped around the crotch area and, in a pinch, it could be unwound and used as a makeshift rope—or garrote.

Hakama: This lower-wear consisted of two independent leggings cinched together at top and ankles, allowing the wearer to easily create an opening for relieving themselves without having to fully disrobe—handy for long stakeouts.

Teko: Distinctive cloth gauntlets that covered the back of the hands for added protection, and coverage of otherwise light-colored skin.

Tabi: Traditional two-toed socks dyed an appropriately dark color. Often cushioned to help mask noise.

Waraji: Traditional straw sandals, sometimes dyed a darker color. Occasionally, spikes or other means of improving traction were woven into the soles.

Seoi: Essentially, a cloth purse. Slung over the shoulder as a backpack.

THE GOLDEN YEARS: 1500-1600

It's no coincidence that the heyday of the ninja largely overlaps with "Sengoku Jidai" – the Era of Warring States.

1550 A.D.

Name: **KATOH DANZO**
加藤段蔵

Birth–Death: 1503?–1557

Occupation: Ninja and Illusionist

Cause of Death: Killed in action

Gender: Male

A.K.A.: Tobi Katoh ("Flying Katoh")
Tobi Katoh ("Raptor Katoh")

Preferred Technique: Cow-Swallowing

Clan Affiliation: Unknown

Existence: Confirmed

The Man

A master of illusion who took the concept of "hiding in plain sight" to a literal extreme, Katoh Danzo didn't practice his art in the shadows but right out in the open as part of a one-man travelling show. A born entertainer, this lone wolf spent his days wowing crowds with magic tricks and his nights putting the same skills of deception and misdirection to work as a ninja for hire.

The sixteenth-century equivalent of a street illusionist like David Blaine, Katoh gained great renown for a performance in which he swallowed an entire cow whole. Described by contemporary sources as employing mass hypnosis rather than misdirection, the origin of the trick appears to be a far older Chinese one involving the illusion (one would hope) of crawling through a horse's anus and out of its mouth.

During one of these performances, a heckler sitting in a nearby tree shouted to the mesmerized crowd that Katoh hadn't swallowed anything. From his vantage point, it was obvious that Katoh was in fact *sitting* atop the cow. Infuriated at having his performance disrupted, Katoh redirected the crowd's attention to a bottle gourd seedling near the stage. Within seconds the plant began growing faster and faster, instantly attaining a height of one meter. Producing a *tanto* dagger, Katoh sliced off a gourd with a lightning-fast flourish. As the fruit toppled to earth, so too did the head of the heckler, having been cleanly separated from his neck despite being many meters removed from the plant and the stage. Katoh used the ensuing commotion to beat a hasty retreat.

The Moment of Glory

His career as entertainer was effectively over. Katoh knew he would need a wealthy patron to make a living. As luck would have it, word of his performances

Flaunting his skills: Danzo

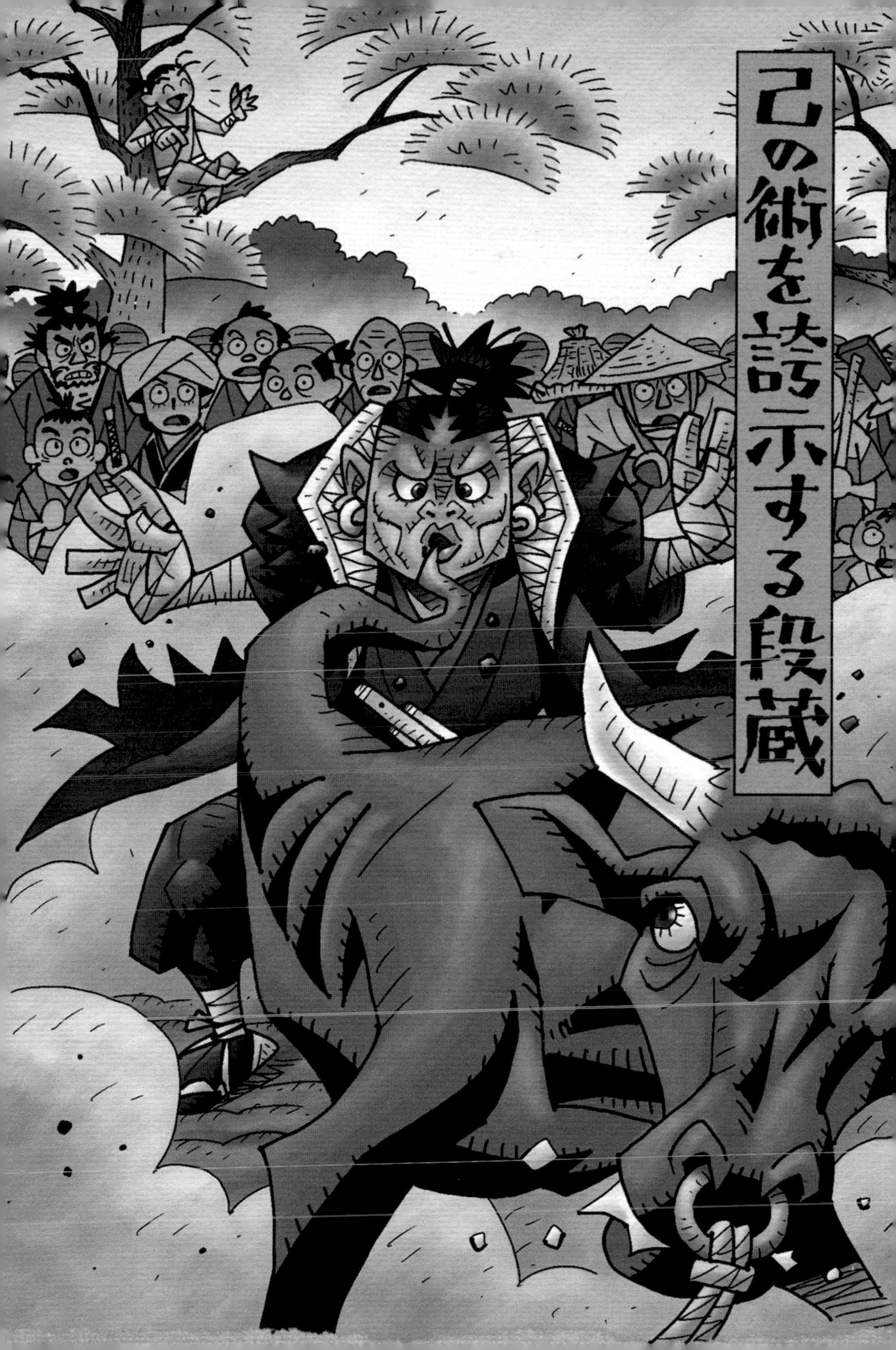
己の術を誇示する段蔵

had attracted the attention of the warlord Uesugi Kenshin, who invited him to his castle, where Katoh boasted of his skills of deception. The prudent Kenshin, however, wanted to test the bold claims. A precious sword, he said, was stored deep within the residence of one of his trusted servants. If Katoh could retrieve it, he would be granted a formal position. The ninja readily agreed.

A trained guard dog patrolled the outer perimeter of the residence, while heavily armed watchmen with lanterns were assigned to banish the darkness from the narrow, winding corridors. Unfazed, Katoh made his move late that evening. Silently dispatching the dog with poison, he worked his way past each of the guards into the inner sanctum, where he rendered a female servant unconscious. Then he scooped up both the sword and the woman and slipped back out, using sleight of hand and misdirection to conceal both himself and his burden from the numerous watchmen.

Unfortunately for Katoh, the sheer audacity of the exploit filled Kenshin not with admira-

A NOT-SO-CLEVER RAPTOR?
Although Katoh is a historical figure, his tale reads like a fable for young ninja. The moral of the story is that it can be detrimental to reveal too much of one's abilities—particularly if they are of the sort that involve sneaking around and killing people. As the old Japanese saying goes, "A clever hawk hides its talons."

tion, but horror. Penetrating a heavily guarded perimeter was one thing. But killing an expensive dog? And kidnapping a woman? Regarding the smiling ninja standing so confidently before him, the warlord knew one thing was certain: he would be sleeping with one eye open for the rest of his life with such a loose cannon under his roof. He quietly signaled one of his best men to kill Katoh.

Sensing the danger, the wily ninja evaded the attack and disappeared from the grounds of the castle. According to one account of the escape, he leapt over a wall several meters high, actually changing direction in midair to avoid the outstretched spears of Kenshin's bodyguards on the other side. Given that ninja may be talented but are as bound by the laws of physics as the rest of us, it is highly likely that this was yet another illusion. Katoh may have pulled this off with the help of a doppelganger—a straw dummy dressed in his clothing, hidden somewhere in the castle beforehand in the event of trouble. Operated with one or more ropes in the manner of a marionette, or even simply hurled over a rampart, in the confusion of a battle even a crude decoy such as this would distract attention from the real target—himself. This form of misdirection, known as *genjutsu*, is a classic ninja trick.

The End

Katoh made his way to the realm of Kai, where he managed to get himself hired as a *suppa* (intelligence agent) in the forces of Kenshin's rival Takeda Shingen. In another misguided attempt to impress a new employer, Katoh stole a one-of-a-kind volume of ancient poetry from Takeda's secret hoard of treasure. But his hubris tripped him up yet again. When the blame fell upon Takeda's top

suppa Kumawaka, he tracked down Katoh to clear his name. Unfortunately, only a single sentence remains chronicling the confrontation between these two highly trained ninja—a lone mention in an official historical record that "on this year [1557] in the area of Kofu, a suppa by the name of Raptor Katoh was exterminated." Perhaps "extinguished" would have been a better word: when it comes to the likes of Katoh Danzo, the only way to fight fire is with fire. ✳

IT'S A DOGGY DOG WORLD

The art of ninjutsu includes a variety of methods for handling guard dogs. Collectively referred to as *Ouken no Jutsu*, literally "Techniques for Dog Encounters," they include:

Goken no ho—Bringing a dog of the opposite sex along, distracting the guard dog with carnal attention.

Inu kuguri no ho—Based on extensive study of canine behavior, this involves exploiting knowledge of dog instincts and habits to avoid disturbing them.

Gukenjutsu—For situations where time is not of the essence, this technique involves sneaking up to a guard dog again and again with treats, getting it used to your scent and appearance before a mission.

One of Katoh's fatal mistakes was failing to exploit any of these techniques before killing Kenshin's beloved dog.

A bottle gourd of the type Katoh Danzo used when assassinating a heckler.

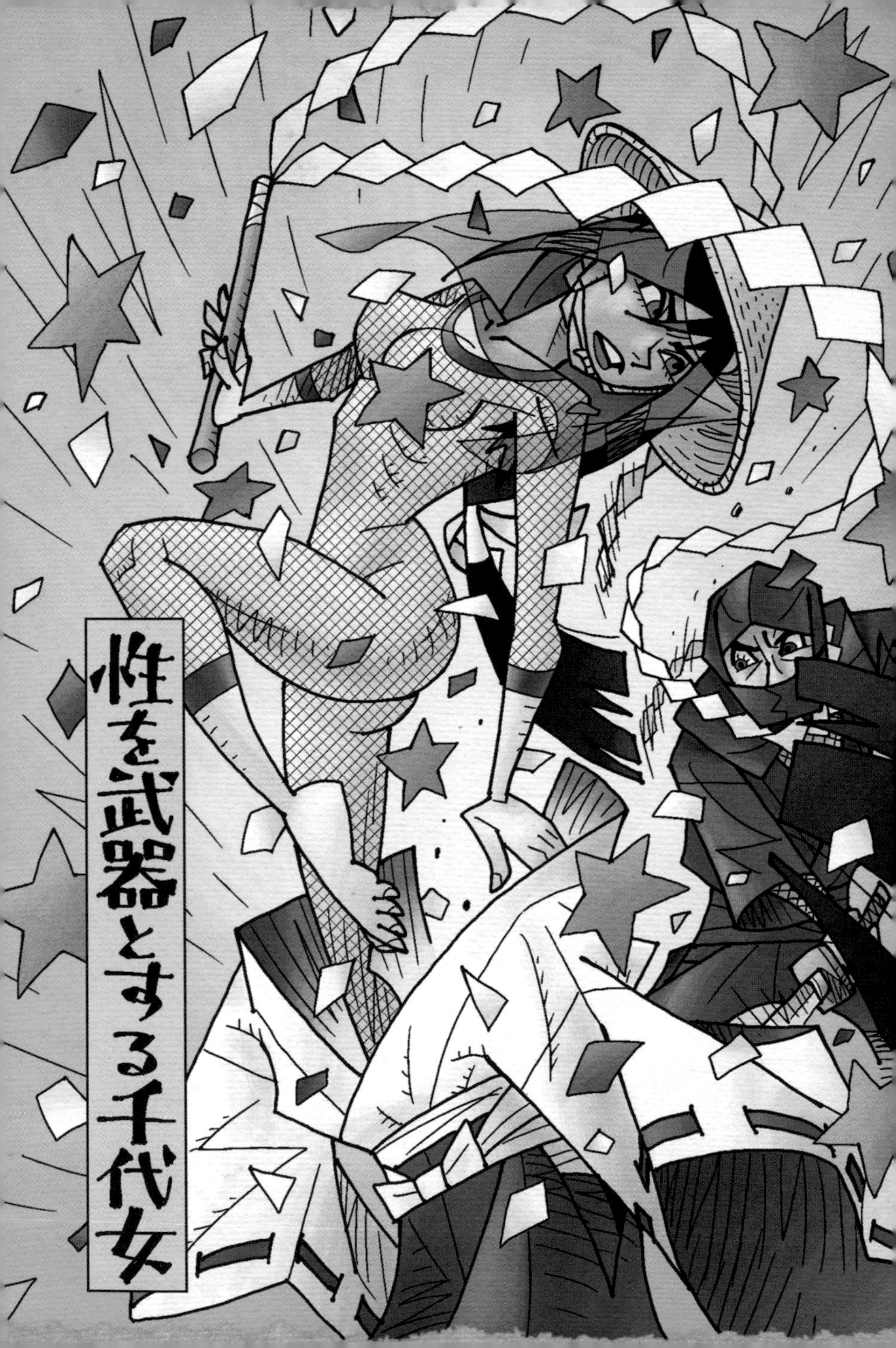
性を武器とする千代女

1560 A.D.

Name: **MOCHIZUKI CHIYOJO**
望月千代女

Birth–Death: 1530s or 1540s–Unknown
Occupation: Ku-no-ichi
Cause of Death: Unknown
A.K.A.: Mochizuki Chiyome (alternate reading)
Preferred Weapon: A small army of highly trained female ninja
Clan Affiliation: Koga / Takeda
Existence: Confirmed

Using sex as a weapon: Chiyojo

The Woman

Mochizuki Chiyojo has attained legendary status as a female ninja for the simple reason that she remains the only female ninja of whom anything is even vaguely known. It is a fact that females as well as males trained as ninja in times of old. But in the man's world that was feudal Japan, the personal achievements of women, no matter how compelling, simply weren't considered on the same level as those of their male counterparts.

Precious little detail about Chiyojo exists in the historical record. Her appearance remains an utter mystery. The precise dates of her birth and death and even the pronunciation of her given name are unclear. It is very likely that she was a descendant of that legendary protector of Koga and all-around ninja innovator, Mochizuki Izumo-no-Kami. In fact, her husband Moritoki, no slouch on the battlefield himself, was a distant relative of Mochizuki's as well. This ninja pedigree must have come with more than just papers, for after Moritoki's death in battle in 1561, the shrewd warlord Takeda Shingen took Chiyojo under his wing . . . and Japanese espionage would never be the same.

The Moment of Glory

Chiyojo earned her place in the history books through her association with Takeda, whose devotion to unconventional warfare—specifically, using ninja to gather information and conduct missions behind enemy lines—was legendary. Realizing the benefits of female as well as male spies, he ordered Chiyojo, who was a distant relative, to secretly build a squad of female intelligence operatives.

Her *aruki miko*, or "walking maidens," are the stuff of legend, not to mention adolescent fantasy. Trained "La Femme Nikita"–style in the ways of the world—religion, martial arts, and sexuality—they crisscrossed the country in the guise of holy women, entertainers, and prostitutes, never arousing suspicion but always keeping an ear to the ground for information of use to their masters. Although *miko* are mainly associated with Shinto shrines today, in Mochizuki's era they performed a different role in society. Rather than being assigned to any specific shrine, a miko wandered the country as a sort of shaman or a spirit medium, dispensing advice and wisdom for the locals she met along the way. Many were legitimate holy women, but the loose-knit order also proved a perfect cover story for the spies Takeda had Chiyojo train for him.

Young girls orphaned or abandoned in the chaos of the civil war raging through Japan provided Chiyojo with ample human resources for her operation. On the one hand, she rescued these lost souls from almost certain death. On the other, she wasn't running a charity. Once trained

as a walking maiden, returning to a normal life was all but out of the question. It is very likely that any who tried to escape faced brutal discipline or worse. It is logical to assume that only those who could be completely trusted to return would be allowed to wander the countryside completely unchaperoned on their information-gathering missions.

The End

No record remains as to how or when Chiyojo met her end, but the fates of her aruki miko were quite likely short and unpleasant. The image of a well-endowed young maiden whisking away her garments to reveal a hidden arsenal is a seductive one, but this is yet another place where hype has far outpaced reality. In spite of what you may have seen in movies, there is absolutely no evidence that female ninja fought alongside their male counterparts, or even engaged in combat of any kind. ✳

PLUS ONE

While the term *ku-no-ichi* is widely used today to refer to female ninja, its actual origins are unclear; some claim it was coined as recently as the 1960s. Whatever the case, it is now a firmly established part of ninja lore. According to one theory, the taboo against the use of female spies led to the coining of the indirect, wink-and-a-nudge word ku-no-ichi, くノ一, which is a breakdown of the individual strokes used to write the character for woman: 女. Another spelling, 九ノ一, translates into "nine and one," referring to the extra, ahem, bodily opening women possess beyond a man's nine (ears, nostrils, eyes, mouth, anus, and urethra).

Kiss and tell is the name of the game for Ku-no-Ichi like Chiyojo. Print by Yoshitoshi, 1875.

CARNAL COMBAT

Many ku-no-ichi techniques are believed to have been explicitly sexual in nature. The following were postulated by the late, great ninja novelist Futaro Yamada.

Mushi-tsubo no jutsu
"The Insect Jar"
Perfect for paternity suits! A technique that allows a woman to choose to have a baby from any partner she's slept with over the last ten months.

Yadokari
"The Hermit Crab"
Who needs a stork? A technique in which an unborn child can be physically transferred from one woman to another without harm.

Tsutsugarashi
"The Tube-Dryer"
Hard to complain: an assassination technique in which a female causes a man to climax so hard that he dies from the experience.

Tennyougai
"Heavenly Clam"
Practice those Kegel exercises: this is the ability to clamp down and prevent a partner from withdrawing during the act.

Kesa-gozen
"Her Ladyship's Vestments"
Swimming upstream? A technique that reverses a man's (ahem) flow back into his body, killing him instantly.

Fukuro-gaeshi
"Flipping the Bag"
Save on plastic surgery bills! This technique involves removing a developing infant from the womb, altering its features as needed, and safely returning it.

Shokuchu-bana
"Carnivorous Flower"
Bust out the baby wipes: a hypnotic technique in which a man is returned to the mindset of an infant, permanently incapacitating him.

Raneki-gyakunagare
"Reverse Egg Flow"
Shades of *The Picture of Dorian Gray*? A technique in which, at the moment of climax, a man sees a vision of himself on his deathbed, paralyzing him with fear.

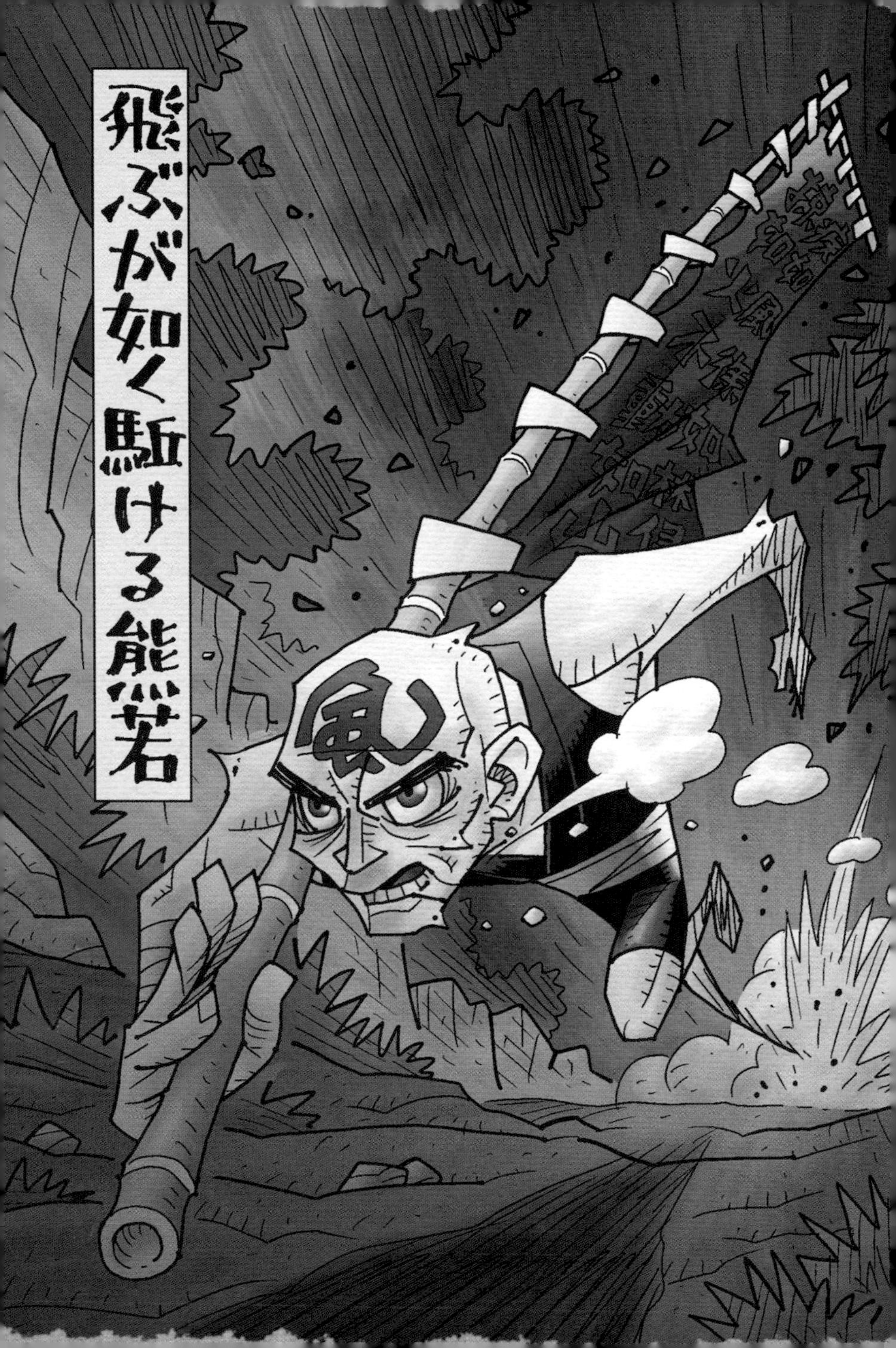
飛ぶが如く駈ける能若

1561 A.D.

Name: **KUMAWAKA**

熊若

Birth-Death: 1540s~Unknown

Occupation: Suppa

Cause of Death: Unknown

Gender: Male

Full Name: Unknown

A.K.A.: "Young Bear" (transliteration)

Top Speed: 128 kph

Special Technique: Legs of steel

Hobbies: Marathon running, presumably

Clan Affiliation: Takeda Shingen

Existence: Believed to be Historical Fact

The Man

A *suppa*—the regional term for ninja in the service of Takeda Shingen—Kumawaka was renowned for his physical endurance. Takeda had created a vast intelligence network built upon individuals with all sorts of extraordinary skills. Some were known for their ability with the sword or for throwing shuriken blades, others for their ability to disguise themselves and gather information undetected. Kumawaka's was his ability to run vast distances at incredible

speeds without tiring—a precious asset in an era before motorized transport existed.

The Moment of Glory

Kumawaka earned his place in ninja history books with two specific incidents.

The first took place in 1561. Takeda's forces were on the march to attack Wari-ga-take castle in what is now Nagano prefecture. Just before reaching his destination, Takeda's field commander realized that he had carelessly forgotten his army's battle pennants in Kai, by this point some 256 kilometers back the way they'd come.

This might not sound like a particularly big deal in the grand scheme of things, but going into battle without pennants simply wasn't done in medieval Japan. Not only did they honorably announce one's appearance and intention to attack to the enemy, they allowed friendly forces to recognize one another in the chaos of battle. Attacking a castle without them would make Takeda look like an ill-mannered buffoon. And so the field commander—undoubtedly realizing his own neck was on the line as well—dispatched Kumawaka, known for his speed, to retrieve the pennants from Kai.

When he returned just four hours later with the pennants in hand, even the field commander

Runs like the wind: Kumawaka

was impressed. Not only had Kumawaka averaged an incredible 128 kilometers per hour, he had neglected to take the travel document proving his allegiance that would get him into the Kai castle where the pennant was kept. How did he get past the castle guards? Kumawaka replied that he had scaled the walls, infiltrated the keep, retrieved the pennants from the commander's residence, and made it back out again without ever being seen. All in the interest of saving time, he explained humbly.

Kumawaka's success earned him praise on the battlefield, but contributed to a misunderstanding that led to the second incident for which he is famed.

The Moment of Glory II

When a priceless, one-of-a-kind volume of ancient poetry went missing from Takeda's stash of treasures, suspicion immediately fell upon the man who had pre-

NINJA RUINS
What little remains of Wari-ga-take castle can be found in the woods of Nagano prefecture today. It is roughly 3km from Furuma station on the Shinetsu Honsen line.

viously managed to infiltrate the castle so successfully: Kumawaka.

Accused of a crime he didn't commit, Kumawaka set off to prove his innocence. By this time, word had spread of a certain ninja nicknamed "Flying" Kato, who had managed to spirit both a precious sword and a beautiful woman out of the private residence of warlord Uesugi Kenshin. Kato's ability to leap great distances mirrored that of Kumwaka, and his propensity for pilfering things from the rich and powerful made him an obvious suspect.

According to a 1666 book by the name of *Otogiboko* (The Enchanted Doll), Kumawaka somehow succeeded in tracking down Kato, killing him, and clearing his own name. No record remains as to how exactly he did it, but one would speculate it involved quite a bit of legwork. ✳

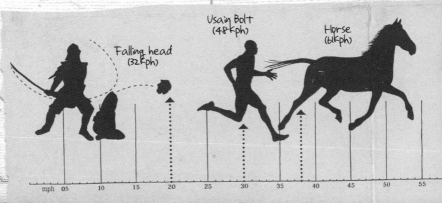

Falling head (32 kph)

Usain Bolt (48 kph)

Horse (61 kph)

mph 05   10   15   20   25   30   35   40   45   50   55

A NEED FOR SPEED

A variety of systems existed to speed the flow of information over long distances in medieval times, including the use of carrier pigeons, smoke signals, and even a simple flag-based semaphore. But these only worked under ideal conditions, and given that horses were restricted to samurai and aristocrats, the speed at which information traveled was generally limited to that of the speed of a human being on foot. Ninja in particular cultivated a wide variety of techniques to enhance their speed and endurance when running.

Techniques:

1) The Iga developed a system of rhythmic inhalations and exhalations to enhance oxygen uptake while running. The breathing pattern is as follows: Inhale, exhale, exhale, inhale, exhale, inhale, inhale, exhale

2) A centuries-old technique called "Nanba running," developed by foot messengers in the Edo period, was said to allow practitioners to run upwards of a hundred kilometers (62 miles) per day without tiring. Long considered a lost art, the basics have been revived through trial and error in recent times. Devotees include professional sprinter Suetsugu Shingo, who credited the technique with helping him win a bronze medal at the 2008 Summer Olympics. In a normal stride, one's arms tend to swing independently of one's legs (with the left arm swinging forward while the right leg is forward, and vice versa.) Namba running is based upon a system of swinging one's arms in time with one's legs (with the left arm swinging out while the left leg is forward, and the right arm swinging out while the right leg is forward.) There is also an emphasis on reducing unnecessary twisting or swinging movements so as to save effort and preserve strength.

3) An old ninja superstition holds that placing a pickled plum inside one's navel prevents fatigue while running. According to tradition, the saltier the plum, the better the performance. (The record is silent as to how those born with "outies" should keep the plum in place.)

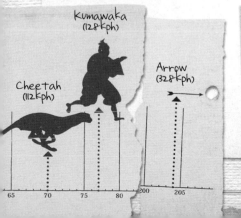

Kumawaka
(128 kph)

Arrow
(328 kph)

Cheetah
(112 kph)

| 65 | 70 | 75 | 80 | 200 | 205 |

NO RELATIONS

Kumawaka, known only by a single name, has no known relation to Hino Kumawaka-Maru, the legendary proto-ninja who assassinated a local leader while still in his early teens. Although their names resemble each other in English, you can see in their files that they are written with different characters in Japanese.

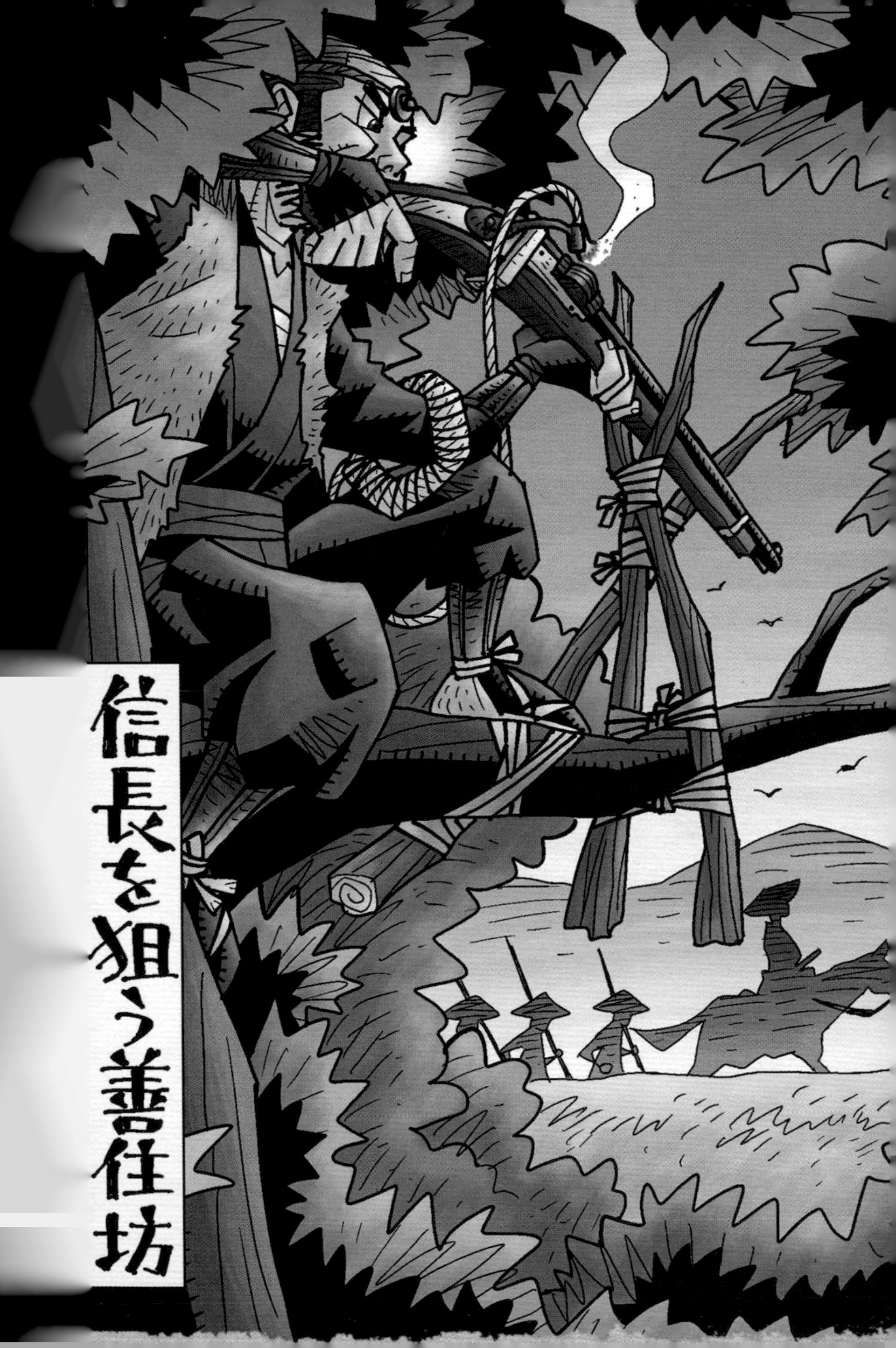
信長を狙う善住坊

1570 A.D.

Name: **SUGITANI ZENJUBO**
杉谷善住坊

Birth–Death: Unknown–1573

Occupation: Sniper

Cause of Death: Execution by torture

Gender: Male

A.K.A.: Zenjubo
The Man Who Shot Nobunaga

Known Associates: Rokkaku Yoshikata

Hobbies: Hunting

Preferred Weapon: Japanese Arquebus (matchlock rifle)

Clan Affiliation: Koga

Existence: Confirmed

The Man

The stereotypical ninja eschews firearms for more traditional forms of weaponry such as blades, bludgeons, and garrotes. Nothing, however, could be further from the truth. Even in the late sixteenth century, during the "golden age" of the ninja, they kept close tabs on technological advances in weaponry to keep their repertoires up to date. In fact, the ninja were, if anything, ahead of the curve when it came to the manufacture and employment of explosives, gunpowder, and firearms. And when it came to technologically oriented ninja, Koga sniper Sugitani Zenjubo was effectively the poster boy.

Born to one of the fifty-three families of Koga, Zenjubo was renowned for his sniper skills with the *hinawa-ju*, or matchlock rifle. So when a local warlord named Rokkaku Yoshikata approached the Koga clan with an audacious plot to assassinate the warlord Oda Nobunaga, there was no question Zenjubo would be picked for the job. In fact the plan was likely hatched with him in mind, as he was already something of local legend for his ability to consistently take down birds in flight with the finicky, relatively low-velocity matchlock.

The Setup

The medieval equivalent of a presidential assassination, the mission was not for the faint of heart. Zenjubo's acceptance shows just how far the ambitious ninja was willing to go in the name of duty.

The crafty Oda Nobunaga was far more dangerous prey than anything Zenjubo had encountered, and failure would rain the warlord's legendary fury down upon anyone even remotely involved. But the Koga ninja had obtained a tantalizing piece of intelligence: Nobunaga's retinue

The man who shot Nobunaga: Zenjubo

A vintage menko game card, circa 1960s.

would pass through the region of Omi that May—and more importantly, they would take the rocky, isolated Chigusa Road to avoid the more direct but tactically exposed Tokaido Road. Travelers inevitably stopped to refresh themselves at Chigusa Pass before pressing onward, and the rough terrain there represented a golden opportunity for an ambush.

Zenjubo arrived many days ahead of Nobunaga's projected arrival, analyzing the area to determine the best location for his sniper's nest. He picked a perch overlooking the road, yet largely inaccessible, something that offered both concealment and ease of escape. The latter in particular represented a prime consideration, as the considerable noise and smoke produced by the matchlock's firing would make the source of the shot painfully obvious.

Alas, no Zapruder-style film exists to document the attempted assassination. But a rough timeline of events has been assembled from several records of the account. On May 19th, 1570, Nobunaga's procession approached Chigusa Pass as planned.

The Moment of Glory

Zenjubo had taken up his position long before Nobunaga's retinue ever entered the pass. Positioned with a perfect view of the road, the barrel of his weapon steadied in a makeshift bipod, he waited for his prey with a predator's calculated patience. Presently the fully armored Nobunaga swung into view, sitting proud atop his horse, flanked by his trusted generals and trailed by his retainers. Zenjubo slowed his breathing as have generations of snipers before and since, taking long pauses between inhales and exhales to clear his mind and steady his aim, firmly fixed upon his quarry's unprotected face and neck. Forty meters. Thirty. Twenty . . . The sound of thunder cracked the stillness of the alpine air as Zenjubo's double-shot streaked home.

Zenjubo knew he had precious moments to escape—but still he waited for the smoke to clear. He had to confirm the kill. Through the haze he could make out Nobunaga's prone form on the rocks below. Mission accomplished . . . wait. No, it couldn't be. The man was stirring.

Zenjubo had never missed a shot, let alone one from this

close. But Nobunaga was struggling back to his feet. He was clutching his neck in obvious pain, but there didn't seem to be any blood. Zenjubo barely had time to curse his luck before first one, then several arrows began thunking into the trees and dirt around him. Amidst the shouts and hail of projectiles, the ninja sniper leapt from his perch and lowered his head into a dead sprint down his exit route.

The End

Although knocked from his horse by the impact, Nobunaga's collar-armor had absorbed the shots. The furious warlord ordered a manhunt, determined to make an example out of his would-be assassin.

Figuring out the triggerman was the easy part. Few would have had the fortitude to even point their weapons at Nobunaga, let alone pull the trigger. And fewer still would have scored an actual hit. Zenjubo's almost-success was akin to a personal calling card. But the investigation stagnated for years. This was no run-of-the-mill bandit. Keenly aware of the painful death he faced if captured, Zenjubo went underground to elude the authorities.

He might have eluded them forever if not for an unlucky break. Zenjubo had taken refuge in Amida-ji, a Buddhist monastery located in the territory of Isono Kazumasa, a rival-turned-uneasy-ally of Nobunaga. (Ironically, the monastery had been founded centuries earlier by that proto-ninja of sorts, Prince Shotoku.) When the word of the assassin's presence somehow leaked out— we'll never know how—Isono gleefully swooped in. Zenjubo represented a priceless opportunity for the warlord to prove his loyalty and curry favor with the increasingly powerful Nobunaga.

In what could be called an origin of the phrase "getting medieval on your ass," Nobunaga personally oversaw Zenjubo's extended execution. He ordered the ninja buried to his neck in sand, and his head slowly removed over the course of many hours (and according to some accounts, days) with deliberately dull-edged blades made of bamboo. ✳

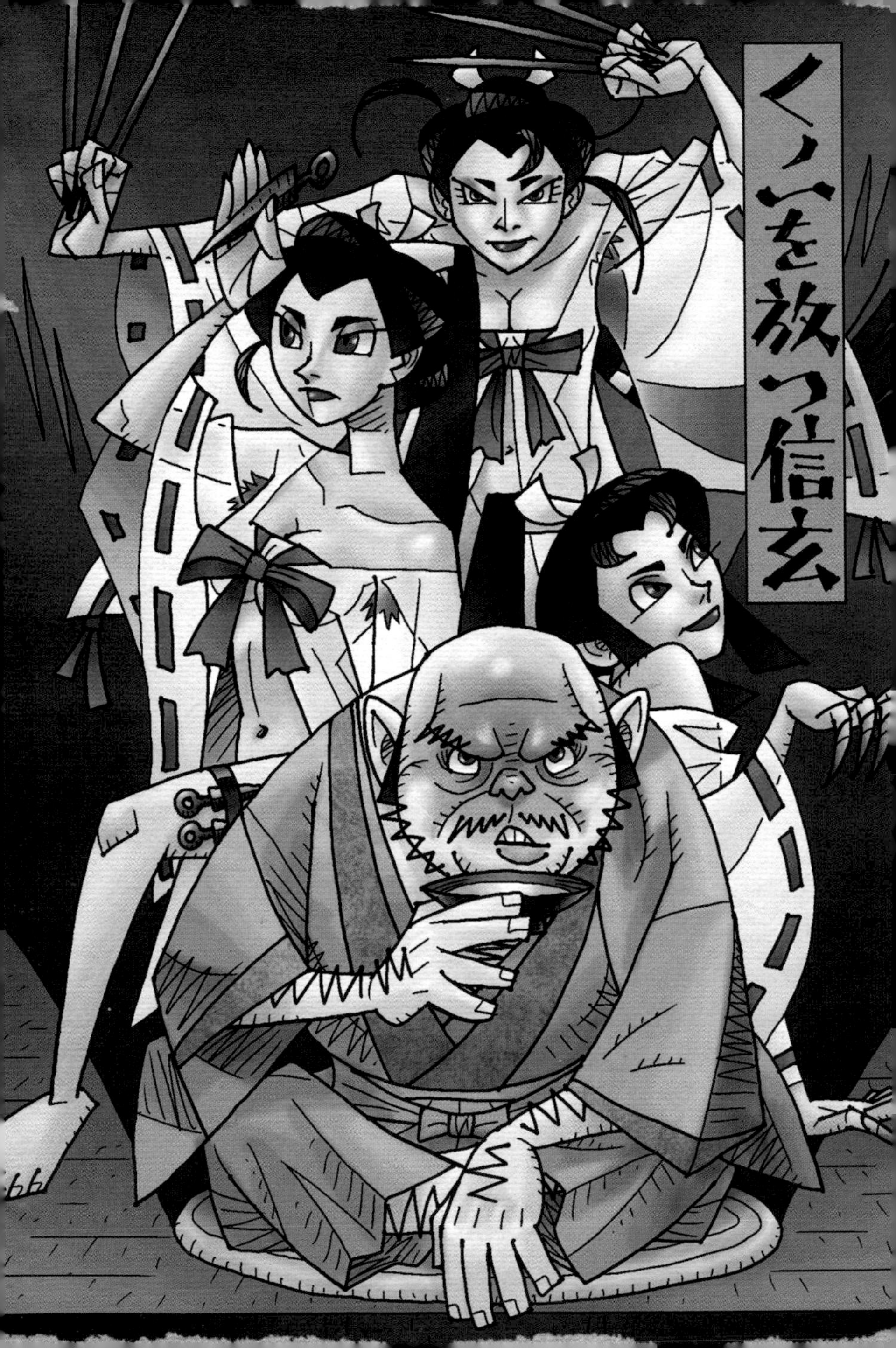
くノ一を放つ信玄

1570 A.D.

Name: **TAKEDA SHINGEN**
武田信玄

Birth/Death: 1521–1573

Occupation: Daimyo (feudal lord)

Cause of Death: Natural causes (illness)

Territory: Kai (Now Yamanashi prefecture)

A.K.A.: Takeda Katsuchiyo
Takeda Harunobu
"The Tiger of the Kai"

Preferred Weapon: Suppa
Mitsumono (another name for suppa)

Existence: Confirmed

FAMILY CREST:

Profile

Takeda Shingen of the province of Kai (today known as Yamanashi prefecture) was one of many aggressive feudal lords vying for territory and glory during the brutal Age of Warring States. What set him head and shoulders above his contemporaries was his vigorous use of *suppa*—the term in local dialect for what we would today call "ninja."

Many great leaders have been inspired by legendary Chinese tactician Sun Tzu's *Art of War*, but Takeda took its chapter on "The Use of Spies" to an unprecedented level. Utilizing travelling priests and shrine-maidens as cover for a covertly trained network of agents, he essentially managed to create a full-fledged intelligence bureau right under the noses of his enemies—centuries before the appearance of modern counterparts such as the KGB or Central Intelligence Agency.

Takeda recruited many of his suppa from the ranks of the *oshi*, itinerant priests who traveled from temple to temple performing religious rites. In an era when most citizens were not permitted to travel freely, the oshi's ability to wander the land without attracting attention made the priesthood a fertile recruiting ground for spies. Other of Takeda's suppa merely used the priesthood as a convenient cover story for their missions. Trained to live by their own wits for extended periods of guerilla warfare, these undercover agents combed the countryside for rumors and information. Other common disguises included those

Releasing the ku-no-ichi: Shingen

of merchants, farmers, doctors, and anything else that would allow them to travel unhindered.

In fact, Takeda's thorough approach to training his suppa earned it a title as an actual school of *ninjutsu*, called Takeda-ryu. So just how good were these guys? One of Takeda's followers, code-named "Jirobo," was capable of consistently felling enemies with his *shuriken* at distances of up to ninety yards.

Perhaps unsurprisingly for someone devious enough to build his own personal spy network, Takeda realized that his highly trained guerillas were a double-edged sword. He kept close watch on field operations, and ensured loyalty by holding wives and children as virtual hostages. Treachery was repaid in kind—by executing the traitor's entire family.

And knowing from firsthand experience that priests and shrine-maidens could well be spies, Takeda expressly forbade his followers from having any sort of contact with them within the borders of his territory.

Speaking of being anal about security, Takeda even ordered that his toilet include a concealed second door for hasty escapes. This wasn't idle paranoia. A popular but unconfirmed legend has it that his fellow warlord Uesugi Kenshin was mortally wounded by a strong-stomached ninja who concealed himself under the sewage in the privy, interrupting the warlord's business with a spear into his nether regions.

The Moment of Glory

What spy network would be complete without a femme fatale . . . or a hundred? Intuiting the obvious advantages—not to mention total awesomeness—of a gender-balanced assassination squad, Takeda retained the services of a *ku-no-ichi* (female ninja) named Mochizuki Chiyojo. Setting up shop in a nearby village, Mochizuki initiated a quiet recruiting campaign specializing in abandoned orphans, prostitutes, drifters, and other lost souls. Training the girls first as female shamans called *miko* (the better to travel the country undetected), followed closely by

---

TAKEDA'S MOTTO
風林火山
Furin Kazan
疾きこと風の如く
Hayaki koto kaze no gotoku
静かなること林の如く
Shizuka naru koto hayashi no gotoku
侵掠すること火の如く
Shinryaku suru koto hi no gotoku
動かざること山の如し
Ugokazaru koto yama no gotoshi

(Swift as the wind
Silent as the forest
Ferocious as fire
Resolute as a mountain)

extensive instruction in deception, stealth, combat, and even sexual techniques, she transformed this motley crew into a full-fledged force of foxy females.

This may sound like the plot of some 1970s ninja-porn flick, but the existence of Takeda's *aruki miko* (walking maidens) is historical fact. They travelled in whatever guise best suited the situation, be it holy woman, entertainer, or even prostitute. They operated with impunity where men feared to (or simply couldn't) tread, gathering intelligence, sowing disinformation, and carrying out the odd assassination or two. By the end of Takeda's reign, his shrine-maiden strike team numbered some two to three hundred strong. The exact military impact of their efforts isn't known, but is there anything cooler than having several hundred ninja women at your disposal?

The End

Takeda was a man who couldn't resist playing the spy game even with a foot in the grave. On his deathbed, he ordered followers to keep his passing secret for three years out of a well-founded fear that the news would spur his many enemies to launch an all-out attack on the clan and its holdings. To this very day nobody is exactly sure where Takeda's remains are buried.

However, a fleeting passage in a 1659 history text called *Koyo Gunkan* claims that Takeda ordered his son to drop his remains in Nagano prefecture's Lake Suwa. In 1986, a routine sonar survey of the lakebed revealed what appeared to be a large man-made object sitting on the bottom, and some experts believe the structure could be the final resting place of Takeda Shingen. ✳

PAPER TIGER
This papercraft replica of Takeda Shingen's distinctive helmet is just the thing for convincing the ladies to join your personal "spy network":
www.yonezawa-naoe.com/images/information/sinngen.pdf

1570 A.D.

Name: TSUNOKUMA SEKISO
角隈石宗

Birth-Death: Unknown – 1578

Occupation: Gunbaisha (Military Strategist/Advisor)

Cause of Death: On Battlefield

Gender: Male

A.K.A.: "The Ninja Weatherman"

Preferred Weapon: The elements

Hobbies: Studying religion, astronomy, meteorology

Clan Affiliation: Vassal of warlord Otomo Sorin (Kyushu)

Existence: Confirmed Historical Fact

The Man

Today, Tsunokuma Sekiso is renowned as one of Japan's top *gunbaisha* – an expert in military strategy. But in his day, he was feared as something more than human. Modern readers might even be tempted to call him an X-File or an X-Man.

A gunbaisha played a key role in any successful Shogun's council of advisors. He was essentially a strategist, determining the deployment of soldiers and their tactics. Practical concerns such as the sizes and emplacements of the opposing forces to the terrain to the weather factored into his calculations. But in an era before science, supernatural elements played a key role as well: the *feng shui* of the battlefield, the alignment of the stars, and the horoscope of the Shogun himself helped gunbaisha determine the most auspicious day for an attack. In other words, the average gunbaisha was part tactician, part astronomer, part astrologer, and part weatherman.

But Sekiso was no average gunbaisha. According to the records of the warlord whom he served, Sekiso possessed the ability not only to read but to control the elements at will.

His trademark attack was conjuring up a swirling hurricane over enemy forces. And this wasn't just any storm, but a whirlwind of *wakizashi* (short swords). Amidst the gusts he conjured innumerable blades that sliced through the hapless troops in a terrifying rain of steel.

He also seems to have had a way with birds. The same records claim he could hail down passing ravens from the sky and

A killer weather man: Sekiso

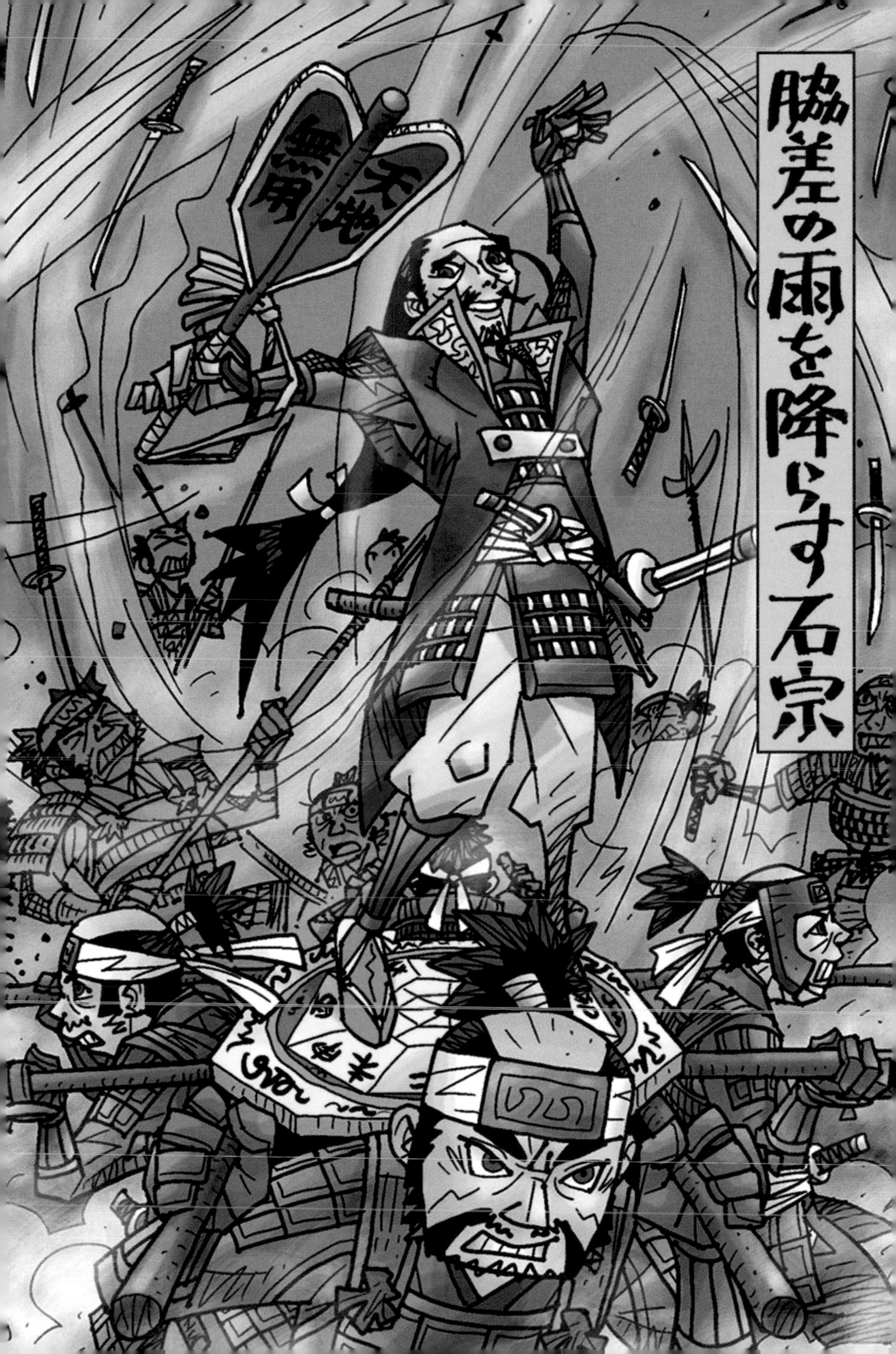
脇差の雨を降らす石宗
天地無用

could snap off a branch upon which a sparrow was sitting, without disturbing said sparrow. While these might seem at first glance to be mere parlor tricks, they can also be considered a bird-oriented version of the well-known ninja *Ouken-no-jutsu* (p. 57) used to pacify and sneak around guard dogs.

The Moment of Glory

Little is known of Sekiso's successes on the battlefield, but there must have been many of them, for legends of his prowess with the elements and his abilities with the sword abound.

He was hailed as a "master of moral teachings and martial arts," and even the Catholic missionaries who converted his master to their religion (see below) had some powerful words of praise for this unrepentant master of the occult. In their reports they called him a "man of reason" who openly shared his wisdom and his weather forecasting techniques with anyone who wanted to learn them. Portuguese missionary Luís Fróis's "History of Japan" (written in 1593, but not made public until 1926), frames his scientific achievements in such glowing terms that some modern Japanese meteorologists consider Sekiso one of their honored ancestors.

But for better or worse, Sekiso's demise is far more well known than his moments of glory.

The End

The Battle of Mimikawa, 1578.

Sekiso's sworn master was a warlord by the name of Otomo Sorin, who controlled a wide swath of the island of Kyushu then known as Bungo (today Oita prefecture). By virtue of his location in the southernmost main island of Japan, Otomo enjoyed a great deal of inter-action with Jesuit missionaries from Portugal, who plied him with gifts in the hopes of strengthening their foothold in Japan. Chief among these were weapons, namely flintlock rifles. In fact, Otomo is one of the very first warlords to have obtained them in all of Japan.

Although a devout Zen monk for most of his life, Otomo had long cultivated relationships with foreigners—particularly those capable of supplying him with the firepower to overcome his enemies. (One of his personal favorites was a massive Portuguese breech-loading cannon he dubbed *kunikuzushi*, or "Destroyer of Nations.")

All of this culminated in his officially converting at the age of 49 in 1578, declaring his intention to create a Catholic state in Kyushu—and eventually all of Japan. The Portuguese lionized him as "good King Francisco of Bungo."

This is precisely when things started to go wrong for Sekiso.

A major part of Sekiso's job as gunbaisha relied on divinations and occult rituals of the sort considered tools of the devil by the Catholic church. And every single one of his prognostications—both practical and supernatural—pointed to Otomo losing the upcoming Battle of Mimikawa.

No matter how correct Sekiso had been in the past, no matter the scope of his powers, his tools ran counter to the teachings of the church. Egged on by the missionaries who urged him to trust in the Lord, Otomo rejected Sekiso's entreaties out of hand, claiming that God would protect them. Like any loyal samurai, Sekiso swallowed his misgivings and followed his master onto the battlefield.

The opposing army slaughtered Otomo's forces, just as Sekiso had predicted. (Historical reports put the number of dead at from three to twenty thousand men—on Otomo's side alone.)

But as it turns out, both sides were actually right. Otomo lost the battle, as Sekiso predicted, but he also made it out alive, as the missionaries had said he would. Whether divine intervention played a role in Otomo's

A gunbaisha's distinctive war fan, which is called a "gunbai," is still used today by the referees in sumo wrestling matches.

survival, we'll never know, but it certainly didn't assure his success. The decimation of his army at Mimikawa all but crushed his ambitions—or at least his ability to carry them to fruition. Although he soldiered along for close to another decade, he succumbed to illness in 1587 with his Catholic empire nothing more than a dream.

The moral of the story: when it comes to war, trust your gunbaisha – particularly if he's a ninja.

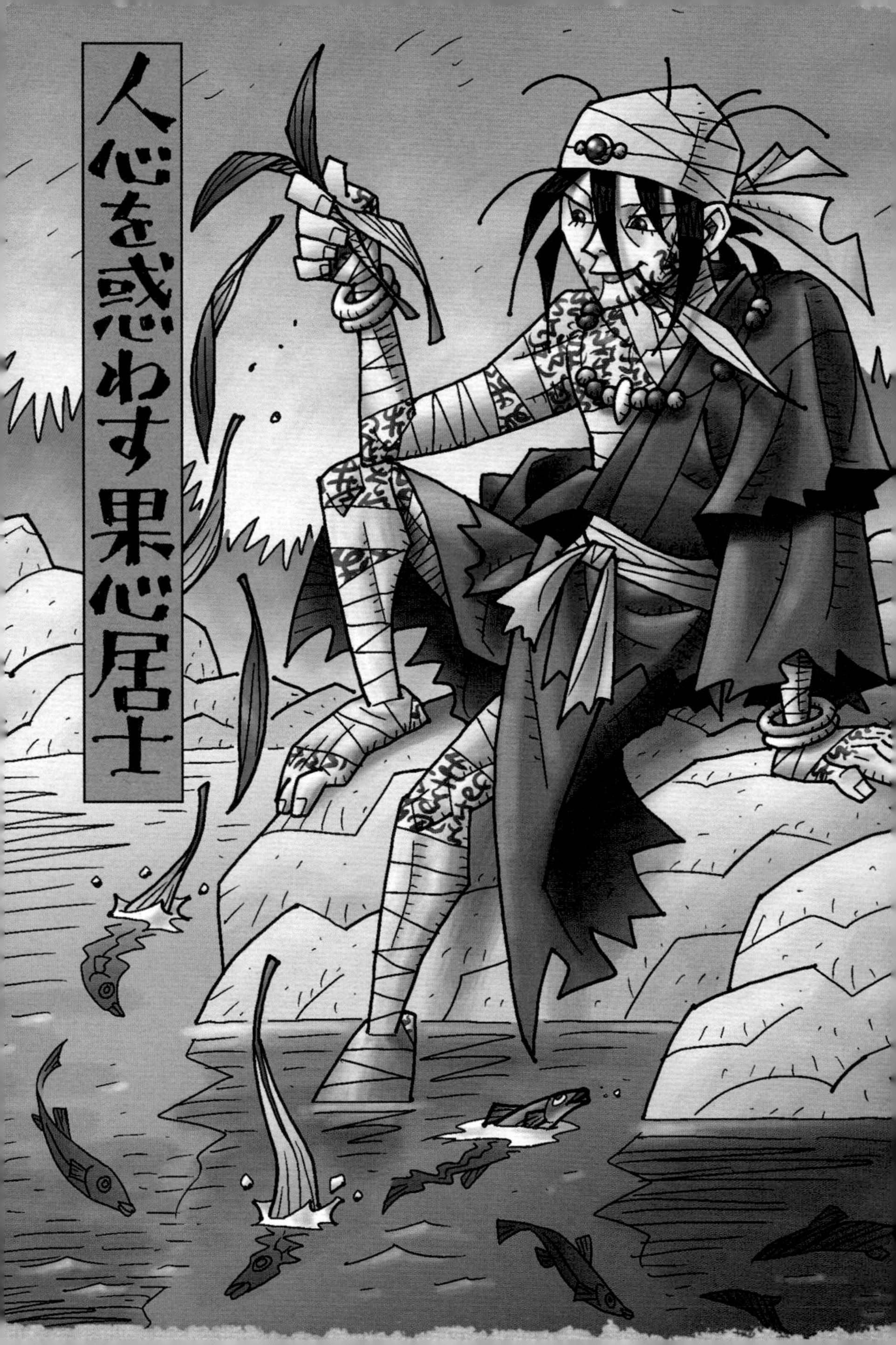
人心を惑わす果心居士

NINJA MAGIC

1574 A.D.

Name: **KASHIN KOJI**
果心居士

Birth–Death: 1524?–Unknown

Occupation: Magician

Cause of Death: Unknown

A.K.A.: Shippo Gyoja "pilgrim of the Seven Treasures"
Kwashin Koji (alt. spelling)

Preferred Techniques: Illusion, misdirection, shape-shifting

Hobbies: Heavy drinking

Clan Affiliation: None

Existence: Confirmed

A rare portrayal of Kashin Koji in his youth.

The Man

Often portrayed as a white-haired, bearded sage in robes—along the lines of a European-style wizard—Kashin Koji most probably never picked up an actual weapon. But his ninja-like ability to deceive opponents with apparitions and illusions let him slip away from any confrontation with the last laugh.

Nothing is known of Kashin Koji's ancestry or childhood. Given that he spent his youth studying the secrets of Shingon esoteric Buddhism on Mount Koya, in what is now Wakayama

prefecture, it is entirely likely that he was abandoned or orphaned. A growing fascination with magic and the occult, however, led to his excommunication from the order. Cut adrift from the only family he had ever known, Kashin Koji wandered from place to place, eventually settling near Lake Sarusawa in Nara, where he began performing as an illusionist. According to an account of one performance, "Kashin Koji made water gush forth between the spectators and made them believe they had go stones in their hands." One of his best-known tricks involved flinging leaves into the lake, whereupon they transformed into living fish and swam away.

The Moment of Glory

In his later years, Kashin Koji turned from simple street performance to a far more challenging avocation: tricking the rich and powerful out of their money.

In 1574, Kashin Koji attracted warlord Oda Nobunaga's attention with a painted scroll depicting the various trials awaiting doomed souls in hell—a fitting sort of artwork for a man who had sent so many people there. It was so exquisitely crafted that it seemed to spring to life, its demons sneering, its tortured

79

souls writhing, and its rivers of blood flowing with such realism that Nobunaga felt compelled to own it.

After a series of lengthy "negotiations" that included at least one attempt on Kashin Koji's life, the mystic agreed to sell Nobunaga the mysterious painting for a fee of 100 ryo—an absolutely astounding sum equivalent to tens of millions of yen in modern currency.

Yet no sooner had the money exchanged hands than the scroll abruptly changed. It looked roughly the same, but lacked the animation of its original showing. As he left, Kashin Koji calmly explained that while the original had been priceless, it currently reflected the value that Nobunaga had paid for it.

Kashin Koji turns on the waterworks. Good luck drying those tatami.

Convinced by the logic if not satisfied by the outcome, Nobunaga grudgingly agreed to let the old man go. Chalk up one for Kashin Koji in a dangerous game of brinksmanship.

Tossed into a Kyoto dungeon for vagrancy in 1582—so much for the riches he'd taken from Nobunaga!—Kashin Koji found himself temporarily sprung from the clink to entertain at a lavish dinner party held by Nobunaga's short-lived successor-assassin, Akechi Mitsuhide. Taking full advantage of his host's hospitality, Koji proceeded to down ten bowls—not cups, *bowls*—of rice wine in rapid succession. In return for the unexpectedly kind treatment, the apparently still completely un-inebriated wizard offered to put on a little show for the assembled guests. Waving his hand at a beautiful folding screen portraying a man rowing a boat on a lake, Kashin Koji caused its waters to overflow, filling the room with a deluge and drawing the illustration of the boat out onto its surface in the room. Clambering on board, he directed the coxswain to head back into the screen, receding into the distance as an illustration once again. When it disappeared from the surface of the screen, the room was dry as though nothing had happened—and Kashin Koji was gone.

You'd think the old magician would have packed his bags and gotten out of town by this point, but he tried his luck at the palace yet again just a few months later.

By this point, Toyotomi Hideyoshi had avenged Nobunaga's death by killing Mitsuhide, taking control of Kyoto for himself. (That this was a busy period in Japanese history is putting it mildly.) Invited to drop by and tell Hideyoshi's fortune, Kashin Koji managed to divine a tantalizing bit of embarrassing information that so enraged the ruler he attempted to kill the old mystic with his own hands. Transforming into a mouse, Kashin Koji beat a hasty four-footed retreat.

The end

Some accounts claim Hideyoshi had the old wizard tracked down and assassinated in 1584. But an intriguing alternate story exists as well. An eighteenth-century book by the name of *Koro Chawa*, or "Tea-Talk of Old," describes an encounter between Kashin Koji and none other than Tokugawa Ieyasu in 1612. The shogun asked the old man his age and was answered "eighty-eight." There is no further mention of Kashin Koji, living or dead, in the historical record. But given his ties to the supernatural and his uncanny, Forrest Gump-like ability to get next to Japan's top leadership, it isn't hard to imagine the bearded old wizard dropping in on the occasional prime minister even today. ✳

KASHIN KOJI'S EXCELLENT ADVENTURES
Kashin's wily wizardry has made him a staple of pop fiction. Portrayals based on him abound in comics, animation, and films, many playing fast and loose with what little reality is associated with him. Some of the more interesting include a short story written by Lafcadio Hearn for his 1901 book *Japanese Miscellany*, the hit manga series "Blade of the Immortal," and the not-quite-a-hit 1982 action film *Ninja Wars* which stars the always-great Hiroyuki Sanada of *Last Samurai* fame.

1579 A.D.

Name: **MOMOCHI TANBA**
百地丹波

Birth-Death: 1512?–1581?

Occupation: Jonin (Master Ninja)

Cause of Death: Killed in Action?

Gender: Male

A.K.A.: Tanba-no-Kami
Momochi Sandayu?
Fujibayashi Nagato?

Hobbies: Polygamy
Planning assassinations of
major leaders

Preferred Technique: Manipulating
things from behind the scenes

Clan Affiliation: Iga

Existence: Confirmed

The Man

At first glance apparently nothing more than a middle-aged farmer, Tanba's humble appearance masked the fact that he personally trained and commanded a vast army of ninja (including, among others, the notorious ninja-turned-thief Ishikawa Goemon). He ruled the Iga clan as part of a council that included Hattori Hanzo and a man named Fujibayashi Nagato, though evidence strongly suggests the latter was merely another alias Tanba used to confuse potential enemies. This was a man so dedicated to subterfuge that he split his time among three separate residences, each with its own wife and family, to throw off potential assassins. (Or that's his official story. A memorial stone for a mistress who was buried alive by his first wife hints that his conjugal arrangements may not have had the blessing of everyone involved.)

By its peak in the late 1570s, Tanba's network of spies had been honed into an exquisite tool, an extension of his own nervous system. His agents prowled the countryside in a variety of disguises, drawing in the tiniest bits of potentially useful information and filtering them back to him.

One can't discuss Tanba without discussing the secluded mountain province of Iga over which he presided. Roughly equivalent in size to the Washington, D.C. metropolitan area, and inaccessible save for an arduous hike over soaring mountain passes, Iga is famed as one of the two birthplaces of Japanese *ninjutsu*. (The other is the adjacent province of Koga.)

A thousand operatives, a thousand data points: Tanba

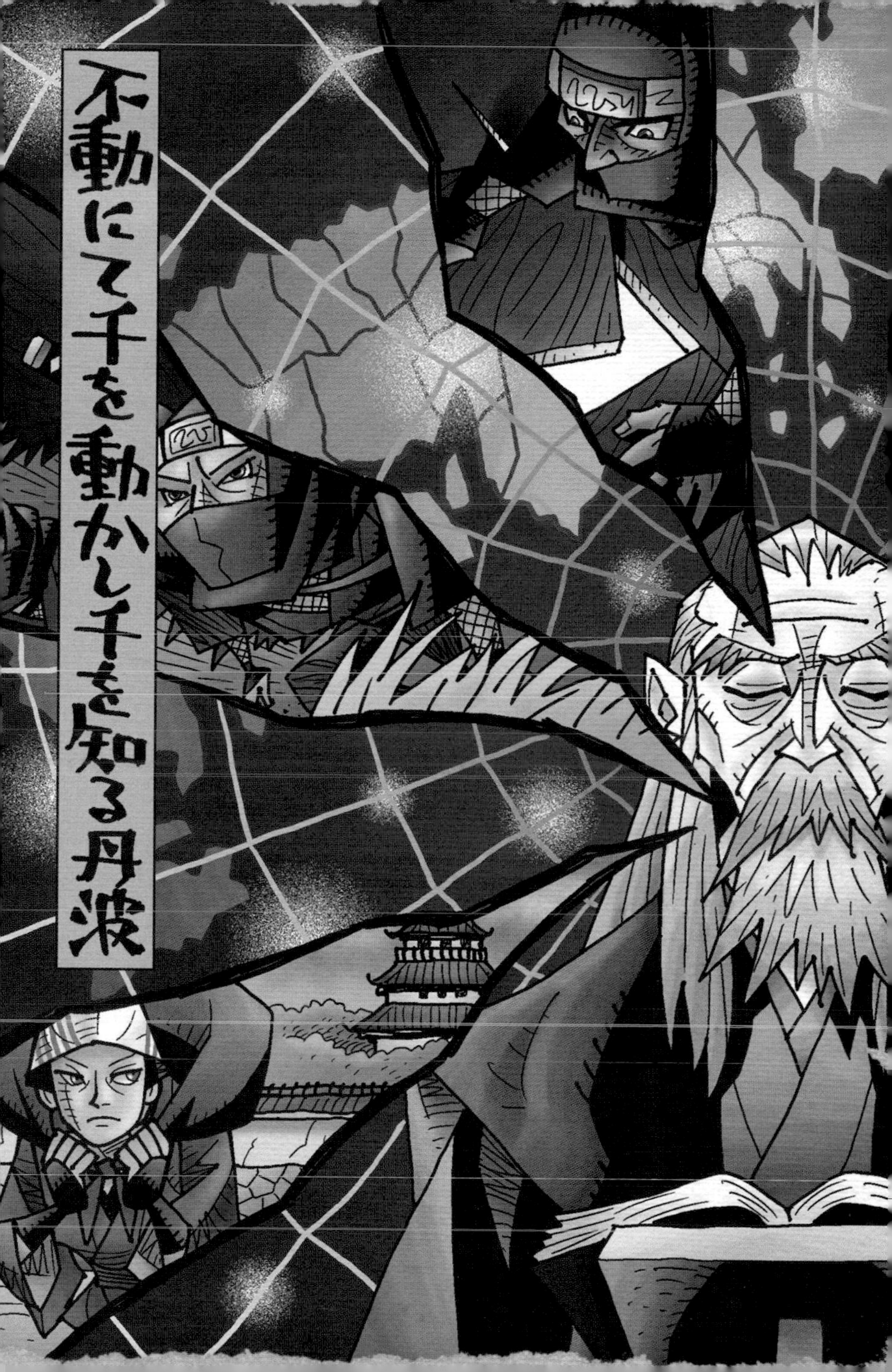
不動にて千を動かし千を知る丹波

The region was known as *kakure no kuni*, or "the hidden country," though its isolation proved a double-edged sword. It hindered invasion by all but the most dedicated enemy, and shielded local affairs from the prying eyes of the government, making it an ideal refuge for those who wanted to start new, anonymous lives, particularly army deserters. But it also ensured that inhabitants would have only themselves to depend on in the event of trouble. Knowing this, would-be defenders of Iga turned to the warrior monks known as *yamabushi* for advice, complementing mainstream martial arts with unorthodox training in wilderness survival, stealth, deception, and concealable weapons adapted from farming implements.

For generations, the fiercely independent inhabitants of Iga lived in a totally self-sufficient ninja commune: farming during the day, training in the evening, and waging vicious battles among themselves at night. They lived, breathed, and died fighting. Centuries of Hatfield-and-McCoy-style feuding, punctuated by temporary alliances forged to deal with occasional foreign intruders, honed the Iga skillset into an exquisitely deadly suite of abilities that came to be known as ninjutsu.

Word of the mysterious Iga talents began to spread, and by the mid-sixteenth century, the highly trained and well-armed inhabitants had established themselves as the definitive go-to guys for clandestine operations, willing to carry out any mission—no matter how dirty—for anyone with the gold to foot the bill. Thus was born the legend of the Iga ninja.

The Moment of Glory

The lesson Momochi Tanba taught the ambitious young Oda Nobukatsu, second son of the ultimate warlord Oda Nobunaga, represents a shining moment in ninja history.

Convinced that the province would be easy pickings for a turncoat ninja with an axe to grind against his own clan, Nobukatsu launched a totally unprovoked, and, in hindsight, really quite ill-advised campaign to invade Iga province in 1579. He began, in traditional fashion, by constructing a fortress on the edge of the region. Fully informed about the impending attacks through his network of *genin* (lower ninja) and *chunin*

NINJA LOVER
Tanba's mistress' memorial stone can still be found in Hojiro in the city of Iga in Mie prefecture today. Blades and scissors are left as offerings by those looking to cut ties with someone in their lives.

(ninja commanders), Momochi Tanba organized a Death Star–style pre-emptive nighttime strike on the compound. A guerilla campaign followed over the next year, and by the time the smoke cleared, Nobukatsu had lost some three thousand foot soldiers, a highly experienced field marshal, and an entire castle. (Note to wannabe conquerors: picking a domain inhabited by thousands of highly trained ninja for your first conquest doesn't exactly speak volumes about your tactical sense.)

The End . . . or Maybe Not?

Daddy to the rescue. Furious at his vainglorious son's abject failure, in 1581 Nobunaga sent some 44,000 troops into the region, armed with a powerful weapon: the *tanegashima* flintlock rifle. His men wove a trail of destruction through Iga, razing shrines and temples, burning farmhouses and fields, and slaughtering any men, women, or children who happened to be in their way. (Never one for doing things halfway, Nobunaga actually instituted a quota, ordering his officers to bring him between three to five hundred heads a day . . . or failing that,

their own.) Overwhelmed by the firepower and sheer numbers of the attacking forces, Momochi Tanba and his dwindling troops made an Alamo-esque last stand at the mountain stronghold of Kashiwahara castle, surrounded by Nobunaga's troops. After a month-long stalemate in which he lost hundreds of men, Nobunaga was forced to negotiate for the surrender of all the ninja inside. All the ninja, that is, save for Tanba, of whom no trace was ever found. According to at least one unconfirmed report, he survived for at least another fourteen years, disguised (or given his origins, perhaps "undisguised" would be more appropriate) as a farmer.

And that traitor ninja who incited the attack in the first place? Recaptured by the ninja defenders during the fighting, he chewed off his own tongue and bled to death rather than face questioning. ✳

Fittingly, the Momochi family crest features two arrows piercing a web-like seven-pointed pattern symbolizing the heavens.

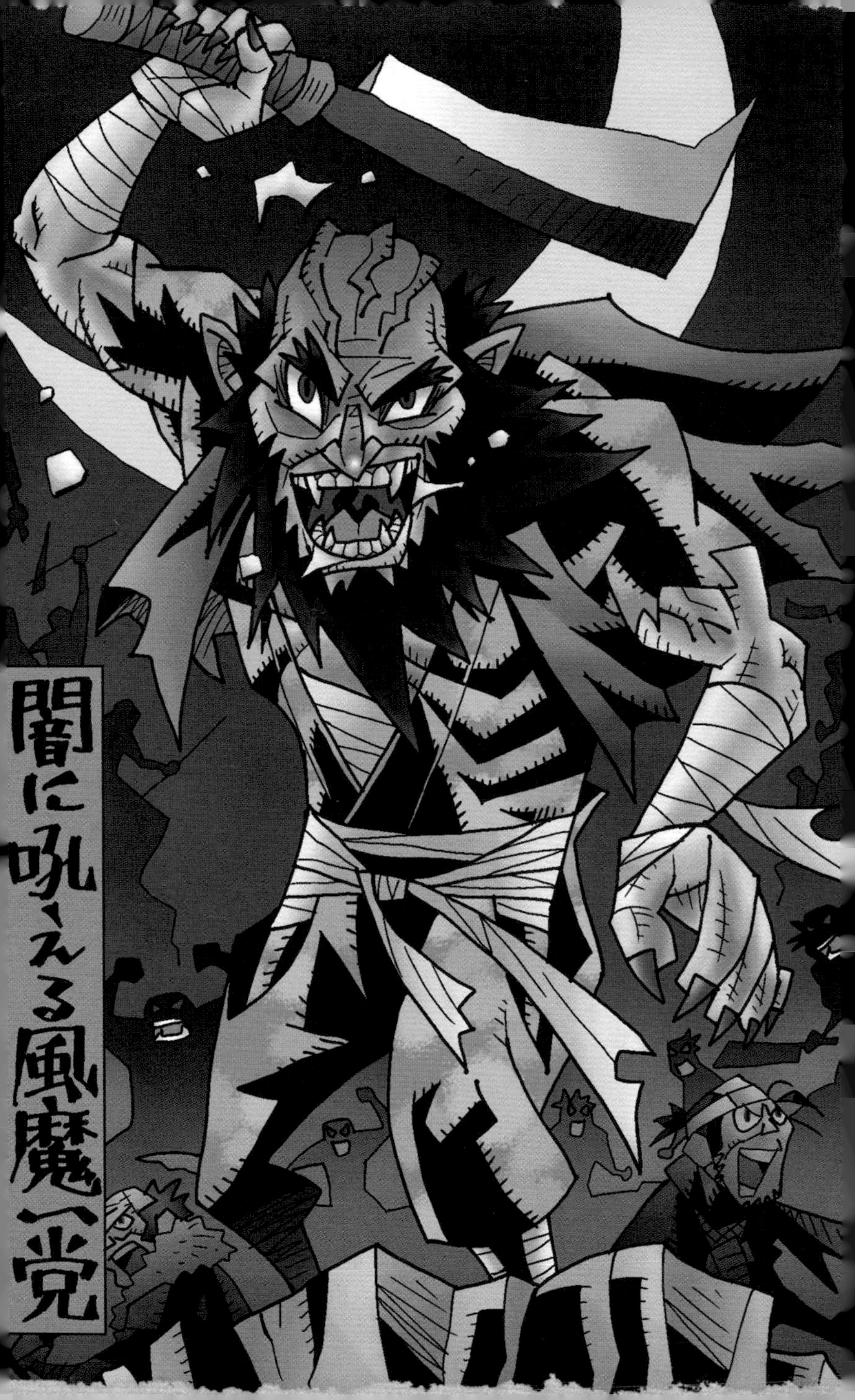
闇に吼える風魔一党

1581 A.D.

Name: **FUMA KOTARO THE FIFTH**
風魔小太郎

Birth–Death: Unknown–1603

Occupation: Rappa

Cause of Death: Execution

Height: 218cm (7 feet)

A.K.A.: Fuma no Kotaro

Preferred Weapon: The Fuma Itto

Clan Affiliation: Hojo

Existence: Confirmed

The Man

Fuma Kotaro V's physical appearance bordered on the demonic—think "Beauty and the Beast" minus the beauty part. Big-boned in the truest sense of the word, he towered some seven feet tall, had limbs and torso roped with thick muscle, and was covered head to toe with knots and lumps earned through decades of hard living. His eyes arched like sharpened sickles, four snaggleteeth protruded beast-like from his lips, and a carpet of black whiskers covered his face. His voice boomed like a *taiko* drum, with a resonance a listener felt in their bones.

The most famous Fuma Kotaro (which transliterates into some-thing like "John Demonwind") was actually the fifth to bear the appellation. The name is actually a title, bestowed upon the latest leader of a gang called the *Fuma Itto* (the Fuma group). The members were *rappa*, a regional term used to describe ninja from the Kanto area of Japan, and they were a rough-and-tumble bunch even by ninja standards (fittingly, the kanji used to write the word are "chaos" and "waves.") Many *rappa* began their careers as bandits, and gangs of these marauding high-waymen often proved fertile recruiting grounds for local warlords seeking "operatives" for any sort of dirty job that required plausible deniability.

Fuma Kotaro's gang was sponsored by the famed Hojo warlords of Odawara, and in contrast to more established Iga and Koga ninja clans, which stressed discipline and an elabo-rate ranking system, the Fuma Itto was essentially a criminal organization. Some two hundred strong, it was subdivided into four groups: *sanzoku* (bandits), *kaizoku* (pirates), *goto* (robbers), and *setto* (burglars).

Sanzoku were outdoorsmen capable of sprinting great dis-tances, leaping from tree to tree like monkeys, and able to conceal themselves as rocks and other innocuous features of the

A howl in the night: the Fuma Itto

やまいぬをつかっ
て
甲賀忍者をた
おす風魔小太郎

A less intimidating Fuma, as seen in a 1960s *Shonen Magazine* article (above) and *menko* card (left).

landscape. Kaizoku were expert combat swimmers and free-divers, capable of piloting nearly any kind of seacraft. Goto were muscle-bound masters of threats and extortion. And setto were expert infiltrators, adept at the arts of breaking and entering. In other words, just your average tight-knit band of highly trained purveyors of mayhem for hire. Part S.P.E.C.T.R.E., part gangster, part guerilla fighter, and all ninja, the Fuma Itto was like a force of nature with criminal tendencies.

The Moment of Glory

The quintessential Fuma Kotaro story concerns the battle of Ukishima-ga-Hara in 1581. In a bold attempt to steal territory from the influential Hojo, the warlord Takeda Katsuyori (son of Takeda Shingen), sent a contingent of forces into the Izu Peninsula on the eastern seaboard of Japan. Perhaps anticipating some difficulties, Katsuyori left the duty of establishing a forward encampment not to foot soldiers but rather a troop of two hundred of his father's *suppa* (ninja).

Rather than staging a head-on confrontation, the Hojo turned to Fuma Kotaro. The results are the stuff of ninja legend.

Fuma and his men snuck into the enemy camp under the cover of darkness, stampeded the stabled horses, set fire to the tents, and sowed the pathways with *makibishi* spikes to lacerate the feet of unwary pursuers. Donning enemy armor stolen during the ensuing chaos, they infiltrated the ranks of Takeda's forces, and launched surprise attacks. In the pandemonium, Fuma and his rappa quietly slipped back into the night. Surveying the carnage at daybreak, the handful of surviving suppa realized that they had spent most of the night hacking their comrades to pieces.

Fuma's guerilla tactics successfully reduced the original contingent of heavily armed invaders to just ten—with few if any casualties on his side. Basking in the glow of another job well done, Fuma Kotaro ordered his rappa to decamp for wherever it is a band of mercenaries in the mood to unwind after a little murder and mayhem go.

The few Takeda ninja left standing planned a counterattack. Taking a page from their tormentors' playbook, they infiltrated Fuma Kotaro's camp in disguise. Unfortunately for them, he was prepared for just such an occasion, and had worked out an elaborate system of codewords that corresponded to specific body movements (i.e., "when you hear 'mountain,' glance up at the sky.") Unaware of the code, Takeda's hapless suppa were quickly discovered and chopped limb from limb. And everyone lived happily ever after. Or did they . . . ?

The End

After the destruction of the Hojo family in 1590, Fuma found himself unable to secure a stable sponsor. After a series of misadventures, including his potential involvement in the death of Tokugawa Ieyasu's right-hand man Hattori Hanzo, Fuma became a man with a price on his head. Reduced to earning a living by running an Edo street gang, he was betrayed in 1603 by a former Takeda suppa named Kosaka Jinnai, who undoubtedly relished the chance for delayed revenge. Apprehended by Tokugawa's forces, Fuma was summarily executed shortly thereafter. ✳

MAKIBISHI
SPIKES

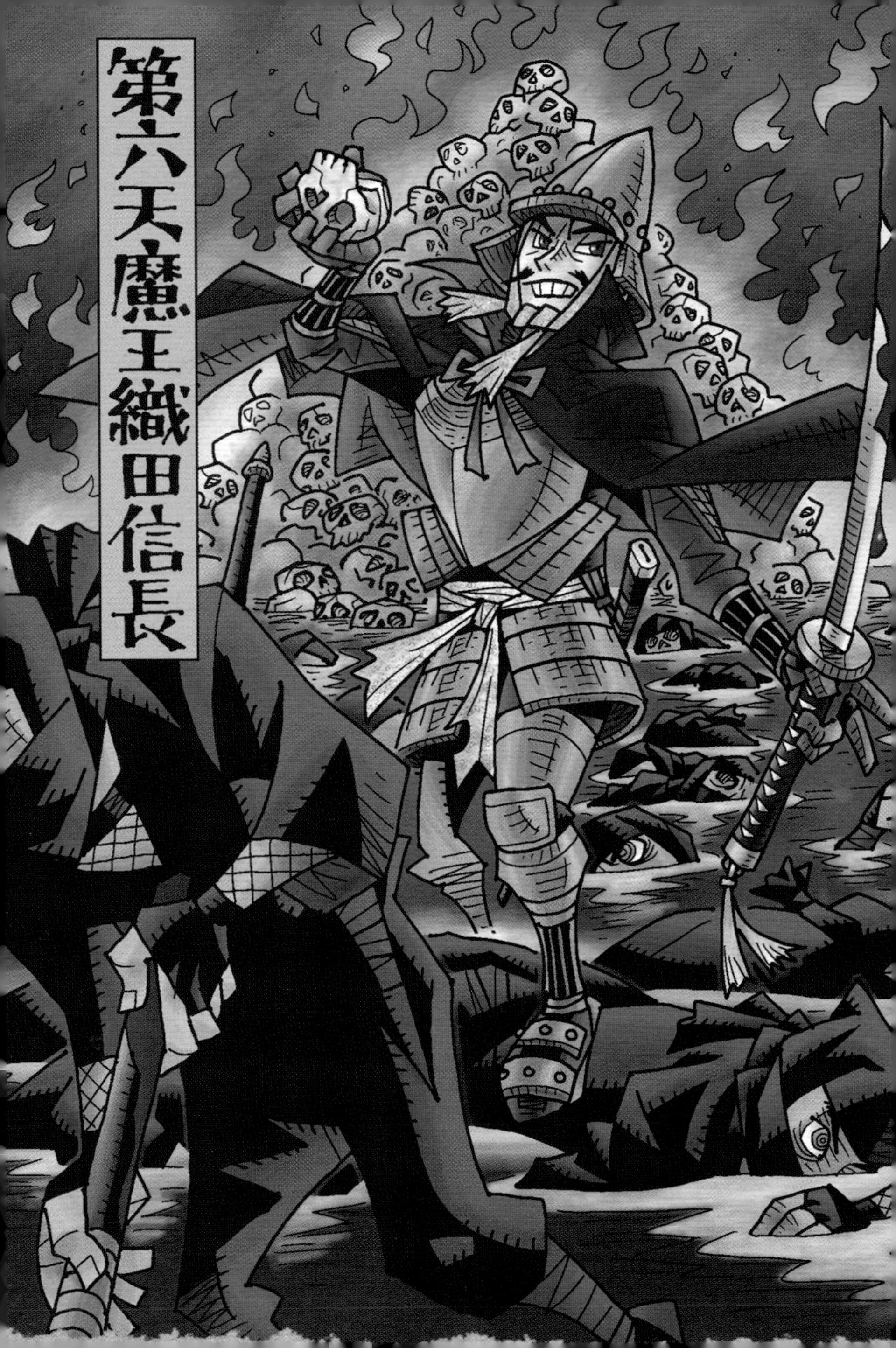
第六天魔王織田信長

THE NINJA DESTROYER

1582 A.D.

Name: **ODA NOBUNAGA**
織田信長

Birth/Death: 1534–1582

Occupation: Daimyo (feudal lord)

Cause of Death: Assassination

A.K.A.: Kipposhi (childhood name)
Saburo Nobunaga
Owari no Outsuke
(The Fool of Owari)
Tenma-O (Demon King)

Hobbies: Fashion Design
Oenophilia
Obliterating all rivals

Preferred Weapon: Massive forces of flintlock-armed soldiers

Existence: Confirmed historical fact

The Man

Babylon had Nebuchadnezzar; China, Sun Tzu; Rome, Alexander the Great; Africa, Hannibal. Japan had Oda Nobunaga, a strategic genius so cunning that his near annihilation of the Iga and Koga ninja clans ranks as a mere footnote in a long list of conquests.

FAMILY CREST:

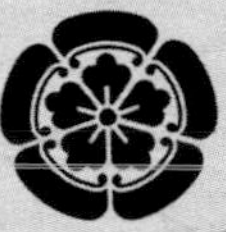

Popular rumor says he was bad to the bone even as a baby, gleefully chewing off the nipples of hapless wet-nurses. As a boy he ran wild with the medieval equivalent of street gangs, raising hell in the town outside his family's castle. As a teenager he disrupted his own father's funeral by hurling incense at the altar and eventually provoked his official tutor to commit ritual suicide out of frustration. Dismissed by rivals as a lost cause and even an out-and-out fool, Nobunaga appeared to be on a fast track to the bottom of a saké barrel. But in reality, the bad-boy shtick was his first of many last laughs: an elaborate ruse, buying time to secretly fortify his family's then-tiny fiefdom before neighboring warlords could move in for the kill.

In an aristocracy dominated by elaborate rules of etiquette, Oda gave his idiosyncrasies free reign. He wore his hair in an offbeat—dare we say punk?—style often compared to a tea whisk. He abhorred the restrictive traditional kimono and personally designed his own flamboyant ensembles. His taste in armor was as unique as his clothing: a modified Portuguese war-helm and cuirass paired with Japanese undergarments and leggings. While his contemporaries swigged saké, he savored red wine. In the midst of an insular culture all but closed to outsiders, he welcomed Christian missionaries and their knowledge with open arms (if not actual piety). While his fellow warlords dismissed firearms as mere playthings, he boldly exploited them to great advantage on the battlefield, building his once-tiny fief into an empire, and quite nearly conquering all of Japan in the process.

Nobunaga stood apart from his fellow warlords when it came to ninja as well, regarding them with ambivalence bordering on hostility. It wasn't that he didn't understand the need for clandestine intelligence gathering. What set this legendary pragmatist's teeth grinding wasn't the concept, but rather the near-monopoly held by the Iga, Koga, *suppa*, and *rappa* ninja clans from which his fellow warlords drew their intelligence services. He knew all too well that they represented a double-edged

sword that could just as easily turn against him. The fiercely independent Iga in particular must have stuck deeply in the craw of someone so dedicated to unifying all of Japan under his iron fist, particularly since they lived in what amounted to his backyard.

The Moments of Glory

When a neighboring warlord named Imagawa Yoshimoto barged through Nobunaga's territory en route to bigger game in Kyoto, Nobunaga turned the humiliation into an opportunity. Initial reports estimated that Imagawa's army numbered from 25,000 to 40,000 men. Nobunaga's total forces, including peasants hastily rounded up and armed with sharp sticks, numbered just 3,000. Yet Nobunaga pressed the "home court" advantage. When he received word that the enemy forces had bivouacked for the night in a nearby gorge by the name of Okehazama, he knew he'd found his chance.

As a timely storm struck, so too did his motley crew fall upon the enemy soldiers, who were fatigued from their long march and totally unprepared

---

A Very Nobunaga New Year

According to an early seventeenth-century history text, Nobunaga greeted holiday visitors on New Year's Day 1574 with a trio of skulls taken from famous defeated warlords—each exquisitely lacquered and decorated with gold leaf. One supposedly featured a removable skullcap, allowing it to be used as a drinking cup. Season's greetings!

for the ambush. By the time the rain lifted several hours later, Nobunaga stood with Imagawa's decapitated head in his hands. Three thousand had defeated nearly ten times their number. Nobunaga was all of twenty-six years old.

The story of his campaign to wipe out the ninja (and citizens) of Iga province after his son failed is recounted on page 85. He engaged a contingent of Koga ninja, while promising lavish rewards to those who provided him with information, and painful deaths for the entire families of those who he believed were holding back. (To this day, the Tensho Shigure Kuyo festival is held annually in the city of Nabari in Mie prefecture to placate the souls of the many individuals—ninja and civilian, man and woman, adult and child—who were killed during the invasion.)

This towering (3 meter!) golden statue of the man stands guard over JR Gifu station.

The End

Disputes between warlords were inevitably expensive, both politically and financially. As such, the frugal often preferred an indirect approach to conflict resolution: hiring ninja assassins. Nobunaga found himself in the crosshairs, sometimes literally, of more than a few during his rise to power.

1570: In the most famous attempt on Nobunaga's life, a trained sharpshooter by the name of Sugitani Zenjubo scored two direct hits, but Nobunaga's armor absorbed the shots.

1573: On orders from his master, a rival of Nobunaga's, the ninja Manabe Rokuro successfully penetrated the walls of Azuchi castle, making his way to Nobunaga's bedroom. Discovered mid-assassination attempt, Manabe killed himself rather than face capture and torture. By breakfast, his body was trussed and displayed in the local marketplace as a warning to other would-be assassins. "Attention, Azuchi shoppers . . ."

1580?: After hiding in the ceiling above Nobunaga's bedroom, ninja-turned-thief Ishikawa Goemon unsuccessfully attempted to poison Nobunaga by dripping poison down a thread. Almost too good to be true, this story is very likely apocryphal.

1581: A three-man fire team led by an Iga sniper opened fire on Nobunaga as he surveyed the destruction wrought by his troops on an Iga battlefield. They missed Nobunaga but killed seven of his advisors.

1582: Nobunaga finally met his end not at the hands of ninja but rather a turncoat general. Cornered by a company of samurai led by Akechi Mitsuhide in a predawn raid on Honnoji temple in Kyoto, a mortally wounded Nobunaga set fire to the building and burned himself alive rather than fall into enemy hands. ✳

弥助
YASUKE, THE REAL "AFRO SAMURAI"

It is a little-known fact that Nobunaga counted among his retainers a man of African descent. Although just a footnote in the pages of history, what little is known hints at an adventure to rival that of any seventies blaxploitation film. As the first and only black samurai, he must have been the source of a great deal of interest from the ninja-spies of Nobunaga's rivals.

Born around 1555 in the vicinity of Zanzibar, he was an unfortunate victim of the Arab slave trade. Sold to the Portuguese in Mozambique, he was transported from Africa to the Far East as human cargo. At some point he became the property of Alessandro Valignano, an ambitious young Jesuit missionary from the Kingdom of Naples. When Oda Nobunaga granted Valignano an audience on April 6, 1581, the missionary brought the African along. By the time the meeting was over, the slave had become Nobunaga's charge. Had that been Valignano's intention all along? Or did the African so intrigue Nobunaga that he demanded Valignano hand him over?

He was a large man by Japanese standards (official records describe

Nobunaga in flames at Honnoji temple, by Yoshitoshi

him as being "roughly 26 or 27, with the strength of ten men, and a complexion as dark as an ox"). But Nobunaga ordered him stripped and scrubbed, to ensure that he hadn't been painted or dyed with pigment. Then, apparently satisfied, Nobunaga took him under his wing. In fact, he was soon made a vassal, quite a leap for someone whose status had been little more than disposable human property—and given the name Yasuke.

Cynics might frame his rise in stature as the result of Nobunaga's desire for a human pet. It's true that Yasuke wasn't precisely a free man, but then again, you could say the same thing about any of Nobunaga's retainers. And for the first time in a long time, Yasuke was being treated as a human being. Nobunaga's family seems to have taken to Yasuke as well; he was apparently a big hit with the children in particular, whom he gave piggyback rides on his broad shoulders and undoubtedly delighted at the dinner table with his inability to master chopsticks, preferring instead to eat with his hands.

Making a black man a vassal was extraordinary enough. But when Nobunaga rode off to do battle with archrival Takeda Shingen just over a year later, Yasuke rode alongside him in full combat regalia. For all intents and purposes, he had been made a

samurai (although likely one without any land or personal holdings).

Within a month, Nobunaga would be dead, felled by the forces of a turncoat. Of Yasuke's fate, no record remains. Legend has it that Mitsuhide turned him loose, declaring that dark-skinned people were akin to animals. If true, his underestimation of a man that Nobunaga saw fit to ride into battle alongside is another example of the short-sightedness that would cost Mitsuhide his own life just two weeks later. ✳

1582 A.D.

Name: **HATTORI HANZO**
服部半蔵

Birth-Death: 1542-1596
Occupation: Jonin (Master Ninja)
Cause of Death: Natural causes?
A.K.A.: Hattori Hanzo Masanari, Oni-Hanzo (Hanzo the Demon)
Preferred Weapon: Spear
Clan Affiliation: Iga
Existence: Confirmed

The Man

Over the years he's been portrayed as everything from a distinguished military advisor to a spymaster to the traditional black-clad, *shuriken*-flinging shadow assassin. Characters in countless Japanese comic books (*Path of the Assassin, Samurai Deeper Kyo*), television shows ("Shadow Warriors"), videogames ("Samurai Showdown," "Samurai Warriors"), and at least one American film (*Kill Bill*) carry his name. And muddying the waters even further, the name became a de facto title for a string of successors, some worthier than others. Will the real Hattori Hanzo please stand up?

The Moment of Glory

The most famous Hattori Hanzo is actually the second to bear the name: Hattori Hanzo Masanari, later known to friend and foe alike as Hanzo the Demon. Member of a legendary ninja family that ruled over the Iga clan, Hanzo was born and raised in Mikawa (currently Aichi prefecture), where his father commanded a garrison of ninja in the service of a young warlord named Tokugawa Ieyasu. At sixteen—an age when most modern young men are worrying about pimples and drivers licenses—Hanzo led a strike team of sixty ninja as they breached the massive stone walls of an enemy castle, and delivered the coup de grace to its master with his own hands. (Naruto Uzumaki, eat your heart out.) The act of leadership and courage formed the cornerstone of a lifelong friendship with the powerful warlord.

The relationship came in handy years later, when Ieyasu found his neck on the proverbial chopping block. Top warlord Oda Nobunaga's 1582 assassination threw the country into chaos and made his right-hand man Ieyasu a prime target, but the well-connected Hanzo quickly assembled a force of bodyguards from several ninja clans and spirited him to safety through

Shadow puppeteer of the Iga: Hanzo

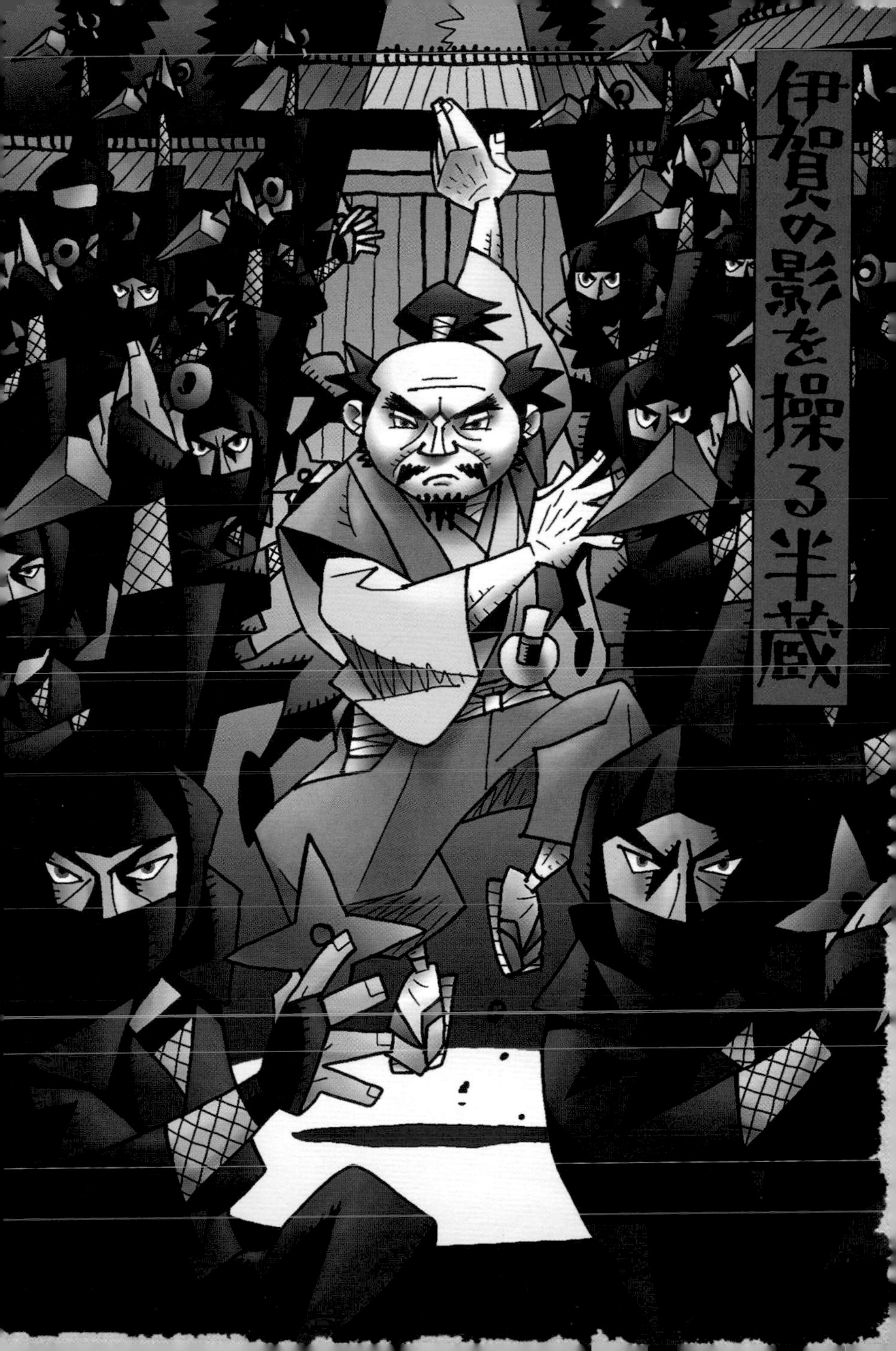
伊賀の影を操る半蔵

dangerous territory. Read more about it on page 107.

From then on, the ninja and the warlord were inseparable. With the financial backing of his new ally, Hanzo armed a crew of three hundred of his already well trained men with state-of-the art flintlock rifles, transforming them from ordinary ninja into the medieval Japanese equivalent of a Special Forces unit.

ON STRIKE:
The Wayward Son of a Ninja
Hanzo's first son, also named Masanari, turned out to be less than a chip off the old block. Although neither trained in *ninjutsu* nor apparently possessing much in the way of leadership qualities, he inherited the Iga ninja strike force that his father had so carefully cultivated. Demanding personal loans and forcing them to repaint his mansion while making crude passes at their wives, Masanari quickly earned the enmity of his men.

After years of abuse, in 1605 the entire ninja garrison barricaded themselves in a nearby temple, and refused to leave until they had Masanari's dismissal or his head. The shogun obliged with the former, and Masanari was officially out of a job. (That he didn't simply have a fatal "accident" somewhere along the way is undoubtedly thanks to his being married to a niece of the shogun.) Historians consider the incident to be Japan's first labor strike. Sasadera temple, where they made their stand, remains in Tokyo's Yotsuya to this very day.

These relentless soldier-assassins wiped out most of Ieyasu's rivals both on and off the battlefield, cementing their commander Hattori Hanzo's reputation as "the Demon"—the undisputed top ninja in all of Japan.

Off the battlefield, the realities of his day-to-day life were

closer to spymaster and master military strategist than a black-clad assassin sneaking along rooftops (which is precisely why the only surviving portrait of Hanzo shows him clad in samurai armor).

Disarming the Demon
In a famous 1579 incident, byzantine medieval politics led Oda Nobunaga to accuse Tokugawa Ieyasu's wife and son of con-

spiring against him. Forced to make a choice between the lives of his loved ones and the utter destruction of his entire family line, Ieyasu ordered the execution of his wife and the *seppuku*, or ritual suicide by disembowelment, of his son. He asked his trusted servant Hanzo to take up his sword as *kaishakunin*—an official "second" who quickly ends the agony of seppuku by beheading the individual. Hanzo found himself too choked up to perform the coup de grace, and an official observer stepped in to make the mercy cut. As the old Japanese saying goes, "even a demon can shed tears."

The End

Unfortunately, Hanzo died in 1596, a few short years before Ieyasu rose to ultimate power as shogun. According to one account, he collapsed while engaged in his favorite sport of falconry. The lack of hard evidence surrounding the details of his death has fueled centuries of overexcited speculation, and though it lacks any actual proof, one theory is such a great tale that we can't

THE ETERNAL HANZO

When Tokugawa Ieyasu moved his base of operations to Edo in 1590, Hanzo followed. The estate Ieyasu bestowed upon Hanzo and the Iga clan faced a palace gate that came to be called Hanzomon—Hanzo's Gate. Now a part of the imperial palace grounds, the gate still stands today. When you ride the Hanzomon subway line in Tokyo, you are indirectly partaking of the legend of this ninja master.

resist spinning it again.

Ieyasu, the story goes, ordered Hanzo and his men to take to the sea and wipe out the forces of another famous ninja, Fuma Kotaro. Fuma learned of the plot and sent snorkel-wearing ninja frogmen and—oh, if only it were true— ninja submarines to disable all of the ninja master's boats. Rudderless and adrift, Hanzo and his men were immolated when Fuma spread an oil slick and set it alight. Or so the story goes.

Hattori's remains are interred at Sainenji temple, near Tokyo's Yotsuya Station, where a helmet and one of his trademark spears are displayed near his gravestone. However he may have died, one thing is certain: without the help of Hanzo and his ninja, Tokugawa Ieyasu would never have lived to establish the shogunate, and Japan would now be a very different place. ✳

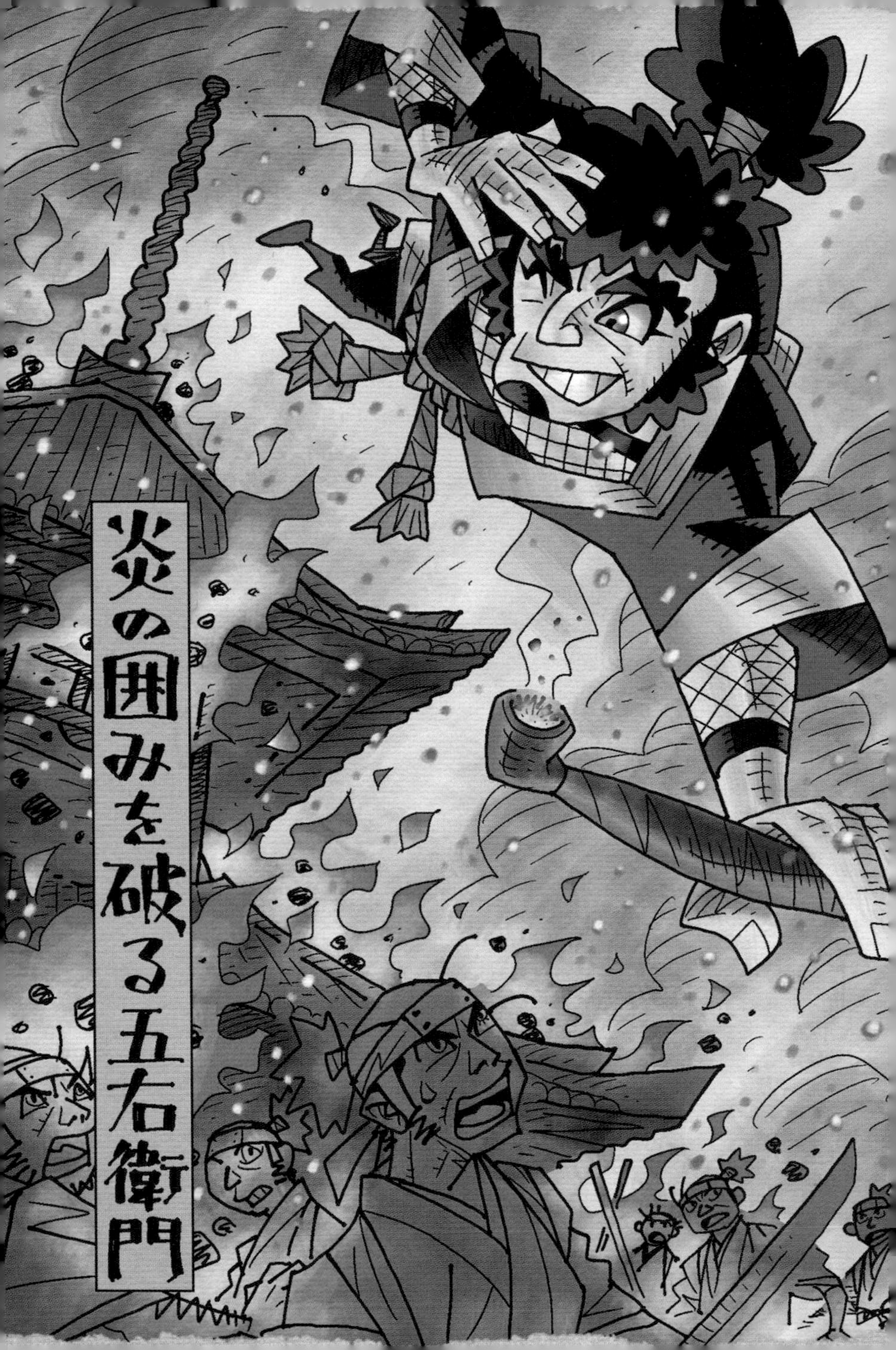
炎の囲みを破る五右衛門

1594 A.D.

Name: **ISHIKAWA GOEMON**
石川五右衛門

Birth-Death: Unknown–1594

Occupation: Nuke-nin (fallen ninja) and thief

Clan Affiliation: None (formerly Iga)

Cause of Death: Execution

A.K.A.: Sanada Hachiro
Ishikawa Bungo (in Kabuki)
Ixicava Goyemon (in Latin)
Simply "Goemon"

Hobbies: Robbin' and stealin'

Preferred Weapon: "The five-fingered discount"

Existence: Confirmed

> **ONLY THE FINE LINE OF DISCIPLINE SEPARATES NINJA FROM THIEF.**
> –From the <u>Mansen Shukai</u> ("All Rivers Flow to the Sea") Iga ninja manual (1676)

The Man

A pop cultural star since before America elected a man named George Washington as its president, Goemon has appeared in virtually every form of entertainment Japan has to offer, from kabuki plays to books to films to anime and manga to video games.

The real Goemon trained under Momochi Sandayu, alias of legendary Iga clan leader Momochi Tanba. The chance to study with the head of the clan must have been quite an honor.

Perhaps Goemon was but one of a larger class of select students; or perhaps Momochi took the young Goemon under his wing because he saw something special in the boy. Whatever the case, Goemon obviously showed potential from a young age.

Oda Nobunaga's invasion of Iga put an effective end to the clan in 1581, scattering its handful of surviving ninja far and wide. Eluding "mop-up crews" charged with hunting down and killing Iga survivors, Goemon fled to the distant province of Kii—what is today known as Wakayama prefecture—taking refuge in Negoroji temple.

Not your average Buddhist temple, Negoroji was home to the Negoro-gumi, an order of warrior monks feared for their skill with firearms. Devoting far more time to gunsmithing and marksmanship than prayer, and reportedly more than a little fond of wine, women, and song, the Negoro-gumi were closer to a special forces unit than a

Escaping the inferno: Goemon

101

cloister of holy men. Armed with their high-tech flintlock weapons and a "train hard, play harder" ethic, the monks must have seemed larger than life to the young Goemon, who had spent his entire life in a remote mountain village. But the fun wouldn't last long.

The Negoro-gumi's "live free or die" philosophy represented a throbbing thorn in the side of the warlords attempting to unify Japan at the time. In 1585, just four years after Goemon's escape from Iga, Nobunaga's successor Toyotomi Hideyoshi launched an all-out assault on Negoroji, setting the temple afire in an attempt to rid himself of the threat the monks posed to his ambitions.

Most had already fled (and would later get their revenge on the battlefield of Sekigahara in 1600, shredding Hideyoshi's forces for Tokugawa Ieyasu), but Goemon happened to be at the temple at the time of the attack. Trapped by the blaze, he shimmied up the temple spire—a height of some 37 meters—and leapt into the forest below. The sight of the young ninja, silhouetted against the flames as he dropped more than ten stories to earth, would have been a breathtaking sight if any had seen it. But his training served him well, and he scampered into the darkness of the mountains completely undetected.

DEATH NOTICE

The circumstances of Goemon's death are historical fact. Although no mention of his name remains in official Japanese records, a Jesuit missionary named Pedro de Morejon recorded in his diary that a man named "Ixicava Goyemon" was boiled alive in oil along with several cohorts.

The Moment of Glory

By the late 1580s, and understandably more than a little fed up with the authorities, Goemon set up shop in the capital of Kyoto. By day he put on the airs of a wealthy daimyo, building an opulent mansion and travelling by palanquin. He was constantly accompanied by a retinue of underlings armed with swords, spears, and muskets, the medieval equivalent of a gangster rapper's posse. He funded the lavish lifestyle with nights spent burgling the homes of the wealthy and by running a school-cum-recruiting-scheme for budding criminals, with instruction tailored to the age and abilities of the student—the very youngest being trained as pickpockets.

Putting one's skills to work for personal gain is a serious no-no in the ninja world. But given the general lawlessness of the era, it's hard to argue that the career move was a bad choice. Had he played his hand quietly, he undoubtedly would have prospered for decades in the shadows. But the quiet life wasn't Goemon's style.

He decided to take down his old nemesis Hideyoshi, who had by this point successfully unified the entire country under his armored fist. Why throw away a life of luxury on such a suicidal mission? Maybe revenge. Maybe money. Or maybe just for the sheer thrill of it. Having reached the top of the ninja and criminal worlds, Goemon may well have been tempted by the challenge.

The End

Born a poor farmer's son, Hideyoshi had clawed his way to the top by sheer willpower, surviving decades of bloody battlefield action and equally bloody political intrigue. Yet it appears he survived Goemon's assassination attempt by sheer luck. After Goemon infiltrated the castle

and made his way into Hideyoshi's bedroom late at night—no mean feat—he accidentally knocked a bell off a table in the darkness, alerting Hideyoshi's guards. (In another version of the story, a bird-shaped incense burner inexplicably began chirping to alert its master.) Captured and sentenced to die along with his entire family and much of his gang, Goemon and company were boiled alive in iron cauldrons filled with oil. To this very day, barrel-shaped one-person tubs are called Goemon-buro ("Goemon baths") in Japan.

Just before his execution, Goemon lashed back at Hideyoshi. "You're the true king of the thieves! You stole the whole damn country!" ✳

Detail of a woodblock print showing Goemon and his son being boiled alive

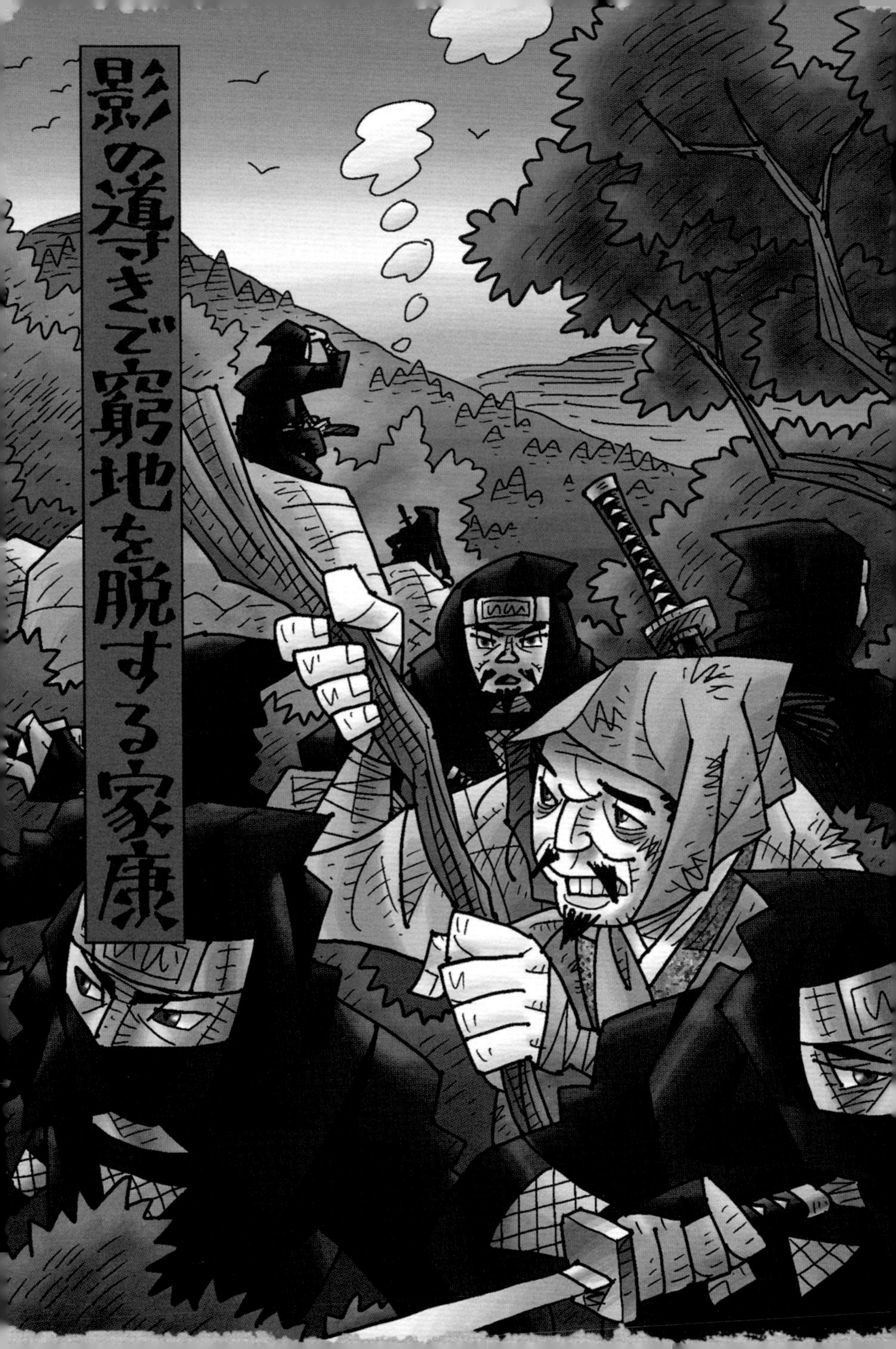
影の導きで窮地を脱する家康

1600 A.D.

Name: **TOKUGAWA IEYASU**
徳川家康

Birth/Death: 1543-1616

Occupation: Shogun

Duration of Reign: 1603-1605

Cause of Death: Natural causes

A.K.A.: Tokugawa Iyeyasu
(alternate romanization)
Matsudaira Takechiyo
(childhood name)
Jirosaburo (nickname)
Matsudaira Motoyasu

Known Associates: Hattori Hanzo

Hobbies: Watching and waiting

Preferred Weapon: See "Known Associates"

Existence: Confirmed

FAMILY CREST:

The Man

It is tempting to call Tokugawa Ieyasu the luckiest man in Japanese history. Simply tallying the episodes in which he should well have been killed in one intrigue or another, in this battle or that, could fill a book. But "lucky" doesn't do justice to a man with the heart of a warrior and a mind as sly as a fox. In the era of constant warfare in which Ieyasu lived, few survived long enough to enjoy a quiet death of old age. That Tokugawa

Ieyasu did—and became shogun of all Japan along the way—is due in no small part to his shrewd use of ninja.

Born Matsudaira Takechiyo, he spent much of his childhood with his head on the proverbial chopping block as a hostage, a pawn in political games playing out between rival warlords. (In keeping with custom at the time, he was well treated and even given a proper education by his captors.) Repatriated to his homeland of Mikawa as a young man, he quickly proved himself a capable military commander.

He first made use of ninja at the age of 21, leading a siege against nearby Kaminogo castle. The enemy had holed up so effectively that a direct attack would have cost the lives of far too many of his own men. The young Ieyasu turned to a trusted advisor, who suggested sending a request for assistance to his contacts in Koga. Before long, a pair of ninja commanders named Banyo Shichiro and Ukai Magoroku, leading a company of some 280 *genin* foot soldiers, arrived on the scene. Late one night, they

Taking a path of shadow through a crisis: Ieyasu

split their men into teams that silently infiltrated the castle's walls, setting fires, slitting a few throats, and throwing the defenders into utter chaos. A potential bloodbath had been transformed into a simple mop-up operation by the ninja, leaving a deep impression on the young leader; it wouldn't be the last time Ieyasu called upon their services.

Pragmatic and calculating, it was always business and never personal with Ieyasu. He weighed every potential alliance carefully, and once even sacrificed the lives of his own wife and son in the interest of living to fight another day. He served those to whom he pledged allegiance, such as Oda Nobunaga and Toyotomi Hideyoshi, with great loyalty. But this shrewd tactician wasn't content to spend his life in the shadow of great men; he was patiently biding his time, determined to become one himself.

The Moment of Glory

Ieyasu's shining moment came on a fall morning in 1600, on a battlefield called Sekigahara. More than eighty thousand of his troops had squared off against those of his rival, Ishida Mitsunari. That the stakes were high was putting it mildly. The fate of the entire country hung in the balance.

Although the forces were evenly matched and Ishida held the tactical high ground, Ieyasu's masterful use of intelligence (swordsman Yagyu Munenori, father of Jubei, funneled reports on Ishida's organization to Ieyasu before and during the battle), counter-intelligence (Ieyasu sent messages behind enemy lines promising riches to any commanders who switched sides), and military technology (in the form of Iga, Koga, and Negoro "shock troops" armed with flintlock rifles) quickly turned the tide to his favor. By the end of the day, he had secured victory—and paved the way for him to become shogun three years later. Ieyasu's success was due in no small part to bringing the entirety of his nation's espionage capabilities to bear.

But on a personal level, an incident close to two decades earlier highlights just how deep his connections to the ninja world ran. In June of 1582, the death of Oda Nobunaga during a coup d'etat threw the nation into chaos. Ieyasu found himself in the crosshairs of potential assassins, both professional and civilian; as one of Nobunaga's closest allies, his head represented a prime opportunity for anyone looking to curry favor with the usurpers. Trapped out in the open along with his retinue, he initially contemplated suicide rather than suffering the dishonor of falling into enemy hands, but was convinced to try returning to his home base in Mikawa.

Using major roads would have been suicidal. Fortunately, Ieyasu had an acquaintance with a few tricks up his sleeve: Hattori Hanzo, who enlisted the services of several hundred Iga and Koga footsoldiers as bodyguards. Their successful flight through Iga's rugged mountain passes, known as "Iga-goé," is the stuff of legend in Japan, akin to Paul Revere's midnight ride or Washington's crossing of the Potomac in American historical lore.

The End

The post-Sekigahara years were kind to the Tokugawa clan. By 1601, some 26 percent of Japan's entire tax revenue went directly to the Tokugawa family and its vassals. In 1603, the emperor bestowed the title of shogun upon Ieyasu, establishing a dynasty that would continue to rule Japan for the next two centuries.

Ieyasu officially ceded power to a son in 1605, both to better rule from behind the scenes and to establish a clear line of authority and succession for his family line. Ieyasu died of natural causes in 1616, for reasons not entirely agreed upon by historical records: some claim illness from spending too much time outdoors with his beloved falcons in the winter; others suggest food poisoning, possibly from tempura; and a few even claim syphilis. One thing is certain: his deft use of ninja over the years played no small part in his avoiding the violent end of many of his fellow warlords. ✳

The Illustrated Ninja
Tools

The six tools of the ninja

A ninja wouldn't be caught alive *or* dead without these handy implements. They were first grouped and described in a 1681 book called *Shoninki* ("A Record of Proper Ninjutsu").

1) Kagi-nawa

The sheer utility of a rope with attached grappling hook outweighed the potential difficulties of trying to explain why one was carrying it if caught.

2) Kasa

A conical straw hat. Used as a sunshade and umbrella throughout Japan at the time, clever ninja armorers often concealed flat blades or arrows along its ribs.

3) Chalk

Used to leave discreet, easily erased messages for fellow ninja along one's path. A standard brush-and-ink set was often carried as well for normal writing needs.

4) Tinderbox

Similar to modern-day matches or lighters, these portable tinderboxes were used for all sorts of purposes, from starting a cooking fire to lighting a matchlock rifle's fuse.

5) Tenugui

Long before *The Hitchhiker's Guide to the Galaxy* recommended them for space-travelers, ninja realized the versatility of the humble towel.

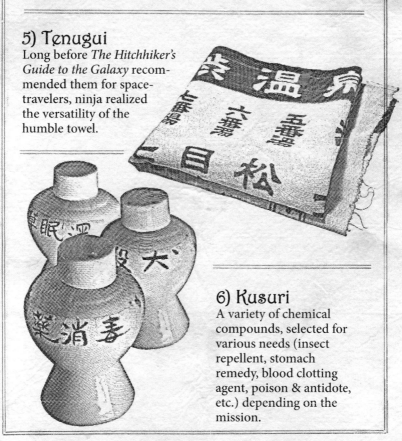

6) Kusuri

A variety of chemical compounds, selected for various needs (insect repellent, stomach remedy, blood clotting agent, poison & antidote, etc.) depending on the mission.

OTHER TOOLS OF THE TRADE

Kunai
A standard field knife. Intended mainly for everyday cutting, scraping, and digging tasks, but can be thrown in a pinch.

Goshiki-mai
These dyed rice grains were used to create discreet trails that could be followed either by the original dropper or by sharp-eyed comrades following behind.

Gandou
A portable lantern using a bucket to focus the feeble illumination of a candle's flame. An ingenious gyroscopic device kept the candle upright no matter the orientation of the bucket—even if hastily placed mouth-down to hide the light.

Michi-hakari (not shown)
A measuring stick allowing a ninja to determine precise distances —often quite useful information for planning an attack.

ADVANCED TOOLS

Shikomi

Airline security may seem like a hassle now, but it was nothing compared to the difficulties encountered by travelers in medieval Japan, who were subject to questioning at any time. Ninja (and other enterprising sorts) occasionally "gimmicked" otherwise innocent-looking items with concealed weapons.

These included (but certainly weren't limited to) items such as swords that appeared to be nothing more than simple walking sticks; wooden or bamboo staffs that were hollowed out and fitted with hidden chains, weighted balls, or blinding powders; flutes that doubled as blowguns; straw hats that concealed blades; and smoking sets that were filled with pepper or other irritants instead of tobacco, which could then be blown or hurled at an opponent.

BREAKING AND ENTERING

Shikoro

A serrated version of the standard *kunai* knife. The curved edge of this tool allowed the user to saw through flat surfaces without needing a starting hole. Folding saws called *hamagari* were used as well.

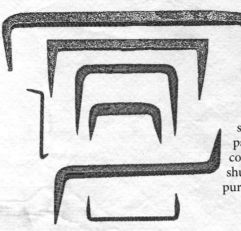

Kasugai

Anchors of a variety of shapes and sizes were inserted into cracks to create handholds on cliff faces or man-made structures such as ramparts or buildings. They could also be used to jam shut doors to delay pursuers.

Tsubo-kiri

This distinctive-looking tool was used like a corkscrew to drill starter openings in walls. The holes would then be widened with *shikoro* or other implements. They were also useful for opening doors locked from within by creating a hole through which the locks could be unlatched by hand.

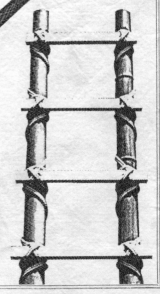

Musubi-hashi, tobi-hashi, uki-hashi

Lightweight ladders made out of bamboo were invaluable tools for scaling walls and other obstacles. *Musubi-hashi* featured a typical construction. *Tobi-hashi* were simple affairs consisting of steps tied to a single pole. *Uki-hashi* were rope ladders designed to be pulled taut across bodies of water as makeshift bridges.

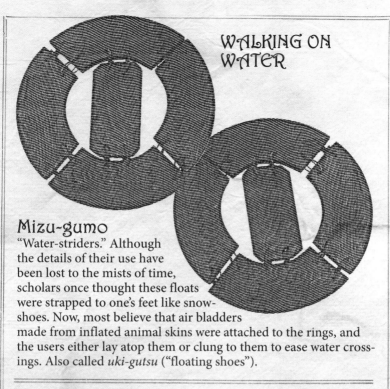

WALKING ON WATER

Mizu-gumo

"Water-striders." Although the details of their use have been lost to the mists of time, scholars once thought these floats were strapped to one's feet like snowshoes. Now, most believe that air bladders made from inflated animal skins were attached to the rings, and the users either lay atop them or clung to them to ease water crossings. Also called *uki-gutsu* ("floating shoes").

Mizugaki

Wooden geta sandals with an angled board extending from their soles, designed to assist the wearer in crossing mucky areas.

Kamei-gata (not shown)

A quick-to-prepare raft made from a bamboo frame over empty clay jars for buoyancy.

THE HIGHER THE WALL

A great many ninja techniques and tools were created to breach Japanese castles—elaborate fortresses constructed from wood and stone atop strategically favorable terrain. The easiest way, of course, was to waltz right in through the front gate undetected, preferably disguised as someone on an official errand of some sort, or barring that, concealed within some sort of cargo being brought inside. But for situations in which time was of the essence, a more direct approach was sometimes necessary.

The first step was scaling the castle's soaring stone base, a steeply sloping structure built from tightly interlocking boulders. In fact, these imposing fortifications were actually nicknamed *musha-gaeshi* (warrior-stopper). Created from interlocking boulders that were carefully cut and fit into place by specialists, and often further surrounded by wide moats for additional protection, they resisted any conventional attack of the time. Yet they also provided numerous finger- and toe-holds for enterprising sorts to attempt climbing them by hand. Tools such as *shikoro*, *kunai*, and *kasugai* (see previous pages) were used as makeshift shims in cases where cracks were too small to work fingers or toes into.

TRANSFORMATIONS: 1600–1860

A period of rapid change for the ninja.

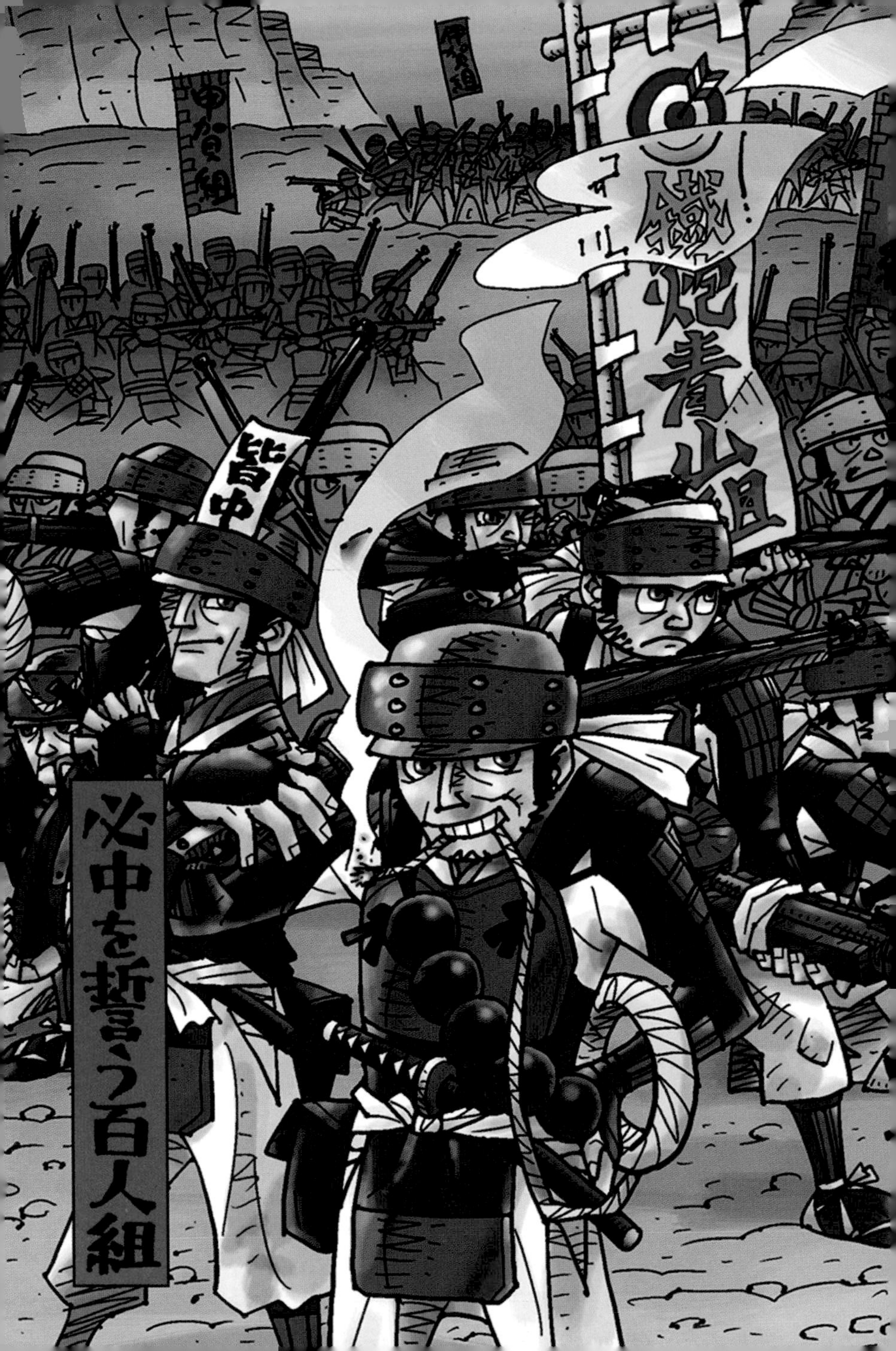
必中を誓う百人組
鐵炮青山組
皆中
甲賀組

1600 A.D.

Name: **HYAKUNIN GUMI**
百人組

First Organized: 1590

Officially Disbanded: 1862

Formed of: Aoyama Gumi Mounted Company
Iga (Okubo) Gumi Rifle Company
Negoro Gumi Rifle Company
Koga Gumi Rifle Company

A.K.A.: "Hundreds Battalion" (English translation)
"The Shogun's Artillery Guard"
Teppo Hyakunin Gumi

Mission: protecting the Shogun
policing Edo (Tokyo)

Headquartered: Edo Castle Grounds

Preferred Weapon: Tanegashima (Flintlock rifle)

Clan Affiliation: Iga / Koga / Negoro mixed

Hobbies: Shooting practice, presumably

Existence: Confirmed Historical Fact

The Battalion

The Hyakunin Gumi was a fighting force composed of ninja from clans across Japan. This may sound like the plot to some B-grade martial arts flick, but it is 100% unvarnished truth. Trust us, these were guys you didn't want to mess with, either on the battlefield or on the streets of Edo.

Its origins date back to the 1582 *Iga-Goe* ("Iga Escape") in which the legendary Hattori Hanzo recruited a team of top Iga and Koga ninja to spirit warlord Tokugawa Ieyasu to safety through enemy territory. Impressed by the resourcefulness of Hattori and his men, Tokugawa retained them as permanent military advisors and bodyguards.

After taking up residence in Edo in 1590, Tokugawa re-organized Hattori's ad-hoc crew into the equivalent of a "special forces" team. Equipping the men with state of the art matchlock rifles, he christened them the Hyakunin Gumi (the "Hundreds Battalion"). If you needed any further evidence that ninja had no qualms about using firearms, this is it.

Organizationally, the Hyakunin Gumi was exactly what the

name implies: a battalion composed of four smaller companies of a hundred riflemen each. The majority were footsoldiers, but at least one company, the Aoyama, consisted of horse-mounted cavalry.

In 1600, the Hyakunin Gumi made their official debut at the pivotal Battle of Sekigahara, where they all but wiped Tokugawa's enemy off the map. After Tokugawa's rise to power as Shogun the following year, they served as castle guards and the equivalent of a secret service, eventually morphing into a police-like organization that ruled over the city for the next two and a half centuries.

The Hyakunin Gumi's transition from stereotypical mercenary-for-hire, to army, to city defense force is a perfect illustration of the changing role of the ninja in Japanese politics from the 15th through the 19th centuries. But while they lasted, they ranked as the single most potent fighting force in all of Japan.

The Moment of Glory

It's hard to pick from a list of "greatest hits." Was it the 1582 escape from Iga they engineered for Tokugawa? The 1600 Battle of Sekigahara? Or was it the quarter-millennium of faithful service and protection they gave the Shoguns and the capitol city?

The End

Ironically, the rise of the Hyakunin Gumi as protectors of the Shogun paralleled an equal decline in their modus operandi as "traditional" ninja.

No longer mercenary outsiders, the former ninja enjoyed an elite status within the Edo social hierarchy. But with this respect and "mainstreaming" came rules, discouraging the innovating culture of ninja tactics that had brought them there. The need for "ninja skills" rapidly dwindled in the relative peace that followed Tokugawa Ieyasu's rise to power, fueling the Hyakunin Gumi's rapid transformation from tactical shinobi strike-teams into strategically deployed conventional soldiers.

Hyakunincho, Tokyo

One of the main areas in which the Hyakunin Gumi troops were headquartered still bears their name today: the Hyakunincho ("Hundreds Town") neighborhood. Located just outside of Shin-Okubo station, one stop from Shinjuku, it is well known as the city's Koreatown today. A large wall mural of a Hyakunin Gumi battalion just outside the train station gates marks the spot.

Besides the name and the mural, there is another aspect of the neighborhood's design that could be called "ninja-influenced." The area was laid out in long, narrow blocks and streets very unlike those in the rest of the city. This layout served two purposes: it accommodated the shape of practice firing ranges, and also potentially hindered incoming enemy soldiers.

And you can actually see the Hyakunin Gumi in action today! A group of local re-enactors calling themselves the *Edo Bakufu Teppo Gumi Hyakunin-tai* (try saying *that* five times fast) holds regular demonstrations of flintlock rifles while dressed in period costumes. Their website can be found at: www.edo-hinawa.com

Escape from Edo

The Hyakunin Gumi didn't just protect the capitol city's (martial) law and order. They served as personal bodyguards for the Shogun himself.

The Tokugawa shoguns lived within a massive castle in the city center (so heavily defended that its moats and other fortifications remain to this very day). But in the unlikely event of a successful attack or invasion, the Hyakunin Gumi were under orders to shift from offense to defense and spirit their ruler to safety outside of the city.

The escape route followed major roads that are still in use today. It involved falling back through the rearward-facing west gate of the castle (not coincidentally called Hanzomon, or Hanzo's gate, named after the Hyakunin Gumi founder Hattori Hanzo). The "convoy" would then proceed down Koshu Kaido through the Shinjuku area and out of the city, eventually reaching Kofu Castle (a.k.a. Maizuru Castle) in what is now Yamanashi prefecture.

Although abandoned in the late 1800s after being ravaged by fires and other mishaps, the castle ruins were turned into a park in the 20th century. Maizuru Castle park remains a popular tourist attraction today, just a five-minute walk from JR Kofu Station.

The reason for picking Kofu Castle was its situation in the midst of a mountain range, giving defenders a tremendous advantage from the terrain. Not coincidentally, prior to the Edo era the castle was occupied by the area's former warlord Takeda Shingen (see p. 70), who was no stranger to ninja tactics himself.

1603 A.D.

Name: **KOSAKA JINNAI**

高坂甚内

Birth–Death: Unknown–1613

Occupation: Suppa

Cause of Death: Execution

A.K.A.: Sakisaka Jinnai (alternate reading of kanji)

Preferred Weapon: The snitch

Clan Affiliation: Takeda Shingen

Existence: Confirmed

The Man

The year was 1600.

Kosaka Jinnai took stock of his situation with a dispassionate clarity born of decades of ninja training. Recruited as a young ruffian scratching out a living shaking down travelers for money, he had been schooled as a *suppa*, an agent in the secret service of warlord Takeda Shingen. In the two decades since his master's untimely death and the resulting annihilation of his clan, Jinnai had found himself reduced to little more than a common mercenary, selling his skills to whoever was willing to pay for them. But Tokugawa Ieyasu's decisive victory at the battle of Sekigahara had silenced a century and a half of bloody strife among the warlords to determine who would rule Japan once and for all.

The unification of Japan under a single all-powerful shogun promised desperately needed stability for its long-suffering citizens. But ninja are products of their environment, and faced with the decidedly unsettling prospect of an era of peace, one can forgive even a normally unflappable ninja for entertaining some trepidation about his future.

One thing was for sure. Now that Ieyasu was in charge, things would be happening in the shogun's little castle town up north. Jinnai made the move to Edo.

The Moment of Glory

The year was 1603.

The moment he had arrived in Edo, Jinnai knew he'd found his new home. The rapidly growing city was a jewel in the rough with a multitude of opportunities for a man of his unique skill set. Pickpocketing. Robbery. Burglary. Even the occasional murder for hire. So many opportunities, in fact, that he had to start hiring help. Recruiting a crew of reliable footsoldiers from his fellow former ninja, he built an organization that began

Laid low by illness: Jinnai

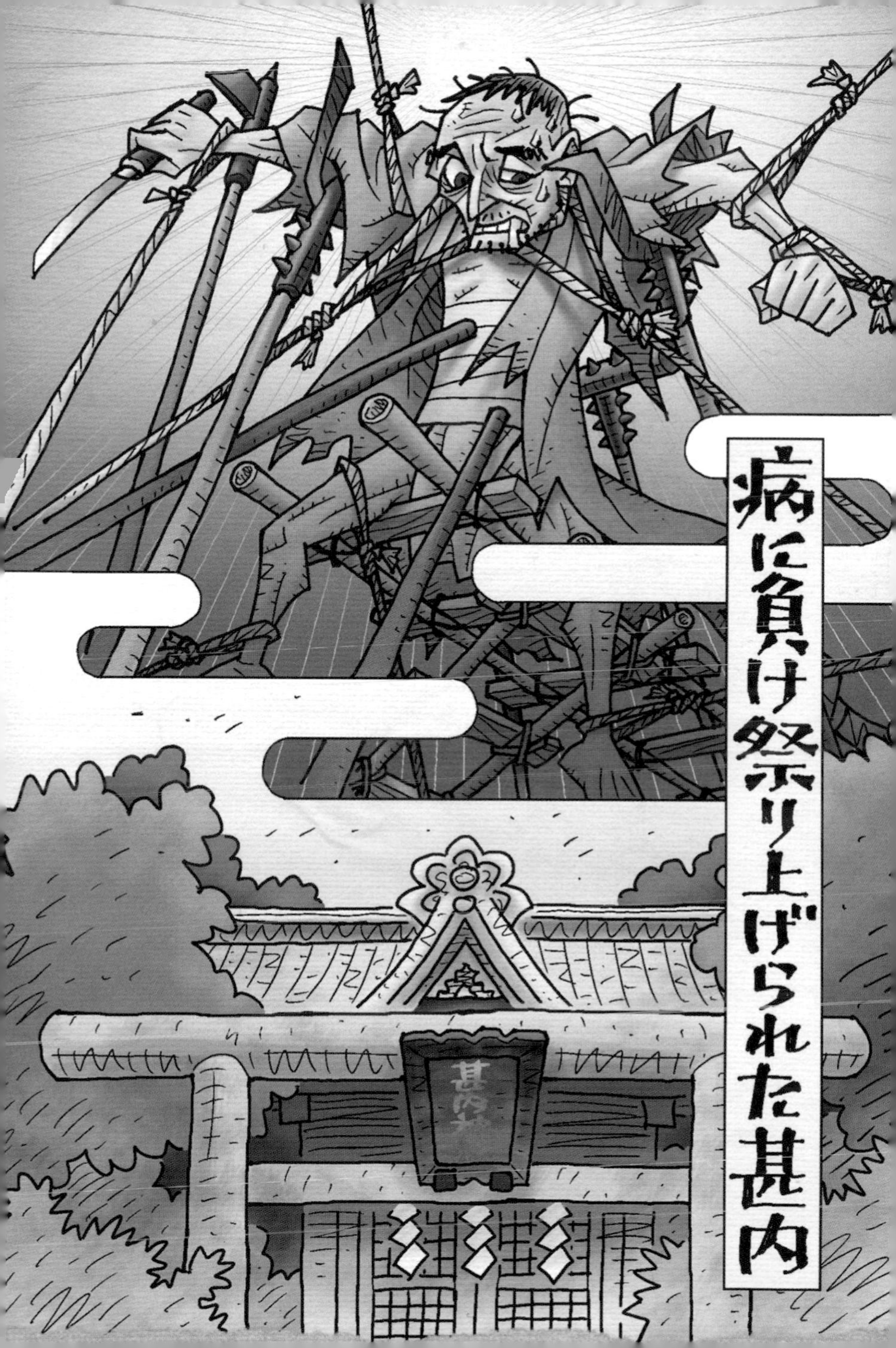
病に負け祭り上げられた甚内

generating riches of the sort he'd only dreamed of during the lean years.

Until that bastard Fuma Kotaro had moved into town, that is. Jinnai knew him well: Fuma's crew of *rappa* ninja foot soldiers had wiped out an entire company of Jinnai's comrades at the battle of Ukishima-ga-hara in 1581. Apparently Fuma had also seen potential in Edo, for he arrived in town with his own crew, setting up shop right under Jinnai's nose, moving in on the same rackets and cutting into profits.

A turf war between two gangs of former ninja would be like another Sekigahara in the streets of Edo. But the crafty Jinnai had a better plan. Infuriated at the crime wave spreading through his fledgling city, the shogun declared a reward of 70 *oban*, "gold plates," to any with information about criminal activities. Jinnai boldly appeared before the authorities, describing an organization the likes of which had never been seen in Edo or anywhere else: some one hundred, one thousand . . . no! Two thousand men strong, immoral beasts run by an incorrigible former rappa by the name of Fuma Kotaro. In the interest of public safety, Jinnai said,

he would be more than happy to show the men of the law where the scalawag prepared for his next foul deed.

Jinnai barely stifled a grin as he watched the resulting raid from a safe remove in the shadows. It didn't take long for the authorities to round up the rappa and pronounce Fuma's inevitable death sentence. The streets were Kosaka Jinnai's once again.

The End

The year was 1608.

The years after Fuma's execution were good. Jinnai took control of the Edo underworld, purchasing an opulent mansion in Akasaka and living like a warlord of old.

But then everything fell apart. A second crackdown netted many of his foot soldiers, who promptly gave up his name under torture. Before long, he found a price on his head. And then came the vicious cycle of sweats and chills: malaria's unmistakable embrace. The shogun's raids robbed his organization of its vitality, while infection robbed him of his. Unable to keep up the delicate dance with the law he'd maintained for so many years, Jinnai was

SWORD SCUTTLEBUTT
According to popular rumor, Jinnai studied swordsmanship for a time under Miyamoto Musashi, but most historians refute the idea as wishful thinking. The spread of the rumor can be seen as a testament to Jinnai's skill with the blade.

captured and sentenced.

On the killing grounds shortly thereafter, he was asked for his last words.

Dazed by fever, he had a sudden inspiration. What better way to stick it to the man than by styling himself as a folk hero?

"You never would have caught me but for the malaria," he said. "Tell those who suffer from it to suffer a thought for Kosaka Jinnai as well, and they shall be cured."

The executioner nodded to the rider atop the horse. Jinnai's ankles had been attached to the saddle by a chain.

Perfectly aware of what was in store, Jinnai undoubtedly prayed without much real hope that he would lose consciousness when the animal yanked him off his feet. Dragged through the streets of the city until the skin was all but flayed off his body, then nailed to a pole, and finally disemboweled with a pair of spears as an open warning to other criminals, Jinnai's public execution served as a brutal counterpoint to his quiet rise to power.

Jinnai Shrine stands in the Asakusa section of Edo, now Tokyo, visited to this very day by those seeking relief from a variety of ailments. ✳

Jinnai Shrine and memorial stone

123

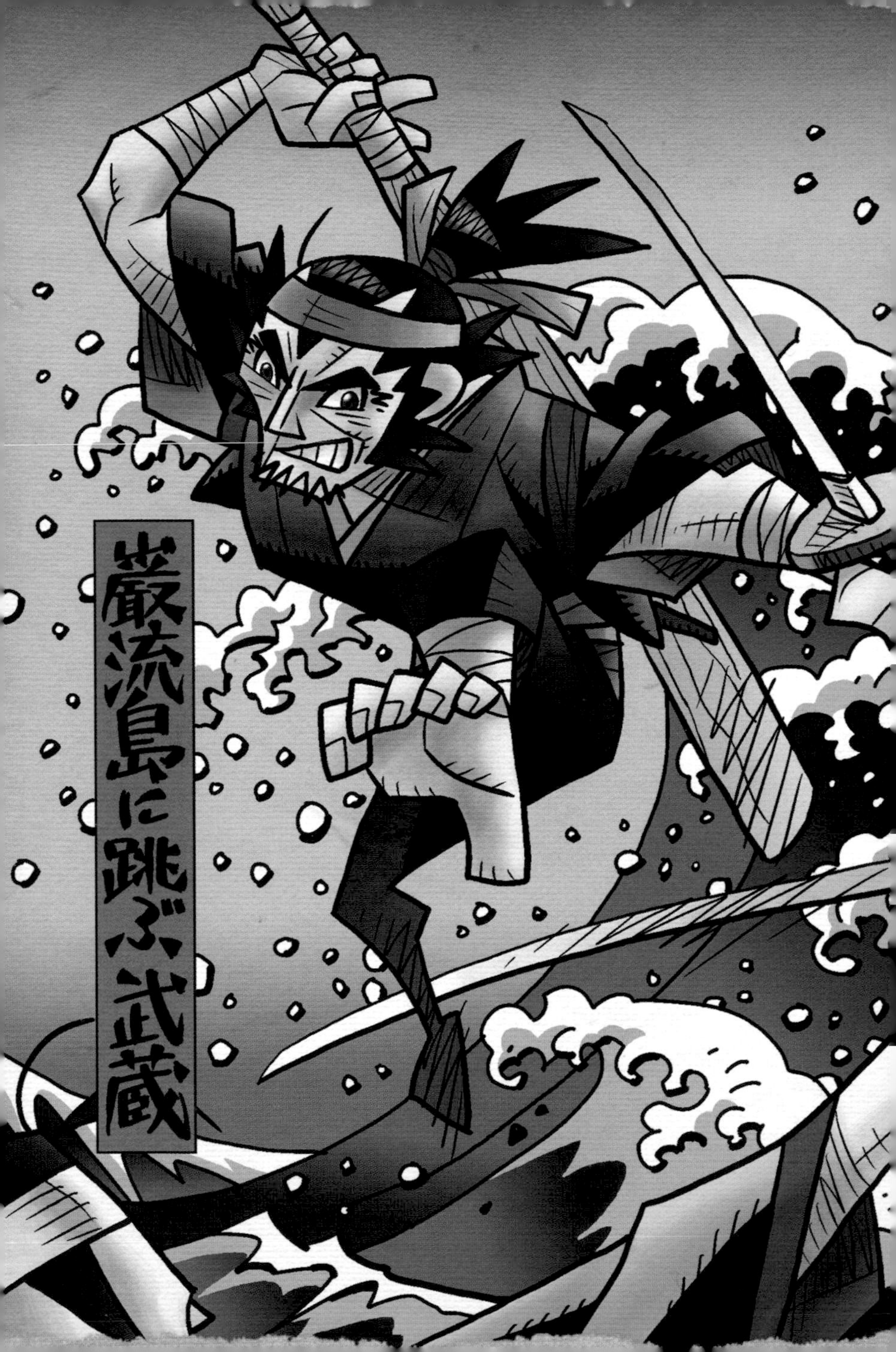
巌流島に跳ぶ武蔵

1612 A.D.

Name: **MIYAMOTO MUSASHI**

宮本武蔵

Birth/Death: 1584–1645

Cause of Death: Natural Causes

Occupation: Shugyosha (wandering swordsman)

A.K.A.: Bennosuke (during childhood) Shinmen Musashi no Kami Fujiwara no Genshin (full name as disclosed in the Book of Five Rings). Niten Doraku (pen name as painter/sculptor)

Preferred Weapon: Wooden sword

Clan Affiliation: N/A

Fighting Style: Niten Ichiryu ("Two Heavens, One Style")

Existence: Confirmed

← Although he is more commonly associated with the *nito-ryu* (two sword) technique, Musashi deliberately avoided relying on any one style of swordfighting

Prologue

Picture this: the year is 1597. Your name is Arima Kihei. You have no home, no possessions to speak of save for the clothing on your back and the pair of swords strapped to your waist. Your days are spent focused on a solitary purpose: seeking out martial artists—the more renowned the better—and killing them. You aren't a stalker or a serial killer. You are a *shugyosha*: a swordsman on a pilgrimage to test your skills in the only way

that truly matters.

It can be difficult to find new opponents. Sometimes you set up shop briefly in an out-of-the-way village, posting a sign on the footpath announcing your intentions to challenge any and all comers to a duel. One day, you notice that the sign you so carefully lettered appears to have been smeared over with sloppy graffiti. Looking more closely, you can make out the vandal's name: "Miyamoto Bennosuke will give you a match tomorrow."

Who the hell? These kanji characters look like they were slathered on by a child! Sure enough, when the rascal shows his face the next day, he turns out to be a teenager. You're unwilling to cut a child down in cold blood, but you can't let the insult go unaddressed, so you demand a formal apology. The public humiliation should be more than enough to teach the lad some manners.

But just when you expect a little groveling, the unrepentant rapscallion attacks. Before you

The Man

From humble beginnings, the untrained Musashi rose through decades of self-directed study and discipline to become the nation's top martial artist. His unwavering self-confidence, with or without his trademark twin swords—long-bladed *katana* in the right, short *wakizashi* in the left, an ambidextrous technique he perfected if not pioneered—has made him a favorite subject of storytellers. An unbeatable swordsman with the heart of a poet, Musashi is the quintessence of the Japanese warrior.

Musashi was an extraordinarily savvy tactician, winning some sixty duels against hardened combat veterans without formal training of any kind, often without a formal weapon.

Though he was not a ninja, his strategic use of psychological warfare to disrupt the concentration of his opponents is the stuff of legend. From simply forcing a foe to stand where the sun would dazzle their eyes, to aggravating those who had demanded duels by showing up far earlier or later than the scheduled time, to overwhelming opponents with the sheer aroma

can draw your sword and give the little scoundrel the comeuppance he so richly deserves, you've been knocked to the ground. By a thirteen-year-old! You're pondering how a fine swordsman such as yourself is going to live this one down when you catch a glimpse of the heavy wooden staff the boy is swinging down with all his might right between your eyes, and that's when it hits you: you won't. Congratulations. You're the first to fall victim to the young Miyamoto Musashi.

of his unwashed clothes and body, Musashi proved willing to use any and every tactic to throw enemies off their game.

The Moment of Glory

In a seventeenth-century equivalent of "turning on, tuning in, and dropping out," Musashi retreated to a remote cave to focus on meditation and committing his teachings to paper. The resulting 1645 treatise on swordsmanship, titled the *Book of Five Rings*, is his crowning achievement as a proponent of the martial arts. Even today, some three-and-a-half centuries later, it continues to inspire and is widely considered Japan's answer to Sun Tzu's *Art of War*.

The Ninja Connection

Given the weapon and the location of the duel, it is likely that Shishido, a *kusari-gama* (sickle and chain) specialist Musashi felled in Iga, was a ninja. Years later, Musashi also fought alongside ninja as a soldier in the siege of Osaka in 1614-1615. Special operations units composed of Iga and Koga ninja worked throughout the siege, at one point sneaking into the heavily fortified Osaka castle dressed in gear pilfered from fallen defenders so as to sow disinformation and discord among the enemy commanders. The castle fell in the summer of 1615.

The End

Musashi passed away shortly after handing the manuscript of his book to a trusted disciple, felled not by a sword or an arrow but rather cancer of the throat. He was 62, a ripe old age by the standards of the day, and particularly by the standards of a wandering swordsman—few of whom ever enjoyed the luxury of dying in their beds. ✳

A BRIEF RESUME

1597 Brains swordsman Arima Kihei with a wooden staff.

1604 Smashes martial-arts school headmaster Seijuro Yoshioka's skull with a wooden sword, crippling him.

1604 Clobbers Seijuro's brother, Denshichiro, with his own wooden sword.

1604 Cleaves Seijuro's son, Matashichiro, from shoulder to waist and slaughters dozens of his henchmen. Yoshioka martial arts school closes.

1607 Impales an Iga chain-and-sickle master named Shishido with a thrown wakizashi.

1608 Bludgeons a wandering swordsman named Gonnosuke with a piece of kindling plucked from the firewood pile.

1612 Caves in skull of legendary "Demon of the Western Provinces," Sasaki Kojiro, with a wooden sword carved from an oar.

1612 Professing that killing is no longer necessary to prove his skills, resolves to only "grievously wound" opponents henceforth.

1645 Pens "Book of Five Rings," his treatise on martial arts.

1615 A.D.

Name: **SANADA YUKIMURA**

真田幸村

Birth/Death: 1567–1615

Occupation: Sho-daimyo (minor warlord)

Location of Territory: Shinano

Cause of Death: Killed in Action

A.K.A.: Sanada Nobushige
Sanada Saemonnosuke Yukimura

Preferred Weapon: The psych-Out

Existence: Confirmed

FAMILY CREST:

The Man

It isn't about winning. It's about exacting a far higher price from your enemy than they ever expected to pay. And Sanada Yukimura was a master at it, becoming the proverbial fly in the ointment, the burr under the saddle, the pea under the mattress of his arch-enemy, Shogun Tokugawa Ieyasu.

Yukimura wasn't even a full-fledged warlord, but a sho-daimyo —literally, a "minor warlord." How did such a small fry become a thorn in the shogun's side? Because what Yukimura lacked in the size of his clan and territory he more than made up for with the ambitious scale of his ideas. He was a master of throwing more powerful opponents off their game—and he relied on a small but dedicated army of ninja to do it.

A David raging against the Goliath of the shogun's rule, Yukimura sifted through gathered intelligence for the tiniest nuggets of information to give him an advantage in the one goal upon which his entire existence was laser-focused: shattering Ieyasu's iron grip on the newly unified Japan. In other words, to quote the title of a rap song from more than three centuries later: fight the power!

The Moments of Glory

In Yukimura's hands, things were never quite what they seemed. Although not a ninja himself, his base in Shinano was home to many ninja, whose "micro" level one-on-one tactics of deception undoubtedly inspired many of Yukimura's "macro" strategies on the battlefield. His shining moments came during the siege of Osaka in 1614–1615, when his outnumbered troops joined forces with

Commander of shadow warriors: Yukimura

影武者たちと駆ける幸村

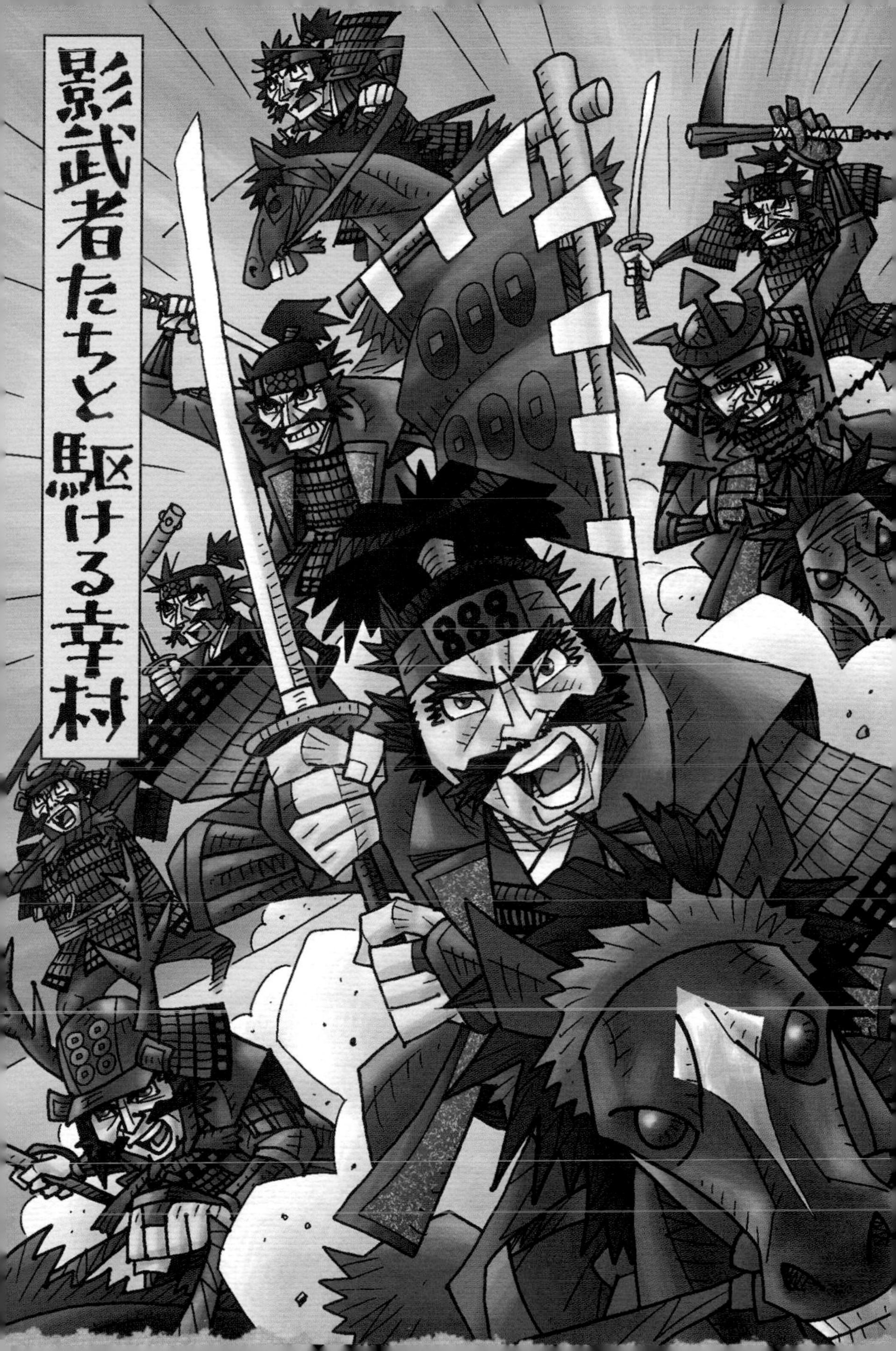

Never afraid of getting his hands dirty, Yukimura stalks his prey through a swamp in this 1872 print by Yoshitoshi.

Yukimura. Prepare to die!" bellowed another. And so on, until each of the seven had identified themselves, in official battlefield protocol, as the one and only Sanada Yukimura. Now this was a head-scratcher. Unsure of who to attack first, the shogun's men turned into sitting ducks for a volley of matchlock fire unleashed by the doppelgangers. It was a Yukimura psych-out at its finest, custom-engineered to give his far smaller army the advantage.

Once, realizing that the shogun's top four front-line field marshals inevitably wore crimson red armor, apparently to make themselves more visible to their troops, Yukimura outfitted his entire army in red armor as well. The simple act of their showing up on the battlefield not only threw enemy communications into disarray but made their leadership prime targets for friendly fire in the ensuing chaos.

And then there was the dreaded *dorenka*. After a hard day of skirmishing, the shogun's famished forces were preparing a long-postponed meal. Just as the food was about to be distributed, Yukimura's special forces launched the dorenka, a primitive artillery shell filled not with explosives but rather a

those of the Toyotomi clan to make a final stand against the shogun's authority.

Here's a classic case in point. Preparing to march, some 100,000 of the shogun's soldiers suddenly found themselves surrounded by seven far smaller contingents of Yukimura's. In front of each of the seven stood a field marshal resplendent in full battle dress. "I am Sanada Yukimura. Prepare to die!" shouted one. "I am Sanada horribly noxious substance. The vile airburst over the encampment all but incapacitated the shogun's troops, sending many into extended bouts of vomiting, knocking others unconscious from the sheer smell, and generally preventing anyone from taking in the nutrition and rest they so desperately needed.

That wasn't Yukimura's only foray into chemical warfare. While stuck inside his fortress during the siege of Osaka castle, his troops mixed their own excrement with chemicals and heated it to create a sticky substance that was hurled at advancing troops to sicken them (and anyone reading about it). The shogun's forces were quite literally in deep shit when dealing with these guys.

And how ninja-powered was Yukimura? At one point during the seige, he led a tiny contingent of forces in a surprise attempt to kill Tokugawa Ieyasu in his own encampment. He came so close to succeeding that the shogun actually began preparations to commit ritual suicide.

A LIFE IN POP CULTURE

The story of Sanada Juyushi, or "Sanada's Ten Heroes," is a fictional account of a Yukimura ninja squad first published in the early twentieth century. Its two most famous members, Sarutobi Sasuke and Kirigakure Saizo, became the subject of uncounted other fictional works as well and remain popular characters today.

A character based on Sanada Yukimura plays a major role in the comic *Samurai Deeper Kyo* (published in English by Tokyopop).

Sanada Yukimura appears as a character in the "Warriors Orochi" and "Samurai Warriors" video game series (published by Koei).

Yukimura's family seal consists of six coins—*rokumon sen*—that correspond to the fare souls pay to be ferried to the underworld. Like a medieval Hell's Angels logo, it was custom-designed to strike terror into the hearts of all who saw it.

The End

Yukimura fell during the final siege of Osaka castle in the summer of 1615. Wounded and greatly outnumbered by the shogun's forces, he was beheaded by an enemy soldier who happened across him during a lull in the fighting. But word of his death only enhanced his reputation. The shogun, whom he had come within a whisker's breadth of killing with his own hands, regarded him as an honored fallen foe, and for generations thereafter, Yukimura would be revered as folk hero among those who chafed against the authority of the shogunate. ✻

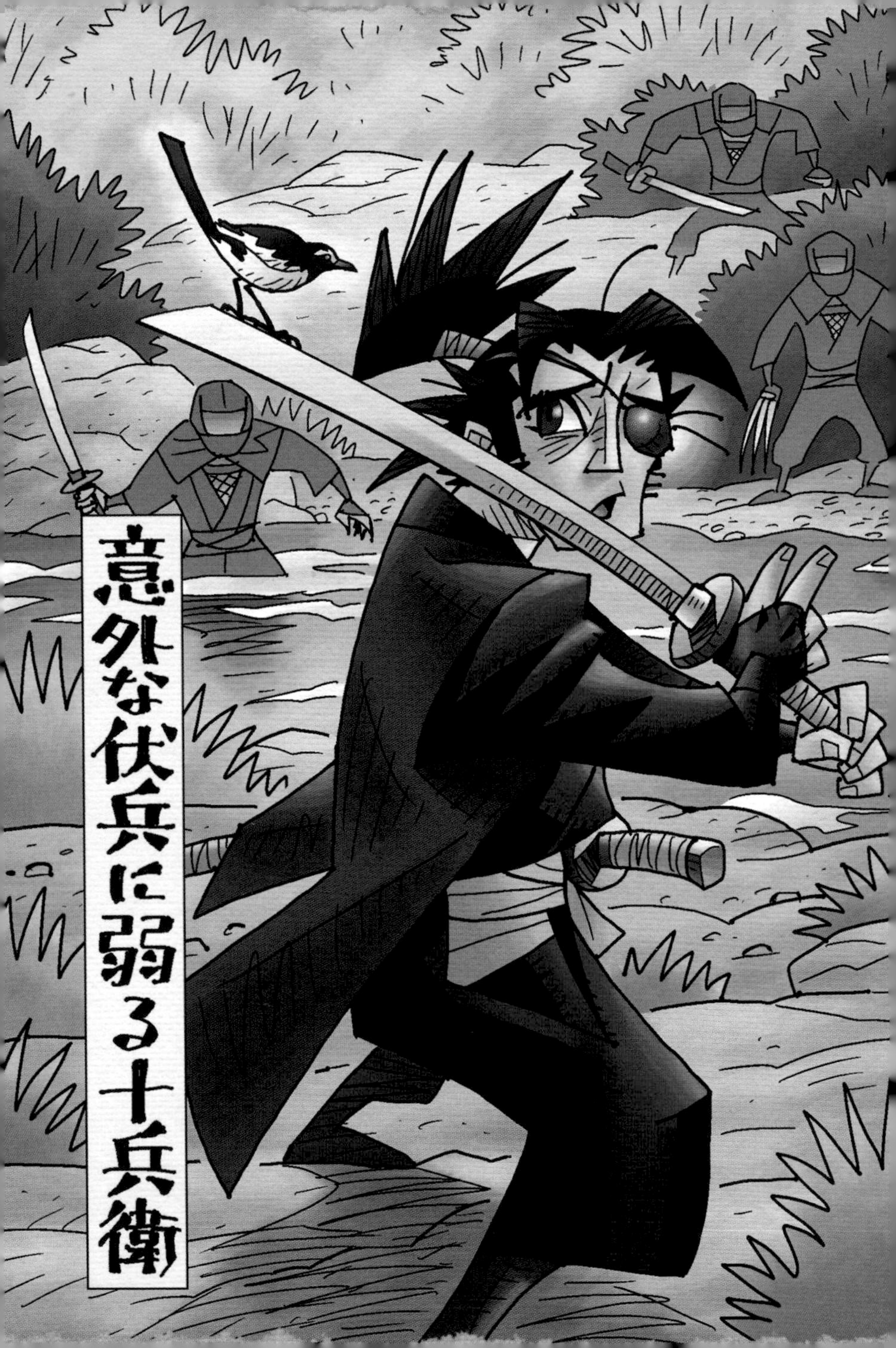
意外な伏兵に弱る十兵衛

1627 A.D.

Name: **YAGYU JUBEI**
柳生十兵衛

Birth/Death: 1607-1650

Cause of Death: Unknown (see below)

A.K.A.: Yagyu Mitsuyoshi (actual name). Shichiro (childhood name)

Known Associates:
Shogun Tokugawa Iemitsu
Yagyu Munenori (father)

Preferred Weapon: Katana

Clan Affiliation: N/A

Existence: Confirmed

The Man

Eye patch. Rakish good looks. A top-notch swordsman since his teens. Very possibly trained by ninja. Oh, yeah, and the ability to stop a sword between the palms of his hands, plus senses honed to unbelievable levels. Is it any wonder that even centuries after his death, the legendary Yagyu Jubei is the star of countless comic books, films, and historical dramas?

Son of master swordsman and politician Yagyu Munenori, Jubei started his career at eleven years old, as a page and later martial arts instructor to Shogun Tokugawa Iemitsu. Just think about that for a second. It's akin to a preteen being named a combination of secretary and exercise trainer to the president of the United States.

Then, at the age of twenty, Jubei decided to sever all ties to his master, hitting the road as a *shugyosha*. This entailed wandering the country "like Caine in 'Kung Fu,'" to paraphrase Samuel L. Jackson, engaging in mortal combat with other ambitious martial artists. The unthinkable (and usually unforgivable) decision to leave must have triggered more than a few, ahem, "heart to heart talks" with his father Munenori, who had spent his entire adult life establishing the Yagyu family as an indispensible asset to the shogunate. That Jubei was actually allowed to leave his master's service with his head still attached to his neck is a testament either to the shogun's respect for him or Munenori's bargaining skills, or both. Jubei's whereabouts remained a total mystery for the next twelve years.

The Style of Attack

No discussion of Yagyu Jubei would be complete without touching upon his distinctive fighting style, *Yagyu Shinkage-Ryu* (Yagyu New Shadow School), perfected by his grandfather, Yagyu Sekishusai Muneyoshi.

A technique with an unexpected weakness: Jubei

Although designed for swordsmen rather than ninja, the style took obvious inspiration from *ninjutsu* tactics. Ruthlessly pragmatic and emphasizing psychological awareness, it was intended to allow practitioners to read their opponents' actions before an incoming attack and to survive the possibility of being disarmed in battle. One of its flashiest moves—the *muto* (no-sword) technique, which involves catching an opponent's blade between one's bare palms—is a common sight in samurai and ninja films.

Equally impressive is the *tsuki-kage*, or "moon-shadow," technique, which Jubei supposedly learned during his twelve years on the road and incorporated into the New Shadow School. This ninja-like skill involves sharpening one's senses to the point where one can fight with eyes closed.

But even the most powerful martial art has its Achilles' heel. According to the chronicles of the Yagyu clan, the distinctive tail-bob of a tiny bird, the white wagtail, is said to resemble a spear technique that can bring even a New Shadow School master to his knees.

EYE WIDE SHUT

Jubei is often portrayed in popular fiction as having only one eye. In many cases he is described as wearing a sword guard in place of an eye patch. According to legend, Jubei lost his eye when Munenori whacked him with a wooden sword during a training session. Yet a classic portrait painted during his lifetime clearly shows both eyes undamaged. Fittingly for a mystery warrior like Jubei, he left us more questions than answers.

The Moment of Glory

Where the heck did Jubei go during that twelve-year hole in his personal history? Nobody knows, but it's far too delicious an opportunity to waste without a little old-fashioned wild speculation. No matter how you slice it, there's no question that Jubei needed to earn money during this period, and he wasn't the sort to get it running a vegetable stand. At the least, it is possible that Jubei sold or traded information gathered on the road, or even engaged in what we would today politely term "murder for hire" to make a living. Did he leave the shogun's service to serve some other master? Or was the entire skipping-out-on-the-shogun thing a ruse, cover for some sort of undercover intelligence-gathering mission? We'll never know. The theoretical conspiracy deepens.

The End

Jubei died in 1650 at the age of 44, while engaged in his favorite hobby: falconry, a popular sport among the aristocracy. (Intriguingly, this is precisely the same manner in which ninja legend Hattori Hanzo is believed to have died.) Perhaps fittingly for a man with such a hazy personal history, nobody is exactly sure how or why. Some claim he was felled by a poison arrow. Others say he suffered a heart attack. Did he fall prey to one of his undoubtedly impressive list of enemies, or did he simply die a natural death? The truth remains a mystery. ✳

POP CULTURE APPEARANCES

"The Yagyu Conspiracy," a 1978 Japanese television series directed by the legendary Kinji (*Battle Royale*) Fukasaku, features a fur-clad, mop-topped Sonny Chiba in one of his most memorable roles. Oh, yeah, and the always drool-inducing Shihomi Etsuko as his sister/sidekick. A theatrical version, re-titled somewhat unimaginatively as *Shogun's Samurai*, hit American theaters in 1984.

The protagonist of director Yoshiaki Kawajiri's 1993 anime film *Ninja Scroll* is an homage to Jubei. In fact, the Japanese title is actually *Jubei Ninpucho* (Jubei's ninja tales).

The second entry in Capcom's "Onimusha" video game series, "Onimusha 2: Samurai's Destiny," stars a character based on a hybrid of Muneyoshi and Jubei, with facial features modeled on the late actor Matsuda Yusaku (*Black Rain*) for good measure. Talk about a composite sketch.

Yagyu Dot Com

This being the twenty-first century, you can visit the official website of the ancestral home of the clan online at http://www.yagyu.com/yagyu/ Now called Yagyu-cho, the area was incorporated into the city of Nara in 1957.

Deep within Yagyu-cho can be found a massive boulder perfectly bisected by a clean vertical slice—the *itto-seki*, literally "one-slice rock." The fist-wide crack was supposedly caused by a stray blow unleashed by Yagyu Muneyoshi in a pitched battle with a Tengu, a ferocious yokai renowned for its skill in the martial arts.

A classic scene early in Akira Kurosawa's *Seven Samurai* in which a talented swordsman is forced to kill a challenger who refuses to admit defeat is supposedly based on a real-life incident from Jubei's travels.

Name: MATSUO BASHO   松尾芭蕉

Birth-Death: 1644-1694   **Occupation:** Poet . . . and spy?

Cause of Death: Natural causes (Dysentery)

A.K.A.: "Banana Tree" (literal translation of "Basho"), Haseo (archaic pronunciation of "Basho" characters), Matsuo Kinsaku (actual name), Matsuo Munefusa (official name), Tosei (pen name), Sobo (pen name)

Known Associates: Kawai Sora   **Preferred Weapon:** The pen

Haiku Composed: Roughly 1,000

Clan Affiliation: Unconfirmed. Possibly Iga.

Existence: Confirmed

Example Haiku:
古池や   Furu ike ya
蛙飛び込む   Kawazu tobikomu
水の音   Mizu no oto

LISTEN! A FROG JUMPING INTO THE STILLNESS OF AN ANCIENT POND!

The Man

One would be forgiven for expressing surprise at finding the undisputed master of the gentle, often playful form of poetry known as haiku in a book about ninja. Those familiar with his work inevitably picture Basho as a wandering composer of verse, an image completely at odds with that of "shadow warriors" of old. But it is this very unsuitability, this ability to travel anywhere without arousing suspicion, that would have made Basho the perfect spy.

The evidence is as provocative as it is circumstantial. Son of a low-ranking samurai, Basho was raised in Iga province, home to one of the most famous ninja clans. Of course, while Iga was rich in ninja tradition, it was also home to many thousands of people who had absolutely no connection to their ways. It only begins to take on significance when viewed as the backdrop of Basho's life as a whole.

By his mid-thirties Basho had built enough of a reputation to support himself as a full-time instructor of poetry, counting some twenty disciples in his school. But for reasons that still remain unknown, Basho chose to abandon his growing fame and

A suspicious traveler: Basho

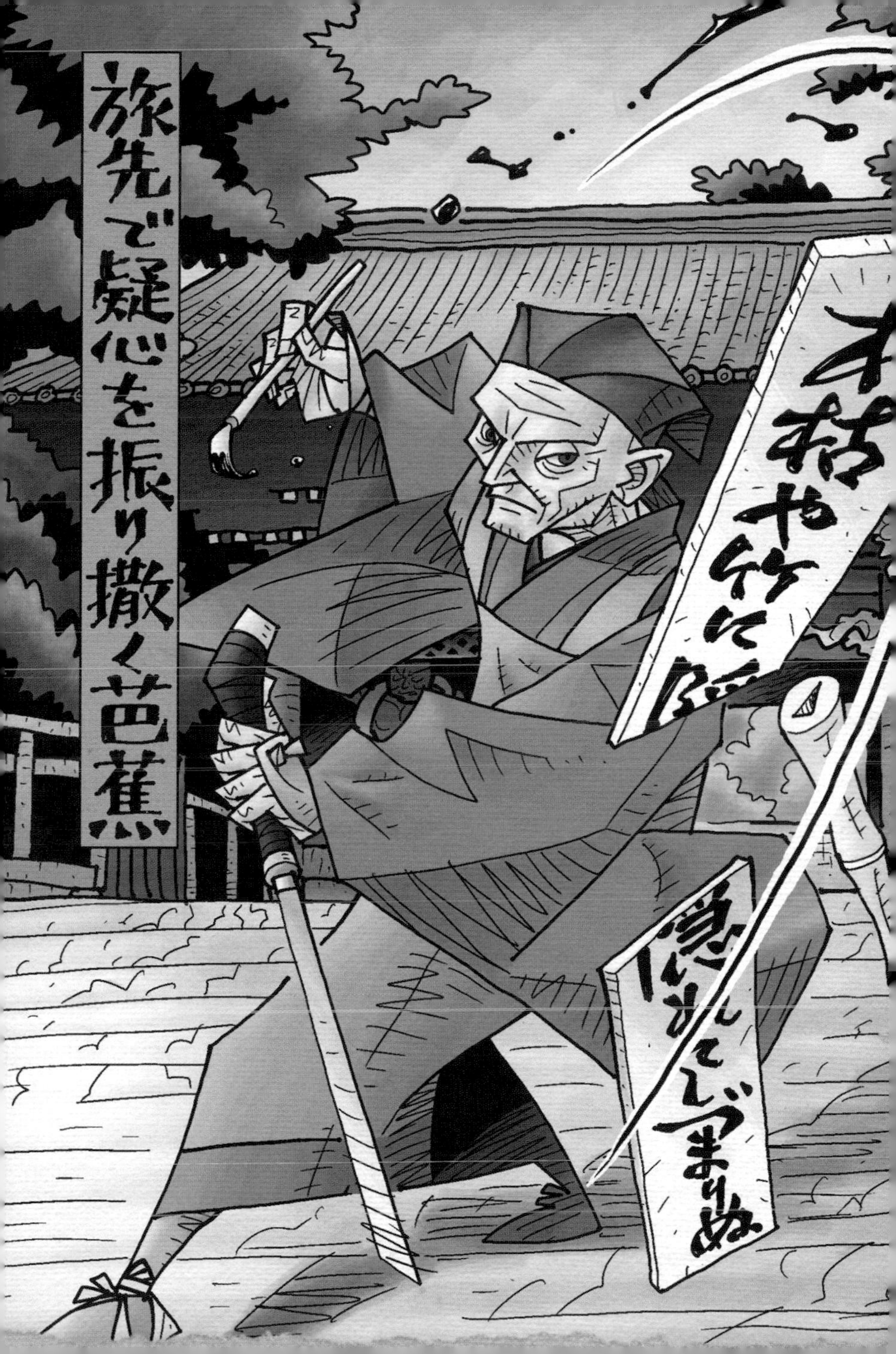
旅先で疑心を振り撒く芭蕉
枯や竹に隠
れてしづまりぬ

success for a life spent wandering the countryside—in essence, a literary version of traveling martial artists like Miyamoto Musashi. And this is precisely where the plot thickens.

The Moments of Glory?

Basho's most famous work, *The Narrow Road to the Interior* (1702), is a log of his most celebrated trip. Basho and his disciple Kawai Sora walked an incredible 2,400 kilometers over the course of just 150 days, occasionally reaching speeds of some fifty kilometers per day. Ninja are known to have utilized a special breathing pattern (in, out, out, in, out, in, in, out) to enhance their oxygen intake and thus their ability to cover long distances, leading to speculation that Basho and his friend may have been utilizing the technique themselves.

The forty-year-old Sora was an accomplished poet in his own right. He was born in Shinano, as it happens quite near Togakushi, one of the cradles of ninja lore. Formally trained as a religious scholar, he must have made an ideal sort of companion for a journey through the shrine- and temple-dotted Japanese countryside. He also happened to keep his own diary of events—an account that differs from Basho's in many surprising ways. In fact, there are some eighty spots in the two diaries that do not match up. Most are discrepancies regarding the dates the pair visited certain areas. Some chalk these up to poetic license on Basho's part; others, more suspicious, see it as an attempt to conceal an official information-gathering mission.

BASHO AND SORA

A statue of Basho contemplating his walk through Japan. It is safe to say that his journey would have turned out quite differently without his faithful companion Sora, who actually went on later in life to become an official investigator for the shogunate. This has led some to speculate that Sora, and not Basho, was the one gathering information at the behest of the government. The truth remains a mystery.

But gathering information about what? Here's a possibility. In 1689, the shogunate attempted to deliberately bankrupt the wealthy and politically powerful Daté clan by ordering them to renovate Toshogu Shrine, an opulent memorial to the late shogun Tokugawa Ieyasu that was located in the city of Nikko. Basho and Sora just happened to pass through the area on the very day that the Daté clan broke ground on their efforts. The coincidence has led some to postulate that the pair was quietly reporting on the Daté clan's compliance with the shogun's orders. (It certainly would have paid significantly better than composing poetry.) In fact one of the most famous differences between *The Narrow Road to the Interior* and Sora's diary concerns Nikko. "How awe-inspiring / on the green leaves, the young leaves / the light of

HOMAGE TO THE POET

The character of Strider in J.R.R. Tolkien's *Lord of the Rings* trilogy is translated as "Haseo" in the Japanese-language version of the book, an obvious tip of the pen to Basho's legendary striding across the country.

the sun!" enthused Basho of his visit to the storied shrine. Meanwhile, Sora dutifully recorded the weather that day as being "rainy." Exaggeration for dramatic effect, or a secret message for parties unknown? We'll never know for sure.

Although Basho's fame would certainly seem a handicap for a ninja, bear in mind that most ninja were far closer to "intelligence operatives" than "assassins." Although homeless in the most literal sense of the word, Basho's reputation afforded him access to the residences of powerful merchants and high-ranking samurai, and his long journeys throughout the cities and countryside would have been an ideal platform to gather local news, rumors, and other information—information of the sort that the government was known to hire ninja to obtain. Secret government backing would also explain how a humble poet could have afforded to spend such long periods without any visible means of support. ✷

HAIKU CODE

The highly contextual nature of Japanese makes it the perfect vehicle for haiku. The subtle, often obscure nature of much of Basho's verse has fueled speculation that his poems and writings may actually contain coded missives. There is little to support this theory one way or another, but it is certainly a possibility—and an intriguing reason to pore over Basho's poetry.

1716 A.D.

Name: **TOKUGAWA YOSHIMUNE**
徳川吉宗

Birth/Death: 1684-1751

Occupation: Shogun

Duration of Reign: 1716-1745

Cause of Death: Natural causes

A.K.A.: Tokugawa Genroku
(childhood name)
The Eighth Shogun
Kome Shogun (The Rice Shogun)

Hobbies: Staying well informed

Preferred Weapon: Highly trained
gardeners

Existence: Confirmed

The Man

By all rights, Yoshimune never should have wound up as shogun. The third son of a daimyo governing the province of Kii, he wouldn't have been a contender except for a series of inexplicable deaths that propelled him to the forefront of Japanese politics. Over the space of a five-month period in 1705, his eldest brother, then his father and another brother died, dropping a substantial fiefdom right into Yoshimune's lap.

His run of luck didn't end there. With the death of the shogun's regent from an apparent poisoning, and the demise of the six-year-old shogun himself after a sudden illness, Yoshimune had become the only real candidate for the post. In spite of having motive aplenty, no evidence of an actual consipiracy has ever surfaced. But perhaps this shouldn't be surprising: after his rise to the top, it became obvious that Yoshimune had been keeping interesting company for quite some time: namely, the local ninja of Kii.

The Moment of Glory

It is one of the most seductive images in Japanese pop culture: a shogun seated alone in his tearoom, apparently conversing with no one, but in reality getting his daily intelligence report from a ninja dressed as a humble groundskeeper trimming the bushes of the garden outside. But in this case, the fiction is actually fact. Upon taking the mantle of Shogun in 1716, Tokugawa Yoshimune established Japan's first true clandestine intelligence service: the Oniwaban, a.k.a. "the gardeners."

It was a watershed moment for ninja in several ways. For one, Yoshimune relied heavily

A Shogun who listened to his gardeners: Yoshimune

御庭番を耳目とした将軍・吉宗

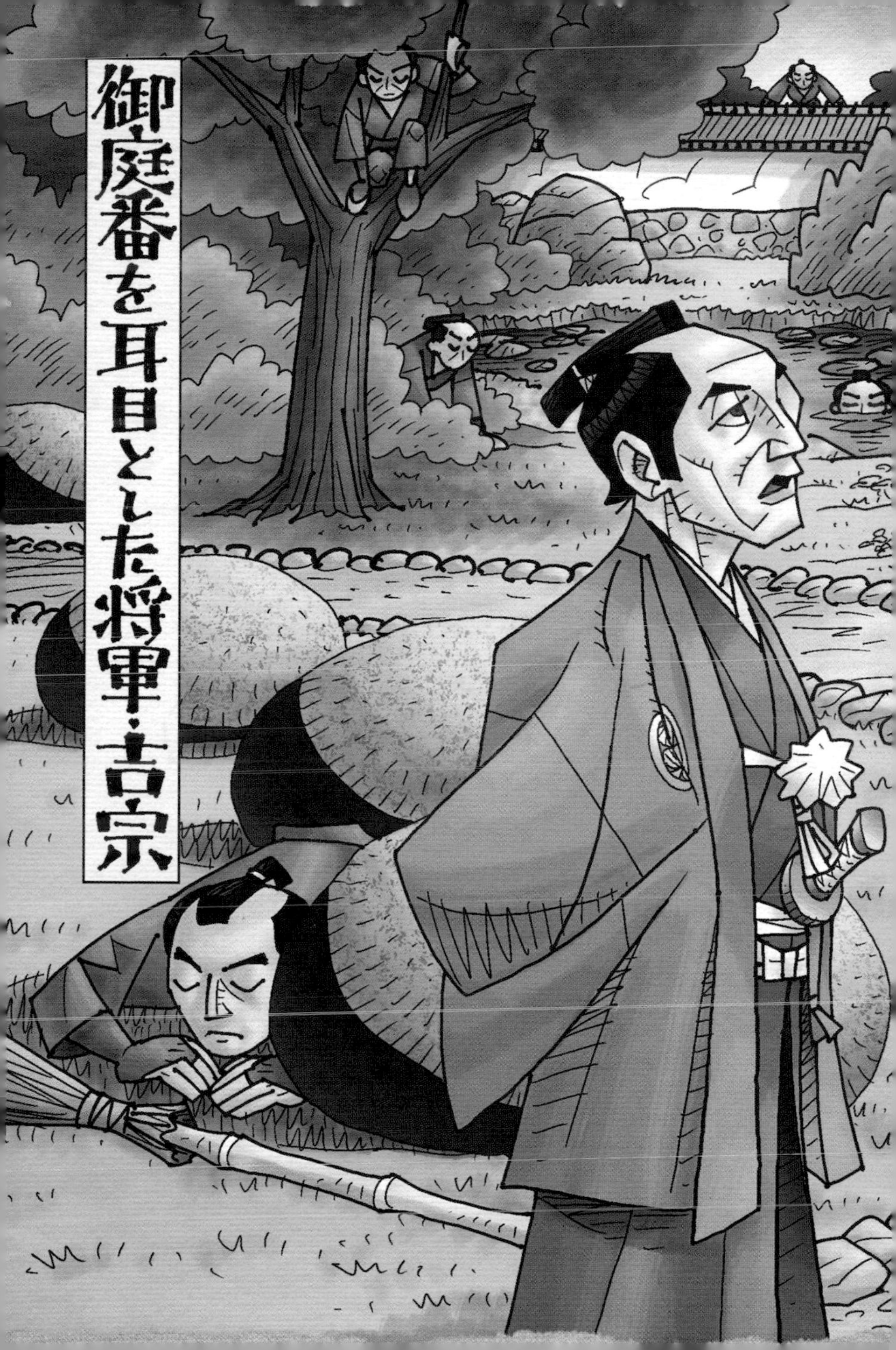

upon operatives from his home province of Kii instead of the traditional Iga and Koga ninja preferred by his predecessors. And, although schooled in traditional *ninjutsu* arts and usually "packing heat" of one kind or another, the Gardeners' mission wasn't simply to kill. It was to protect the shogun by any means necessary–both physically and strategically, by gathering information from around the country. Taking a page from the "best defense is a good offense" playbook, dealing with potential threats or rivals via quiet "accidents" behind the scenes was well within their purview. But the real trick was that they did it right under the noses of the other residents of the castle, completely undetected.

On the grounds, dressed as gardeners and other innocuous servants, they kept a close eye on the comings and goings of visitors, ready to spring into action in the event of danger. But on the orders of their master, they reported to a certain nearby store downtown prepared

THE SEVEN DEADLY COSTUMES

The Oniwa-ban relied on a variety of techniques to make their way through Edo-era Japan unhindered and undetected. They made copious use of tricks to physically alter their appearances: tumeric powder to simulate the dark pallor of a sick person, poisonous herbs to deliberately swell one's skin, or inserting fish scales as makeshift contact lenses to simulate cataracts. They also used a wide variety of costumes to disguise their identites. In no particular order, these included the following guises.

1) *Komuso* (Silent monk—see below)
2) Buddhist priest
3) *Yamabushi* (Shugendo practitioner)
4) Merchant
5) Street performer
6) Stage performer
7) Normal civilian plainclothes

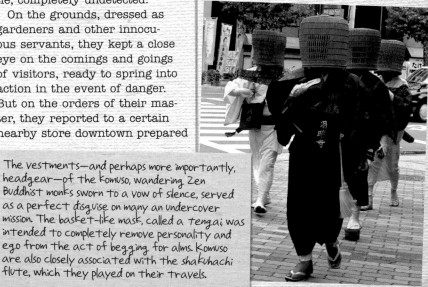

The vestments—and perhaps more importantly, headgear—of the komuso, wandering Zen Buddhist monks sworn to a vow of silence, served as a perfect disguise on many an undercover mission. The basket-like mask, called a tengai, was intended to completely remove personality and ego from the act of begging for alms. Komuso are also closely associated with the shakuhachi flute, which they played on their travels.

specially for their needs. Ostensibly just a normal clothing shop, it served as a front to a vast warehouse of costumes and props that the Oniwa-ban were authorized to use on undercover missions.

They proved their worth in a spectacular fashion in August of 1720, when they executed what could well be the world's first coordinated undercover sting operation. Disguised as beggars and vagrants, the Oniwa-ban shadowed a vicious criminal by the name of Sazanami Denbei, waiting until they had him totally surrounded before brandishing concealed weapons and taking him down. When it came to Yoshimune's Edo, you really couldn't judge a book by its cover: anyone, no matter how harmless-seeming, was another potential agent.

Oniwa-ban, live in the USA! This engraving shows President Buchanan welcoming Muragaki and comrades on their first visit to the United States in 1860. Their exotic outfits and beautiful swords caused a sensation wherever they set foot. Congress allotted $50,000 ($1.5 million in modern dollars) to entertain them.

The End

Although Yoshimune retired in 1745 and died in 1751, his Oniwa-ban organization lived on to serve generations of shogun. In fact, when the Japanese government sent its first official delegation to the United States in 1860, an Oniwa-ban named Muragaki Norimasa was among their number. It's tempting to view this as an act of espionage. In actual fact, however, Muragaki's exquisitely detailed reports of the journey—which included stops in Hawaii, San Francisco, Washington DC, and even an audience with President Buchanan—were proof that the ability to fling a *shuriken* had long since been eclipsed by a good memory and the ability to wield a pen. ✳

ONIWABAN IN POP CULTURE

Yoshimune and his Oniwa-ban rose to prominence in modern times thanks to the popularity of a seventies television series called "Abarenbo Shogun" (The Wild Shogun.) Gloriously over the top in the way that only seventies Japanese television dramas can be, it features Yoshimune and his ninja sidekicks crossing swords with countless villains in battles that may not be based in reality, but sure are a hell of a lot of fun to watch.

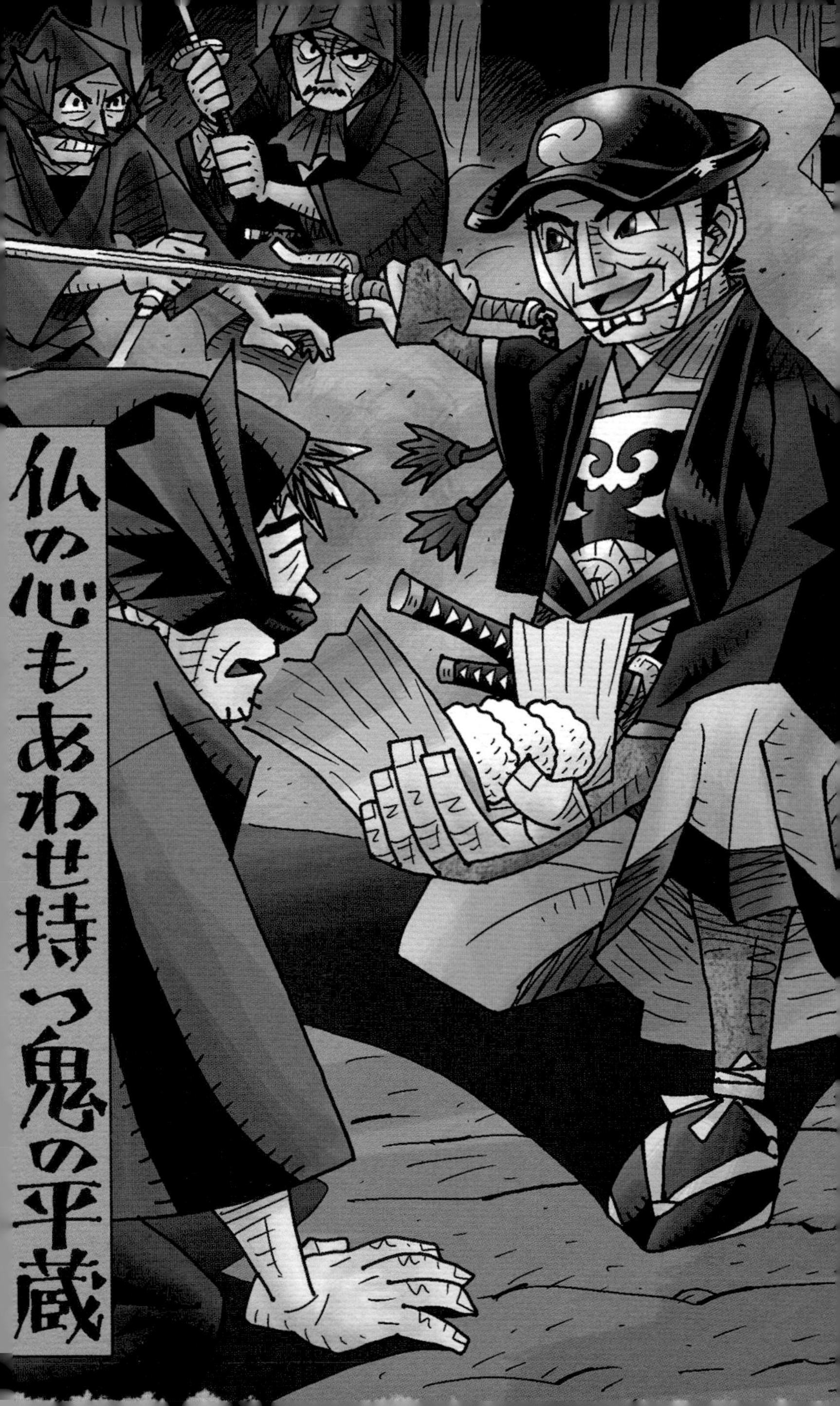
仏の心もあわせ持つ鬼の平蔵

1787 A.D.

Name: **HASEGAWA HEIZO**

長谷川平蔵

Birth/Death: 1745-1795

Occupation: Crimebuster

Cause of Death: Overwork

A.K.A.: Hasegawa Tetsusaburo (birth name)

Hasegawa Heizo Nobutame (actual full name)

Positions Held: Head of Arson-Thievery Task Force. Head of Edo "halfway house" facility.

Number of Arrests: 201

Preferred Weapon Jutte

Affiliation: Edo Shogunate (Government employee)

Existence: Confirmed

The Man

The 1780s weren't particularly good years to be a citizen of Edo. Famine caused by a series of cold summers, exacerbated by the massive eruption of Mount Asama in 1783, devastated Japan's agricultural base and flooded the capital with uncounted numbers of desperate farmers and villagers. Utterly poor and devoid of any skills that would allow them to make a living in the big city, many turned to crime out of desperation. In 1789 alone, there were close to a thousand cases of burglaries and out-and-out attacks on rice shops, wealthy merchants . . . even the residences of samurai. The situation was rapidly spiraling out of control.

In 1787, the shogunate handpicked a man by the name of Hasegawa Heizo to head up the Arson-Thievery Task Force, a totally independent unit that was something like the FBI, a SWAT team, and a paramilitary special-forces crew all rolled into one. This may sound like a plum job, but in reality the much-loathed position was seen by most as little more than a necessary penance for advancement in the Edo government. It didn't even pay so much as expenses until a case was proven, making it closer to "bounty hunter" than "detective." Few remained longer than a year at most. But Heizo kept the job for close to a decade, and redefined what it meant to be a lawman in a near-lawless city.

For the next nine years, he kicked ass and took names in a town overrun by robbers, burglars, and thieves of every

Demon with a heart of gold: Heizo

conceivable background, mostly of the petty variety but undoubtedly some of whom—like Kosaka Jinnai, who ran wild in Edo close to two centuries before—may well have been fallen ninja.

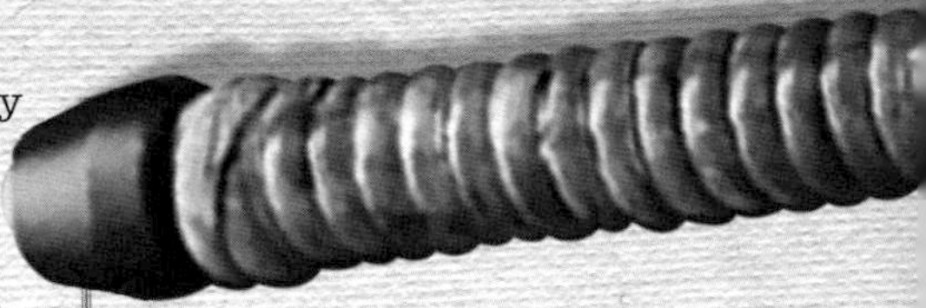

The Moment of Glory

In his years of duty Heizo saw his share of dramatic takedowns and collars, for he firmly believed in meting out punishment to those who deserved it. But don't let the fact that he ran Edo's premiere strike team fool you: in fact, his approach to crime-fighting emphasized brains over brawn. In the Age of Warring States two centuries earlier, many a warlord spent vast sums of money building extensive intelligence-gathering networks. Heizo pulled off the same trick in downtown Edo—all for the price of a cauldron of rice.

Every night, Heizo had his servants boil up a huge pot of fresh rice that was turned into *onigiri* rice balls for distribution to Edo's massive indigent population. He actively welcomed any and all who needed a bite to eat—those down on their luck, of course—but even those who may have drunk or gambled their money away. This proto-soup kitchen wasn't set up purely out of the goodness of his heart; he calculated that the more of these people he fed, the less they would turn to crime to fill their stomachs. Call it the beginnings of criminal psychology.

Most of Heizo's compatriots wouldn't have been caught dead associating with this bottom rung of humanity, but his strategy paid off handsomely when the city suffered a surge of unusually well-planned and-executed burglaries. Learning that a swordsman named

FRESH HAND-MADE ONIGIRI RICE BALLS

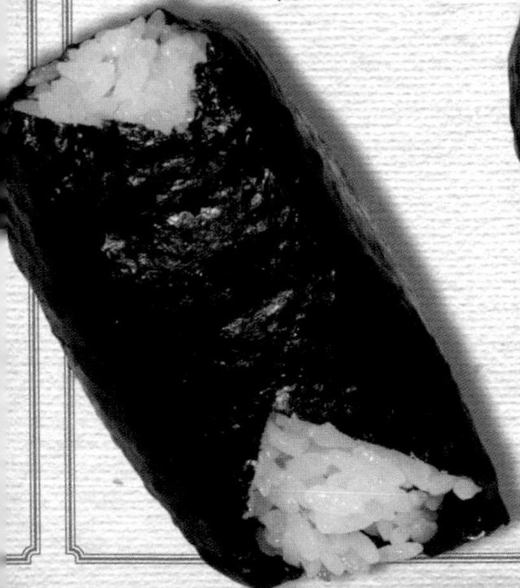

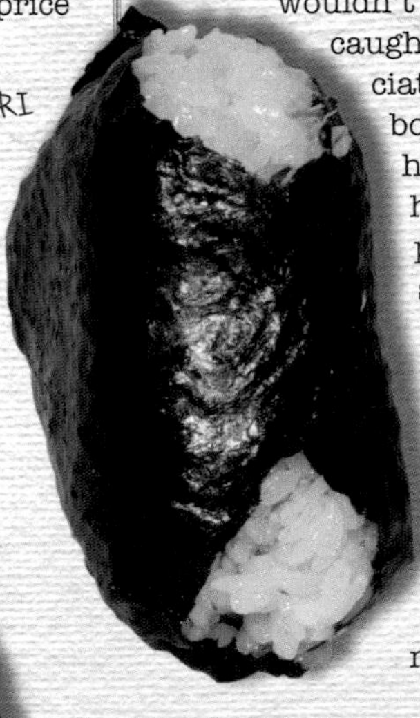

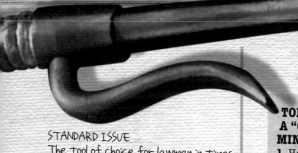

STANDARD ISSUE
The tool of choice for lawmen in times of old, a *jutte* could be used to catch a foe's blade and twist it out of their hands.

Shinto Tokujiro was behind the thefts, Heizo used his rice-ball informants to piece together a disturbing picture. Shinto's crew had somehow managed to obtain the outfits and official lanterns carried by lawmen. Using their ill-gotten credentials to scout out hundreds of likely targets—temples, shops, homes, warehouses, and even the occasional ship—they returned at night to strip anything of value, then fenced it at pawnshops for cash. Heizo's ear to the street gave him the intelligence needed to get the drop on Shinto and his men, putting an end to the crime wave and restoring the streets to something resembling order.

The End
Heizo's dedication and determination proved to be his downfall. In 1795, he collapsed and died of an unspecified illness that modern historians attribute to what is now commonly called *karoshi*—death from overwork. He was only 51. ✳

TOP 5 REASONS HEIZO WAS A "GOOD COP, BAD COP" MINUS THE "BAD COP" PART

1. He established one of the world's first true "correctional facilities," intended to rehabilitate and return criminals to society.
2. He always took the accused's circumstances into consideration, carefully meting out sentences that matched the actual criminal and crime.
3. He checked in on convicts from time to time, and saw that they received training appropriate to their abilities: carpentry, stonemasonry, shoemaking, even massage.
4. He never took a single vacation, as far as the historical record shows.
5. He made a mean rice ball.

HEIZO, MEET "ONI-HEI"
In modern times, a parade of popular films and shows based on Shotaro Ikenami's historical-fiction novel series *Onihei Hankacho* (*Hei the Demon's Crime Log*) has inextricably linked the real-life Hasegawa Heizo to the fictional nickname Oni-Hei (*Hei the Demon*). In reality, it is extremely unlikely that he was ever actually called that.

黒船内を探る澤村保祐

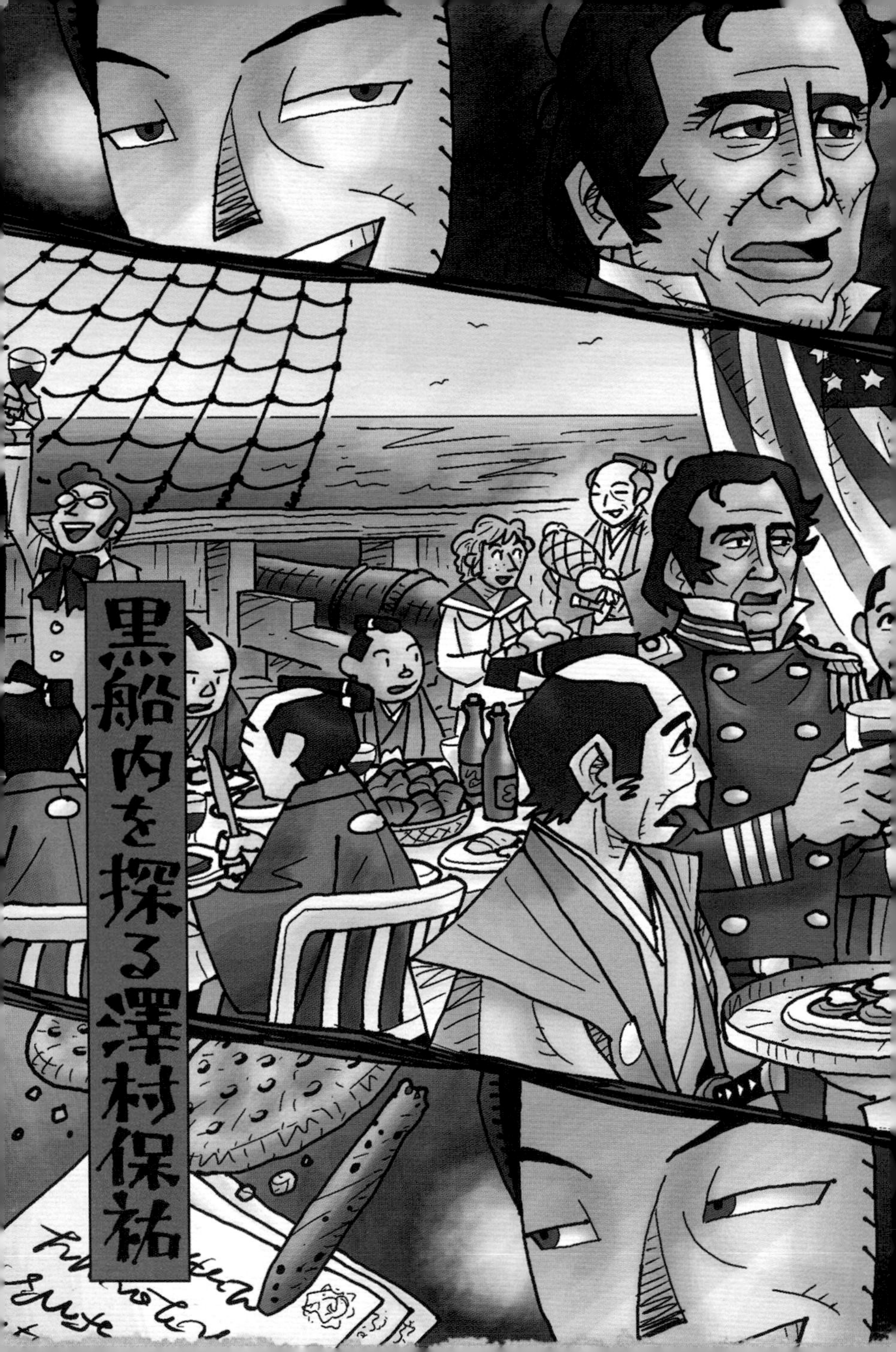

1853 A.D.

Name: **SAWAMURA JINZABURO YASUSUKE**

澤村甚三朗保祐

Birth–Death: 1820s ~ Unknown

Occupation: Intelligence Operative

Cause of Death: Unknown

Gender: Male

A.K.A.: "The Last Ninja"

Preferred Weapon: Capricious sleeves

Clan Affiliation: Iga?

Existence: Confirmed

The Man

In 1853, four heavily armed, state-of-the-art American warships sailed unannounced into Uraga Harbor, just south of the Edo capital. Their appearance signaled the end to some two hundred and fifty years of isolation and threw the rapidly weakening Tokugawa Shogunate into turmoil.

Commodore Matthew Perry, who commanded the successful expedition, described the reception thus:

The Japanese were as yet too suspicious of foreigners not to resort to their favorite system of espionage ... but they never came near the squadron.

Au contraire, Commodore. You just never knew about it. Meet Sawamura Jinzaburo Yasusuke, a man often described as Japan's "last ninja." For it was Sawamura to whom the Japanese government turned to get desperately needed info about the American forces in its harbor.

Iga-born and raised, Sawamura had ninja in the blood. His family had lived in the area for more than a millennium by the time he was born. While questions remain about his knowledge of *ninjutsu*, his ancestors were among the few local survivors of Oda Nobunaga's Iga-no-Ran wars of 1579 and 1581. According to local history, the family continued serving in an official capacity for local leaders for the next several centuries. Officially described as *musokunin*, essentially low-ranking samurai, the Sawamura family was also part of a loose confederation of local families called *shinobi-no-shu* (something like "the espionage group"), each of which specialized in a different aspect of unconventional warfare. Sawamura's orders came through the Todo clan, who then ruled the Iga region. Whether this was at the behest of the Tokugawa government, or simply represents a local

Searching the Black Ships: Sawamura Jinzaburo

149

bureaucrat wanting his own take on the mysterious foreigners who had appeared in Uraga Bay is unclear.

The Moment of Glory

Although precious little hard information remains about his mission, it is a fact that Sawamura successfully gained entry to one of the American ships and returned with items from it. The official tally of his spoils, according to Japanese sources, includes two loaves of bread, two cigarettes, two candles, and a two-page document. Hardly a king's ransom, but then again, even the most mundane of items can take on extraordinary significance in the context of getting to know one's opponent.

The big question is, how did he get them? More than a few Japanese sources intimate that Sawamura snuck on board the ships in classic ninja fashion, and we'd be happy if we could believe them. But an obscure passage in Perry's *Narrative of the Expedition to the China Seas and Japan* hints at a more prosaic answer. On

the evening of July 15, 1853, the commander of the flagship USS *Susquehanna* entertained an informal party of Japanese officials that had come aboard. Of the gathering, Perry's diary records:

> *Quite a convivial scene ensued, in the course of which abundant supplies of ham, ship's biscuit, and other stores, washed down by plentiful draughts of whiskey, quickly disappeared. [The Japanese guests] desired to bear away some substantial mementos of the pleasant feast, and . . . they carried off in their capricious sleeves pieces of bread and ham, wherewith to refresh their memories and their future appetites.*

So we have a record on both sides of bread being carried away. It appears the Americans might well have given Sawamura, who was conceivably assigned inconspicuously to the boarding party, the items he took back to his masters. This certainly makes more sense than his swimming, knife

MAN OF MYSTERY

In spite of Sawamura being the most recently living individual covered in this book, there is surprisingly little official information about him on public record—another bit of evidence that suggests his mission may have been purely a local interest. His descendants, apparently a bit touchy about being associated with shadow warrior lore, take pains to convince anyone who asks that Sawamura was not a stereotypical ninja or assassin. The family still occupies the same fortified homestead of their ancestors, though it is not open to the public.

clenched in teeth, from shore and then somehow boarding the heavily armed and constantly guarded war-frigates without anyone noticing. And unromantic though it may be, it fits perfectly with the ninja modus operandi of always blending in. What better place to hide than among the members of an envoy with permission to come aboard?

In reality, Sawamura's role was probably closer to that of a secretary asked to keep his eyes and ears open during a critical meeting than of an Edo-era James Bond. Yet it is also a perfect illustration of just how times had changed for the ninja. Although feared as shadow warriors during the Age of Warring States some two hundred and fifty years earlier, ensuing centuries of relative peace essentially robbed them of their raison d'être. Sawamura's mission represents the end of an era—perhaps lamented by the ninja, but undoubtedly a boon for the average citizen of Japan. Perry successfully concluded treaty negotiations in 1854, opening Japanese harbors and ushering in a new era of modernization and prosperity for the nation. And regardless of the actual strategic value of the items Sawamura spirited off of the Black Ships, his remains the last official ninja mission on record. ✳

Susquehanna, the "Black Ship" that Sawamura visited

THE PURLOINED LETTER

The two pages Sawamura obtained from the *Susquehanna* are written not in English but rather in Dutch—unsurprising, as Dutch (along with Portuguese) was a lingua franca between the West and Japan during its period of isolation from the outside world. In fact, the Sawamura family retains the papers to this day. According to the Iga-Ryu Ninja Museum, the content is more banal than strategic: one page consists of the phrase "Still waters run deep." The other muses on the perfection of British ladies in bed, French in the kitchen, and Dutch in housekeeping. One can only speculate that this information came in handy on the nation's first official diplomatic mission to Europe several years later.

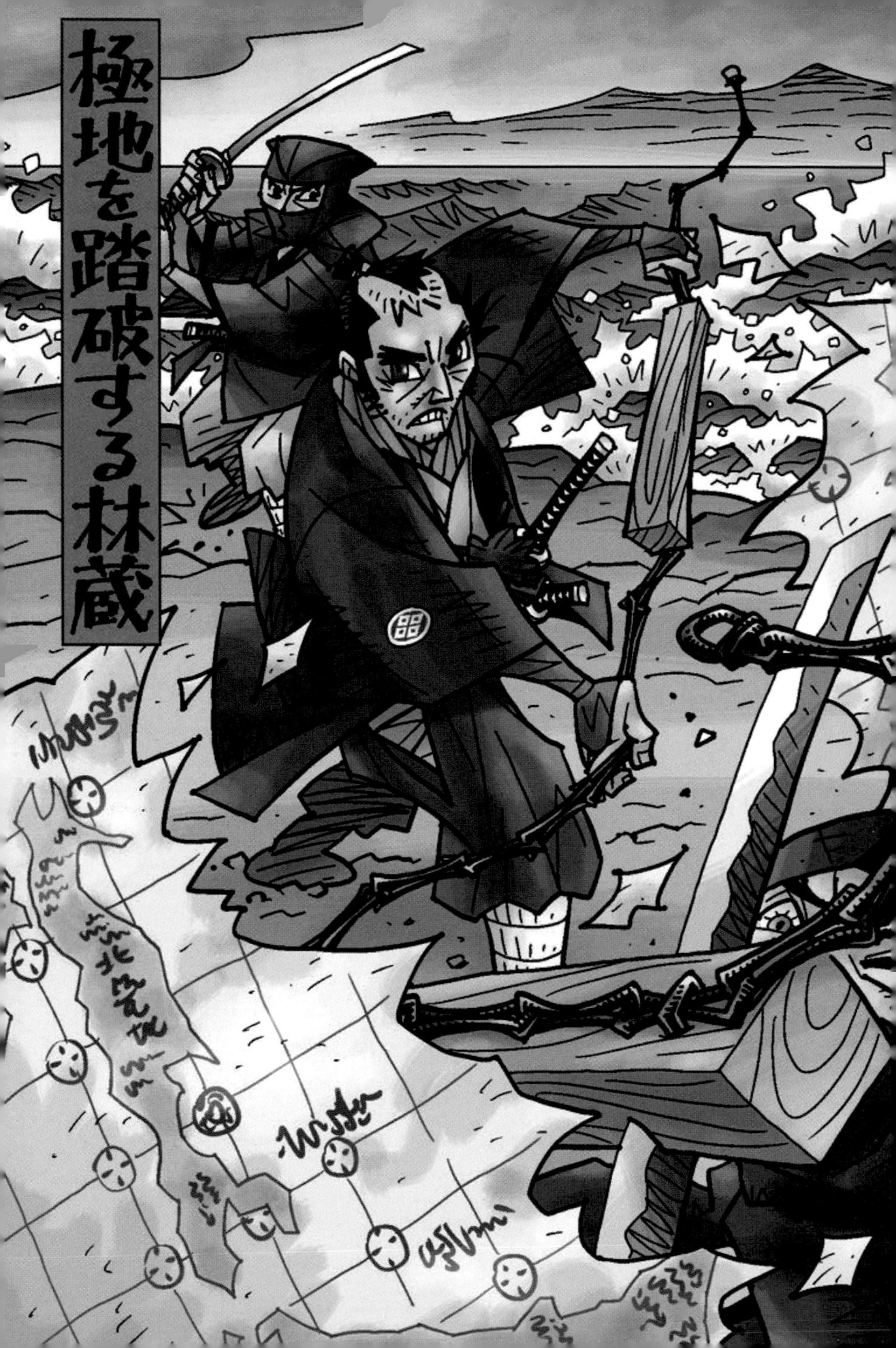
極地を踏破する林蔵

1830 A.D.

Name: **MAMIYA RINZO**
間宮林蔵

Birth–Death: 1775~1844

Occupation: Surveyor, Explorer, Informer, Secret Agent

Cause of Death: Natural causes (Illness)

Gender: Male

Hobbies.: Extreme nationalism

Preferred Technique: The sounding chain (see below)

Clan Affiliation: Tokugawa "Onmitsu"

Existence: Confirmed historical fact

The Man

Mamiya Rinzo never trained as a ninja, nor would have used the word to refer to himself. But he earned his place among their ranks through an incredible feat of espionage: infiltrating the virtually sealed-off domain of Satsuma in southern Kyushu and bringing back valuable intelligence for the Shogun. But in order to understand Mamiya, first you need to understand...

Map Mania

In an era of handheld global positioning systems, it can be easy to forget that maps of the world were once filled with large areas to which no one had ever gone before (or at least never returned from to tell the tale).

In the 1700s and 1800s, maps represented power. Often treated as state secrets, they held the keys to binding nations together: defining borders, opening trade agreements, fighting wars. Maps are the stuff empires are made of.

Thanks to an official policy called sakoku (literally, "locked country") Japan remained a virtually shut-in society between the years of 1639 and 1854. But the "powers that be" knew the strategic value of accurate maps. The Shogun, unsatisfied with the accuracy level of his charts, ordered a formal re-survey of the entire country in 1801. Twenty-six year old Mamiya Rinzo, who had been trained by the nation's top cartographer, was delegated the responsibility for exploring the northernmost reaches of Hokkaido (then known as "Ezo"). He and a partner penetrated forbidding wilderness for months on end without any outside support, living off the land while they did their work.

Mamiya's crowning glory as a polar explorer came in 1809,

Breaking new ground: Rinzo

when he successfully circum-navigated Sakhalin by foot and canoe, conclusively proving theories that it was an island rather than a peninsula of the Asian mainland. (The narrow bit of water separating the two is known as the Mamiya Strait even today.)

This far-flung and virtually uninhabited chunk of real estate existed in a precarious political tug-of-war between Japan and Russia. Japan would set up colonies that were blown to pieces by cannon-fire from Russian ships; in turn, the Japanese would capture Russian sailors and throw them into the 19th century equivalent of Guantanamo Bay. Mamiya occasionally participated in their interrogations, foreshadowing his future as a spy rather than explorer.

The Siebold Affair: 1829

For all his rugged determination, Mamiya had a dark side that would come to define his life.

Vain, boastful, and nationalistic to an obsessive degree, he harbored a deep distrust of foreigners and anyone who came into contact with them. Although his own surveying techniques were largely of foreign origin, he justified his studies as being for the "public good," while denouncing those of rivals as "disloyal."

He secretly tallied any mentions of foreign communications or foreign texts he saw on the shelves of fellow cartographers. No exchange was too small to be reported. When in 1828 a fellow geographer passed along a parcel from visiting German botanist Philip Frantz von Siebold to Mamiya, Mamiya turned it over to the police unopened. It turned out to contain nothing more than a friendly letter of introduction, but the simple act of communicating with foreigners outside of official channels violated the Shogun's sakoku edict.

Mamiya watched the resulting witch-hunt of Siebold and his "conspirators" with satisfaction. Local scholars were interrogated and imprisoned; meanwhile Siebold, a Japaonphile who really had only been interested in intellectual exchange, was tried and then deported. Even the Shogun's personal physician fell into the dragnet. It turned out he had given Siebold a gift in exchange for information about treating a common eye disease. In spite of the obvious value of this treatment to Japan, the doctor was stripped of his title and assets.

The geographer who had first passed along Siebold's letter to Mamiya was thrown into prison, where he collapsed and died. The authorities were so incensed that he died before they could make a public example of him that they embalmed the corpse

A statue of Mamiya erected on Cape Soya, the northernmost point of Hokkaido.

and put it on trial anyway, beheading it for treason.

The Moment of Glory: 1830

All of this skulking around culminated in the Shogunate giving Mamiya his most dangerous assignment: penetrating Satsuma, a powerful fiefdom located in Western Kyushu. This was the equivalent of a "007" mission. Although not precisely "sovereign," Satsuma's distance from the capital coupled with a long-held exclusive monopoly on foreign trade gave it the wealth and power to operate by a different set of rules than other domains. Its internal goings-on

were essentially a black hole to the Shogun.

Satsuma was legendarily hostile to outsiders of any kind. It even had its own regional dialect that was (and still is) largely impenetrable to non-locals. In order to successfully penetrate Satsuma's borders, let alone its highest echelons, Mamiya went back to square zero. He snuck across in the rags of a vagrant and then apprenticed to a paper-hanger for three solid years, soaking up local flavor as he studied a trade that he banked would gain him access to the Satsuma castle.

Posing as a lowly day laborer must have required superhuman patience for a man with as big an ego as Mamiya. But blending in was a matter of life and death. Mamiya made it back to Edo with critical information about Satsuma concerns engaging in prohibited trade—information that couldn't have been gathered in any way other than painstaking, dangerous observation and eavesdropping.

> **TOOLS OF THE TRADE**
> The wood-and-chain device Mamiya is often portrayed as carrying is called a *ken-nawa*. It is a sounding line designed to measure depths and distances over water, but in a pinch undoubtedly came in handy in other ways.

The Illustrated Ninja
Tricks & Techniques

Ninja relied on more than just martial arts; they were keen observers of the world around them. Their techniques span a wide variety of disciplines, from natural sciences such as biology, chemistry, and meteorology to psychology.

THE ART OF CONCEALMENT, OR KAKURE-JUTSU

Noroshi-no-jutsu:

Concealment via smoke. In the movies, ninja are often portrayed as tossing rapid-acting smoke grenades to mask a quick exit; more likely, given the limited explosives technology of the pre-modern era, they carefully placed and ignited smoke-pots to fill an area with smoke to conceal their movements before or during an operation. Simple firecracker-like noisemakers were occasionally employed to disorient opponents as well. It is said that over the centuries, the various ninja schools created some two hundred types of gunpowder and chemical-based smoke and noise diversions. Mochizuki Izumo-no-Kami was a master of this particular technique.

Kitsune-gakure-no-jutsu: the fox technique (not shown). Submerging oneself in water, or using water to mask the scent of one's trail.

Kannon-gakure-no-jutsu: the Kannon Goddess technique (not shown). Pressing oneself flat against a wall or other static object, covering one's face with sleeves or other material, and remaining absolutely still.

Uzura-gakure-no-jutsu: The quail technique.
Derived from the defensive posture of the bird, this involves balling oneself up, slowing one's breath, and stilling all movement. Reduces silhouette and noise, enhancing the effect of limited cover.

Tanuki-gakure-no-jutsu: The *tanuki* technique.
Involves taking cover in a high place, often within the branches of a tree. Exploits the fact that humans often fail to look above when searching for something. Forty-five degrees above the normal line of vision is said to be the ideal "blind spot."

Ninja Spells
The concealment techniques were often used in conjunction with what are euphemistically called "ninja spells." In reality these are not magic but rather more akin to self-hypnosis, used to still one's heart and breathing to further enhance the effectiveness of concealment. Specifically, the (quiet!) chanting of multi-syllabic mantras such as "On-anichi-marishi-ei-sowaka" is said to calm one down even in a tight spot.

Noon
10   14
7   17
5   23

The Cat's-Eye Clock

Regardless of ambient light conditions, a cat's pupils dilate in a regular pattern throughout the day, allowing the observant to "read" them like a clock. Two catches: you need a cat, and it needs to be friendly enough to let you get a good glimpse of its eyes.

5:00am
Pupils are egg-shaped.

7:00am - 10:00am
Pupils are oval, but narrowing.

12:00pm - 14:00pm
Pupils are very narrow, almost needle-like.

14:00pm - 17:00pm
Pupils are becoming more oval.

23:00pm
Pupils take on an egg shape again.

The Eyes Have It

In an era before corrective lenses, binoculars, or other forms of visual enhancement, ninja paid exquisite attention to attaining and maintaining their vision. Physical training included rapidly moving between dark and bright spaces (emerging from a shuttered room into the afternoon sunlight, for example) to train their pupils to expand and contract more quickly, staring at candle flames, and counting the number of pinpricks in the sides of paper lanterns. According to unconfirmed reports, they also consumed boiled peppercorns in a belief that the spice improved night vision. The standard "dose" is said to be three a day.

Reading Emotions

Ninja learned to properly judge—and use—the emotional states of those around them. A 1681 book of ninja lore, *Shoninki*, describes five basic emotions and five needs that can be exploited for one's gain: happiness, anger, sadness, enjoyment, and fear being the emotions, with hunger, sexuality, vanity, money, and hobbies being the needs. The last in particular might seem strange at first glance, but the idea of feigning interest in a field of study, work, or pastime is a classic method of getting close to a subject.

The Science of Snoring

When sneaking around in the dead of night, the ability to determine whether someone was actually sleeping or just faking was a crucial skill. The most adept could even discern critical clues about an individual from the pitch and rhythm of their snoring.

Healthy individuals not suffering from pain or emotional stress tend to snore with a stable rhythm. (The tone will vary depending on the individual, however.) The snoring of manual laborers tends to be louder and more erratic than that of people with less physically demanding jobs. The ill—particularly those with athsma or syphilis, a common complaint in an era before penicillin—tend to have a duller-sounding snore than the healthy.

Individuals feigning sleep tend to overly vary the pitch of their faux snores, making them high and low, loud and quiet. The unnatural "accent" of a forced snore is key to determining if someone is actually awake. The swallowing of saliva, sighing, or skipping of breaths are other clues.

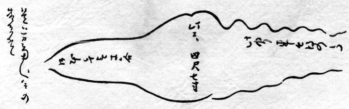

This doodle was created by Matsuo Basho to describe the intensity of an average snore. It is another tantalizingly circumstantial piece of evidence linking him to the world of the ninja.

THE NINJA DIET

Weight Training

Ninja watched their weight carefully, as one might expect for people who spent inordinate amounts of time hanging from rafters or crouched beneath floorboards. The ideal weight was said to be no greater than a full sack of rice: 60kg (132 pounds).

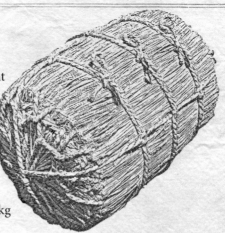

You Are What You Eat

Body odor was a significant issue for ninja, as a strong scent could lead right to one's hiding place. They generally avoided highly aromatic foods such as garlic, chives, or onions, and meat. In addition to bathing fastidiously, ninja ate a well-balanced, protein-rich, low-calorie, low-fat diet long before the concept took off in the mainstream. Tofu, miso, pickled plums, vegetables, brown rice, wheat, buckwheat, and potatoes formed the basis of the ninja diet.

Combat Rations

Umeboshi (pickled plum)

The humble pickled plum, a staple of boxed lunches even today, was a potent culinary tool in medieval times. Used in a similar manner to sports drinks today, the nutritious, pungent plums were popped as a perk-up. They also served to get one's saliva flowing, acting as thirst-quenchers when water was unavailable.

Kata-yaki ("ninja biscuits")

Similar to the hardtack served to ship's crews in the west, these biscuits were designed to be durable and spoil-resistant. In fact they were so hard that they needed to be cracked into pieces with a knife- or sword-pommel before eating.

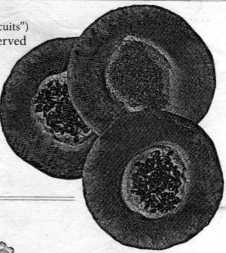

Hoshi-ii (dried rice)

The simplest preserved food: rice, steamed and then dried. They needed to be soaked in water, preferably warm, to rehydrate before eating.

Kikatsu-gan (hunger and thirst-quenching balls. Not shown)

The medieval equivalent of an energy bar. A mixture of dried carrots, buckwheat, wheat, yam, licorice, and sticky rice was ground into powder and soaked in saké for three years. The slurry-like material left behind after the evaporation of the saké was rolled into balls roughly the size of a peach pit. On missions, three were consumed over the course of a day.

Hyoro-gan

(ration balls. Not shown)
Wheat powder, saké, honey, sticky rice, and carrots were mixed and cooked into a mash that was then molded into small balls. Thirty of these balls equaled a single day's nourishment, and were consumed as needed while in the field.

Wild Vegetables & Herbs: Sansai and Yakuso

These are excellent sources of nutrition, ninja or not. Still widely consumed even today, pleasantly bitter-tasting wild vegetables (known collectively as sansai) can be found in alpine regions during the very early spring, just after the snows retreat. Generally picked as soft shoots, soaked to remove bitterness, then steamed or boiled, they are considered a seasonal delicacy throughout Japan. For ninja who spent long days and weeks outdoors, they were an excellent supplement to rations in certain seasons.

Some sansai are also known as *yakuso*—medicinal herbs. Dried, powdered, made into poultices, or even used in baths, they were important tools in the ninja bag of tricks. Koga was (and is) fertile ground for these sorts of herbs, and the ninja from this region were known to be particular knowledgeable about where to find and how to use them. The following smattering of common selections represents the tiniest fraction of nutritional and medicinal herbs found in Japan.

Yomogi
"Japanese mugwort"
A perennial flowering plant of the daisy family. It can be boiled, steamed, or fried and consumed directly as food, or dried for use in a variety of medicinal applications.

Tsukushi
"Horsetail"
Often found near *fuki*, horsetail shoots are boiled either alone or with rice to make a tasty dish.

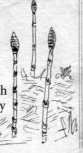

Fuki
"Butterbur"
Soaked in water to lessen their bitterness, butterbur stalks are chopped into short lengths and boiled for use as a side-dish or topping on boiled rice.

THE LEGEND BEGINS 1860~

In an era of peace, story tellers unearth and embellish ninja tales of old for entertainment.

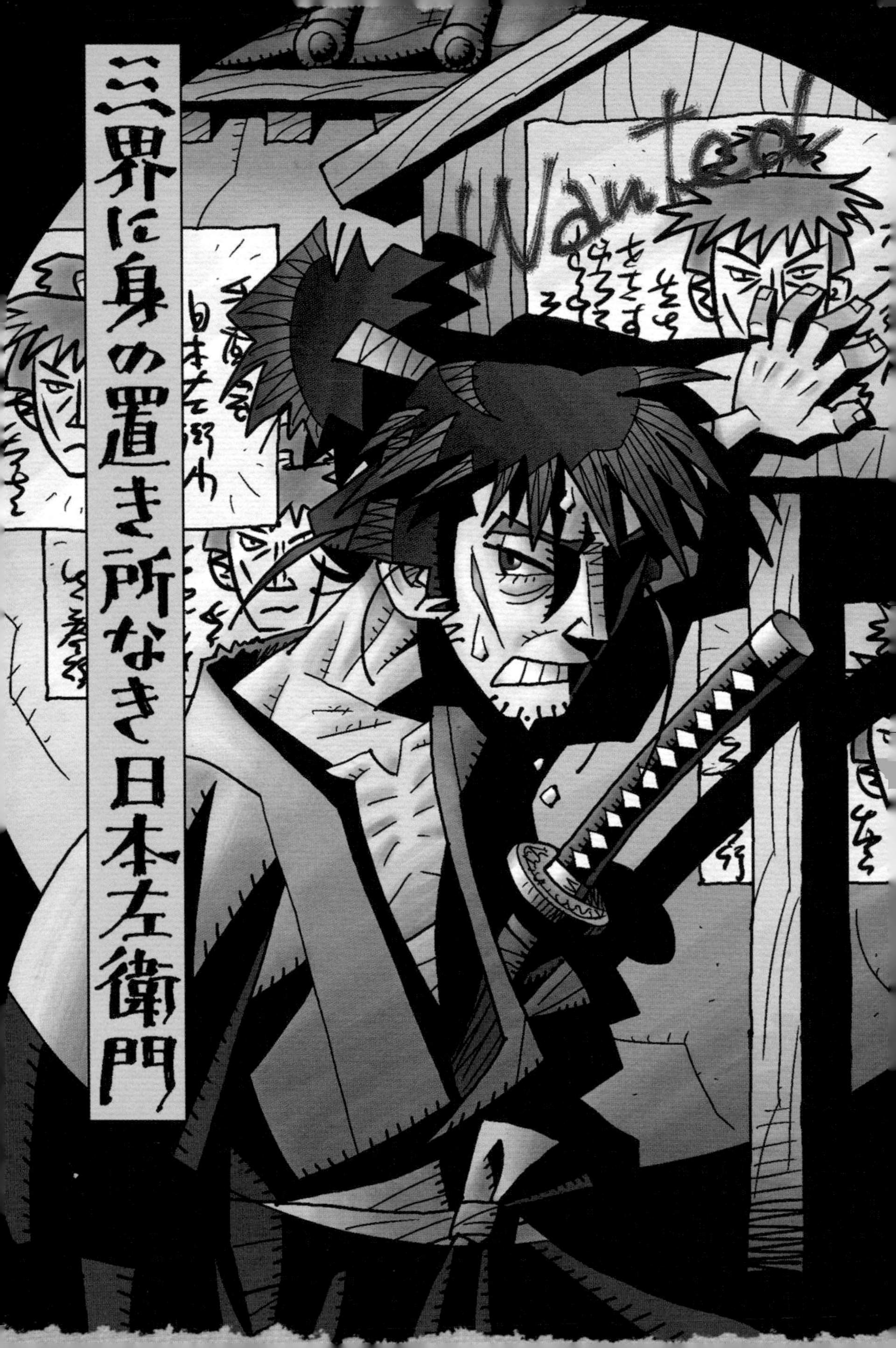
三界に身の置き所なき日本左衛門
Wanted

1746 A.D.

Name: **NIPPON ZAEMON**
日本左衛門

Birth–Death: 1719-1747

Occupation: Gizoku (Honorable Thief)

Cause of Death: Execution

A.K.A.: Hamashima Shobei (birth name)
Chikushi (Haiku pen name)
Nippon Daemon (in Kabuki)

Preferred Technique: Swordsmanship

Hobbies: Composing Haiku

Gang Affiliation: "The Shiranami Five"

Existence: Confirmed

The Man

This natural-born swordsman who preferred a life of crime to that of a martial artist dubbed himself Nippon Zaemon—essentially, "Mister Japan." Operating out of what is now Shizuoka prefecture, he and his gang terrorized a wide swath of the countryside west of Edo. As fond of sticking it to the Man as he was of the stick-up itself, Zaemon's penchant for shaking down the rich while steadfastly refusing to physically harm any of his victims made him a folk hero (think John Dillinger with a katana instead of a Tommy gun).

Like Dillinger, his notoriety quickly earned him public enemy status and the questionable honor of being the subject of Japan's very first wanted poster, which only helped cement his rep as a bad-ass with a heart of gold. While he wasn't a true ninja, he and his pals took a big page from the ninja playbook.

He targeted the upper crust: successful farmers, merchants, heirs and heiresses, and those transporting money on their behalf. It's officially confirmed that he stole some 2,622 ryo of gold (2.2 million US dollars in modern currency) over the course of his career, an absolutely astounding sum of money at the time.

It helped that Nippon Zaemon surrounded himself with the criminal elite. His right-hand man Nakamura Sazen, a talented strategist and a dandy to boot, actually managed to secure a job with the imperial family in Kyoto. He used his position to send Nippon Zaemon official lanterns marked with the royal crest, the Edo-period equivalent of a secret-service badge and a virtual free pass to anywhere in the country.

The Moments of Glory

Not one to lurk in shadows, Nippon Zaemon pounced on his victims in broad daylight, dressed to the nines. He would begin

Nowhere left to run: Nippon Zaemon

with a bold declaration of whom they were having the honor of being robbed by, and depart with a promise that everything stolen would be used to help the poor. Word of his antics struck a chord with "the other half," who conveniently ignored

A statue of kabuki hero Nippon Daemon in Asakusa, Tokyo

the fact that he never seems to have actually distributed any of this ill-gotten wealth to the needy. (This probably says more about class relations at the time than it does about any actual belief in him as Japan's answer to Robin Hood.)

Only two crimes truly warranted the full attention of the authorities in the hierarchy-obsessed Edo period: murdering one's parents or murdering one's master. Nippon Zaemon changed all that. Fed up with the local enforcers' inability to tame "Mister Japan" and his merry men, the shogunate released a

detailed wanted poster, complete with a "police sketch" of his appearance in 1746. It was a first in Japan.

Shaken by the sight of the poster, Nippon Zaemon went into hiding. Dropping out of his criminal network, he began staying at the homes of friends he had made, penning and exchanging haiku verse of the sort popularized by Matsuo Basho. And rather than going underground, he hid in plain sight, touring the many countryside "haiku roads" (tourist paths that led to scenery conducive for producing poems).

The End

On January 7, 1747, Nippon Zaemon surrendered himself to the authorities in Kyoto, and on March 11th, he was executed, his head displayed on a garrote for all to see. But his legend lived on. In 1862, more than a century after his death, a kabuki play starring a character based on Nippon Zaemon as the leader of a gang of five super-bandits called the "Shiranami Five" opened to raves. (Pop-cultural historians cite the play as the direct historical ancestor of the "Power Ranger" style kids'

The protagonist of the 1862 kabuki play Aoki Zoshi Hana no Nishikie (The Glorious picture Book of Aoto's Exploits) is called "Nippon Daemon" — an obvious nod to Nippon Zaemon.

show so popular in Japan and abroad today.)

Which is all fine and dandy. But it begs a question. Why on earth would such a flamboyant iconoclast, a bad-to-the-bone rebel, turn himself in so willingly? The fact is that the wanted poster represented just the tip of the iceberg. Given the large amount of personal info it contained, it is likely that the frustrated authorities were rounding up and detaining family, friends, acquaintances, and anyone else who might know Zae-

mon's whereabouts.

Trust us, the last place you wanted anyone you cared about to be was an Edo-period detention center–where the food was literally rotten, and the guards solved prison issues such as fighting and overcrowding by killing prisoners based on little more than a whim of the moment. When word reached Zaemon that sidekick Nakamura Sazen had been arrested and transported to Edo, he knew he couldn't live with the blood of his friends on his hands. ✳

Japan's Most Wanted

Actual text from Zaemon's *ninso-gaki* (wanted poster).

- Height: Roughly 5 *shaku* and 8 or 9 *sun* (roughly 177cm)
- Age: 29 years (but 31 or 32 in appearance)
- Hair on scalp grown out; has a scar.
- White, well-aligned teeth
- Straight, well-defined nose
- Oval-shaped eyes
- Elongated face
- Head tends to cock slightly to the right
- Hair: Average-sized topknot, swept back and tied
- Last seen wearing a reddish-brown, quilted kosode jacket. The jacket featured a round crest with a tachibana (mandarin orange) motif. Lower body: yellow-green silk bottoms with similar crest. Undergarments: white silk.
- Armed with single *wakizashi* (short sword)

Sword guard: gold rim, luxury type. Brass temper line. Nanako style inlay, animal pattern. Kogai dagger: plain copper. Grip spacer and collar mount: gold. Scabbard: Black lacquer; Silver-leaf tip.
- Yellow-green felt purse
- Gold lacquered medicine case with bird motif

This pimped-out short sword is Edo-era "bling-bling," the equivalent of a chrome-plated sawed-off shotgun.

If you encounter this man, tell the owner of the property at once, and present yourself at the local magistrate's office. Those discovered to be aiding or harboring this man will be punished as criminals.

Ordered
October, 1746

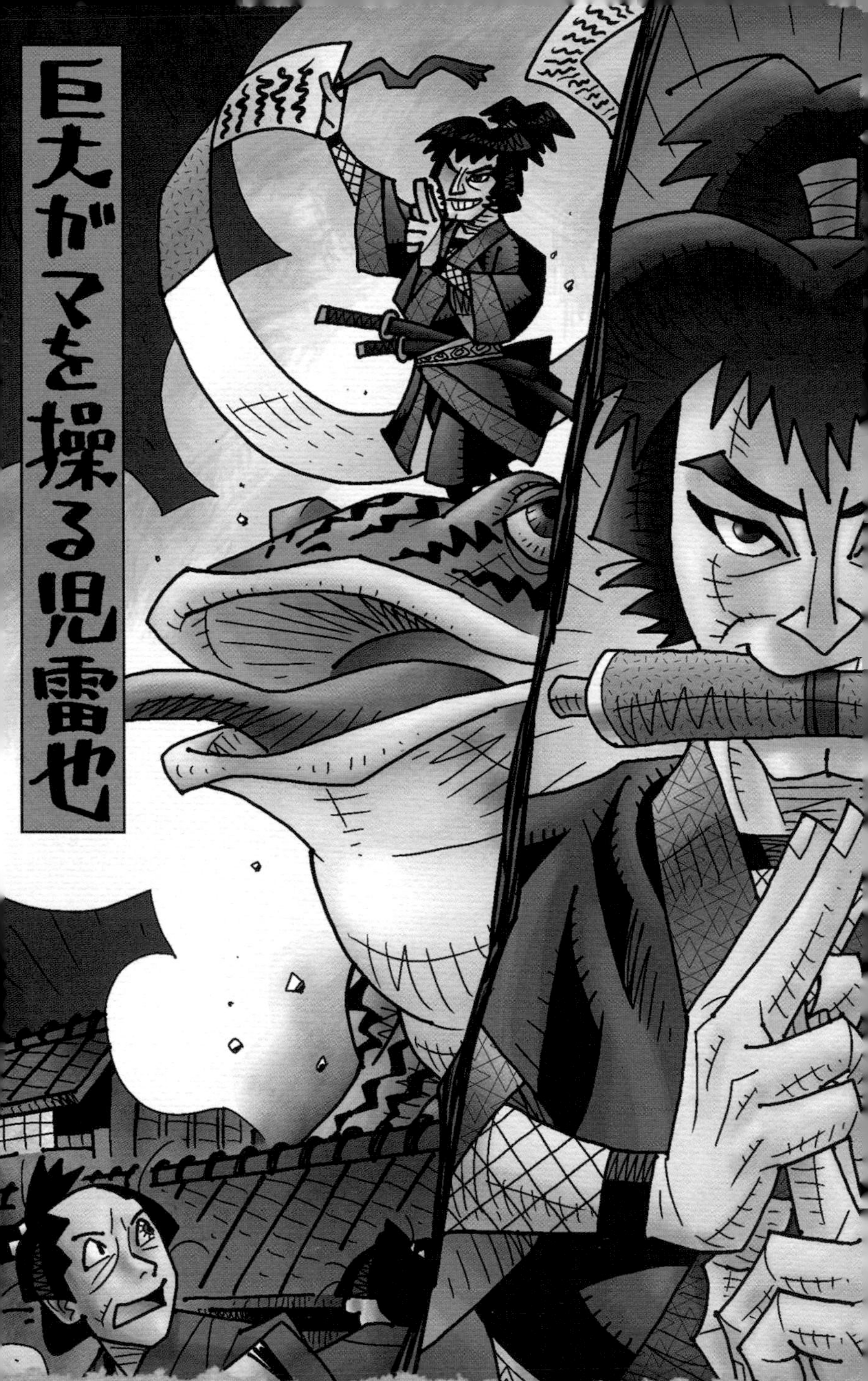
巨大ガマを操る児雷也

1806 A.D.

Name: **JIRAIYA**
児雷也

Debut: 1806
Occupation: A chivalrous thief
Cause of Death: N/A
A.K.A.: 自来也 (different kanji, same reading)
Ogata Shuma (alter ego)
Known Associates: Orochimaru, Master of Snakes
Tsunade, the Slug Princess
Preferred Weapon: Toads of Terror
Clan Affiliation: None
Existence: Fictional character

The Man

Now famed worldwide as a character in the "Naruto" anime series, Jiraiya has been a staple of Japanese pop culture for well over two centuries. This outlaw with a heart of gold and the ability to conjure up giant phantom toads debuted in an 1806 book entitled *Jiraiya Setsuwa* (The story of Jiraiya), written by Onitake Kanwatei.

Accompanied by his sidekick, Tsunade, the slug-princess, Jiraiya uses his powers to fight injustice and foil the evil plans of Orochimaru, the master of snakes. In the book, toads are weaker than snakes, snakes are weaker than slugs, and slugs can be defeated by toads, establishing a rock-paper-scissors conundrum that should be familiar to anyone who's ever played a round of Pokemon.

While the ability to summon a fat toad might sound like something of a let-down as a super power, think of Jiraiya as "Knight Rider" with an amphibian sidekick instead of a souped-up sports car, and it all starts to make sense. This toad's no slouch, either, capable of belching forth enchanted smoke, for example, that can coalesce into a solid object. A favorite move of Jiraiya's is using his pal's emissions to create a phantom bridge over a valley to escape, then dispelling it to send hapless pursuers tumbling to earth like Wile E. Coyote.

But he's more than just a man with a warty four-legged friend. Although theoretically a bad guy—he's a thief, after all—Jiraiya is also more "Superman" than safecracker. He's a guy with a moral code, more than happy to take on even the biggest, baddest bad guys in the name of justice. Quite often, his targets are powerful men who use their political weight to make life miserable for those beneath them.

Master of toads: Jiraiya

Iwate-Ishidoriya Festival

The Moment of Glory

Here's the very first Jiraiya story. When a young woman's husband is tossed into debtor's prison for his inability to pay taxes, she turns to prostitution to support their young child. Things only get worse when her father-in-law, who looks after the baby while she works, is attacked, robbed, and killed by a brigand called Gundayu, who drop-kicks the tyke into a deep gorge for good measure. Fortunately, Jiraya, at this point just your average guy, happens upon the scene and rescues the boy.

Fast forward several years. Jiraya encounters a huge toad being tormented by an even bigger snake deep in the forest. He uses his trusty flintlock rifle to drive the nefarious serpent away, earning the gratitude of the mysteriously large amphibian, who in turn instructs him in the magical ways of polliwog power.

Meanwhile, Gundayu has risen to become the right-hand man of the local daimyo, living in splendor in his castle. The boy's mother and father, now out of jail, launch a daring raid against

GRAFFITI OF LEGEND

Jiraiya creator Onitake Kanwatei was inspired by a real-life thief and jailbreaker from Song-era China called Garaiya, so named because he carved the word "Garaiya" (我来也)—"I was here"—onto the walls of his victims. Onitake tweaked the spelling to 自来也, and a new hero was born.

the former brigand to exact revenge, but are killed in the process. Enter the Toad: Jiraiya, now fortified with magic, steps in, obliterates Gundayu, and justice is served.

Prosititution, firearms, mystical amphibians . . . It may not sound like a tale for the ages, but it apparently struck a chord with Edo-era readers. An 1839 graphic novel series based on Kanwatei's work, called *Jiraiya Goketsu Monogatari* (Tales of brave Jiraiya), proved so popular that regular installments continued for nearly three decades.

Meiji period woodblock print of Jiraiya ↷

The End

There's really no end in sight. The Jiraiya story was updated yet again in the late 1980s as *Sekai Ninja Sen Jiraiya* (World Ninja War Jiraiya), a live-action television series produced by "Power Rangers" creators Toei. It even co-starred Dr. Masaaki Hatsumi, the current grandmaster of the Togakure-ryu school of *ninjutsu* pioneered by Daisuke Togagushi. And the popularity of "Naruto" pushed Jiraiya to all-new heights in the first decade of this century. When it comes to pop culture, anyway, this ninja is nobody's toady save his own. ✳

No.7

MOVE OVER, TURTLES
Toads and ninja continue to enjoy a strange degree of association even today, as can be seen from this 1976 Takara die-cast toy.

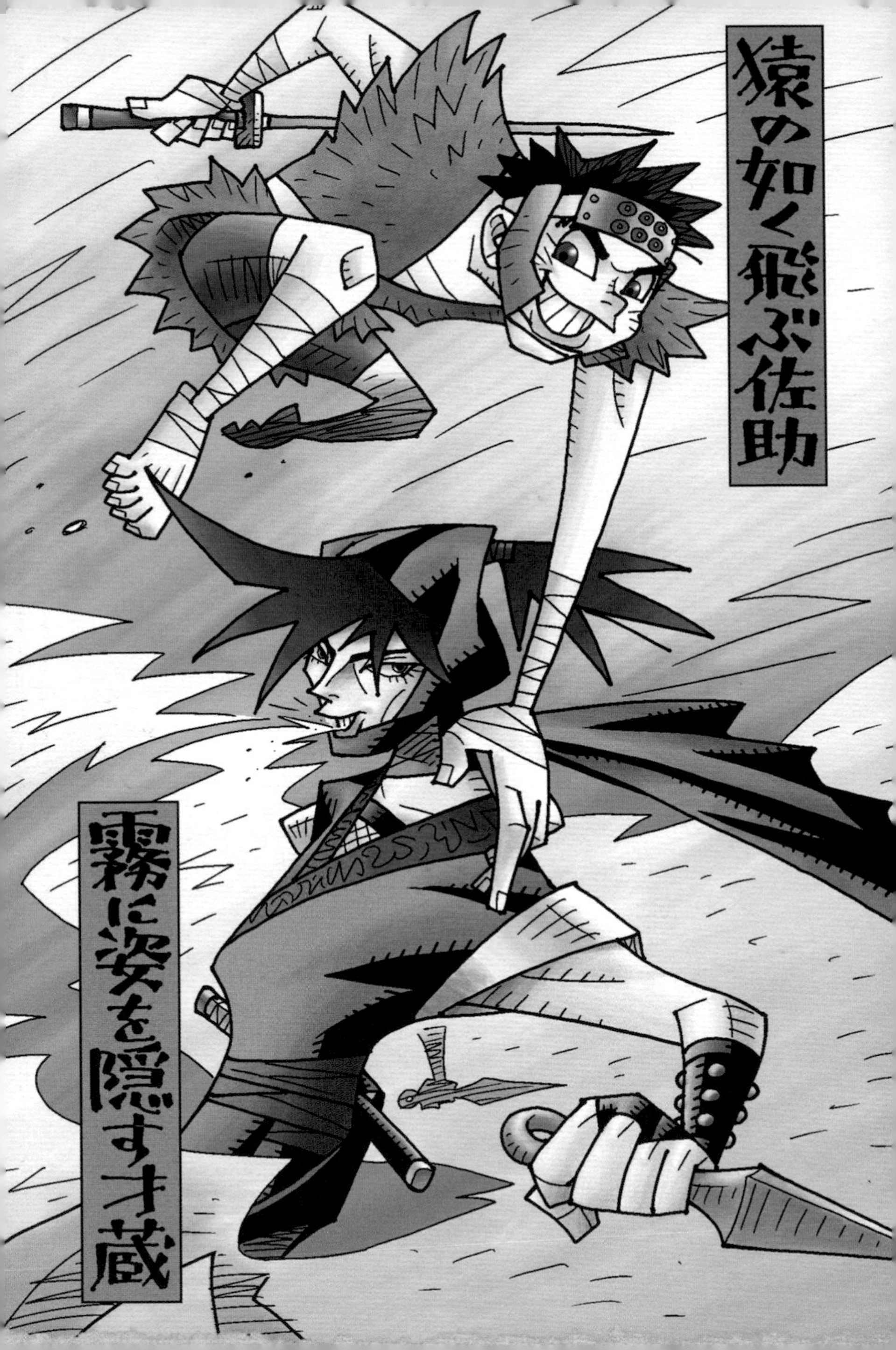

猿の如く飛ぶ佐助
霧に姿を隠す才蔵

1912 A.D.

Name: **SARUTOBI SASUKE**
猿飛佐助

Name: **KIRIGAKURE SAIZO**
霧隠才蔵

Debut: 1912/1913

Occupation: Ninja

Cause of Death: N/A

Gender: Male

A.K.A.: Washizuka Sasuke (actual name)
"Leaping Monkey" (literal
translation of "Sarutobi")
"Cloaked in Mist" (literal
translation of "Kirigakure")

Known Associates: Sanada Yukimura

Preferred Technique: Jumping (Sasuke),
Illusion / Deception (Saizo)

Clan Affiliation: Sanada's Ten Heroes;
Koga (Sasuke) Iga (Saizo)

Existence: Fictional Characters

The Men

Sarutobi Sasuke and Kirigakure Saizo represent ground zero for the worldwide popularity of ninja today. A matched pair of eternal ninja rivals in the service of warlord Sanada Yukimura, they first appeared in an early twentieth-century series of juvenile novels called the *Tachikawa* *Pocket Books*, captivating children and touching off a fad for ninja-related entertainment that swept Japan and, eventually, the world.

Until their debut, ninja in popular fiction had been portrayed as antiheroes at best— "ninja gone bad" like Ishikawa Goemon, or magical thieves like Jiriaya. But Sasuke and Saizo shattered the stereotype. Their creators, a group of writers working under the collective name Sekka Sanjin, pioneered the concept of the ninja as hero. Inspired in parts by China's *Journey to the West* (a historical fable that not coincidentally also featured a monkey-themed hero) and tales of real-life ninja, they singlehandedly established Saizo and Sasuke as poster boys for the Iga/Koga rivalry, and ninja as a potential force for good. They were so successful at it, in fact, that Sasuke remains the de facto stereotypical name for a ninja in Japan today. (It is no coincidence that one of the main characters in the anime "Naruto" shares the name.)

Leap like a monkey, hide in the mist: Sasuke and Saizo

Sarutobi Sasuke

Sasuke was raised, à la Tarzan, by monkeys in the mountains of Togakushi (also, incidentally, home of ninja legend Togakushi Daisuke). An elderly ninja master happened across the wild lad, took him under his wing, and tamed his savage heart by instructing him in the ways of Koga *ninjitsu*.

When warlord Sanada Yukimura later encountered Sasuke on a trip through the area, he was taken by the boy's mischievous attitude and incredible skills. Inviting him to join his retinue, Sanada codenamed the lad "Sarutobi" ("leaping monkey") for his ability to jump effortlessly from tree to tree, and eventually promoted him to the top of a super-secret special-ops squad known as Sanada's Ten Heroes.

Sasuke's association with the iconoclastic Sanada, who tried but ultimately failed to shake Tokugawa Ieyasu's stranglehold on the country, established his character as an underdog and counter-cultural hero. Splitting his time between missions for his master and personal quests to rescue the weaker and less fortunate from the powers that be, Sasuke evolved into a Superman-styled fighter for truth, justice, and the Japanese way.

Some say Sasuke is loosely based on a pair of real-life Iga ninja brothers named Shimotsuge Kizaru and Kozaru, whose nicknames translate into "Tree-Monkey" and "Little Monkey," respectively.

Kirigakure Saizo

Supposedly the brother of Ishikawa Goemon, and trained alongside him by Iga master ninja Momochi Sandayu, Kirigakure Saizo played the nihilistic foil to the wildly upbeat Sasuke. In his debut story, he was scratching out a living as a bandit in the mountains near Himeji until Sasuke recruited him to be one of Sanada's Ten Heroes. Although his portrayal differs wildly from book to book and film to film, Saizo often has the ability to harness the power of clouds, fog, lightning, and thunder to distract opponents and mask his comings and goings, making him the ultimate infiltrator. (His first name, Kirigakure, translates into "cloaked in mist," after all.)

Taking the proverbial horse by the hooves, Kirigakure Saizo shows off his strength on the cover of his debut novel.

The End?

Sasuke and Saizo's original adventures culminated at the bloody siege of Osaka, a real-life battle in which shogun Tokugawa Ieyasu's forces pummeled the last vestiges of resistance to his rule. The basic story has Sasuke and Saizo meeting their ends there alongside other valiant anti-Tokugawa warriors. Other stories claim that they quietly slipped away during the aftermath. But whatever the case, there is no question that their legends lived on.

While Sasuke's playful antics were a big hit among kids, Saizo's brooding demeanor and troubled past made him perfect fodder for a generation of post-war adult novelists and manga artists. Reinvented in dozens upon dozens of books, graphic novels, and films, he is arguably the more popular of the two characters today. ✱

LITERARY LICENSE

The *Journey to the West* connection means that Sarutobi Sasuke is the first Japanized version of Monkey King Sun Wukong, who in turn formed the basis for Goku in Akira Toriyama's "Dragonball" series. What a tangled web we weave.

A 1959 Toei animated film called *Sarutobi Sasuke* was released in English as *Magic Boy*, apparently because the word "ninja" hadn't entered the English language at the time; another, the 1979 series *Manga Sarutobi Sasuke*, came out in the eighties as the rather unimaginatively titled *Ninja the Wonder Boy*.

The protagonists of the 1994 kids' TV show "*Ninja Sentai Kakuranger*," a live-action spectacle of fisticuffs, monsters, spandex, and giant robots, include the descendants of Sarutobi Sasuke, Kirigakure Saizo, and Jiraiya. Action scenes from the show aired abroad as part of the "Mighty Morphin' Power Rangers" series.

✄

Kirigakure Saizo is the antagonist of Kazuaki Kiriya's 2009 film *Goemon*.

BASED ON FACT?

While Kirigakure Saizo is a purely fictional creation, there is a historical record of Sanada Yukimura having employed a ninja by the name of Kirigakure Shikaemon, who is believed to be the inspiration (in name if not actual biography) for the ninja character.

The Illustrated Ninja

The Ninja Home

The old proverb "a man's home is his castle" is known throughout the world, but the expression took on quite the literal meaning in feudal Japan. Perhaps no aspect of the ninja lifestyle has attracted as much attention as the ninja *yashiki*, the uniquely gimmicked redoubts in which the leaders of the shadowy clans sometimes lived. In order to rule their territories and protect themselves from attack during the chaos of the Age of Warring States in the early to mid sixteenth century, local leaders in certain areas redesigned their homesteads into fortified compounds. Early measures took the form of surrounding normal domiciles with simple physical fortifications such as high earthen berms and deep moats. Over the long years of civil unrest gradual modifications such as trapdoors and tunnels accrued,

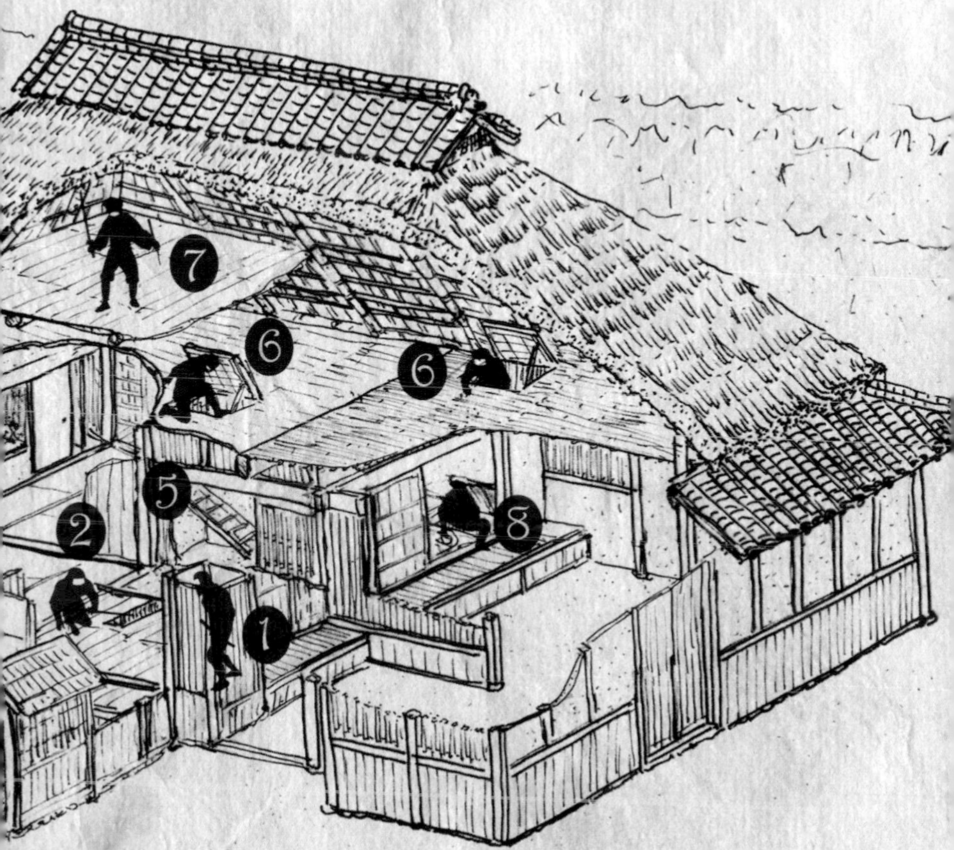
7
6
6
5
2
8
1

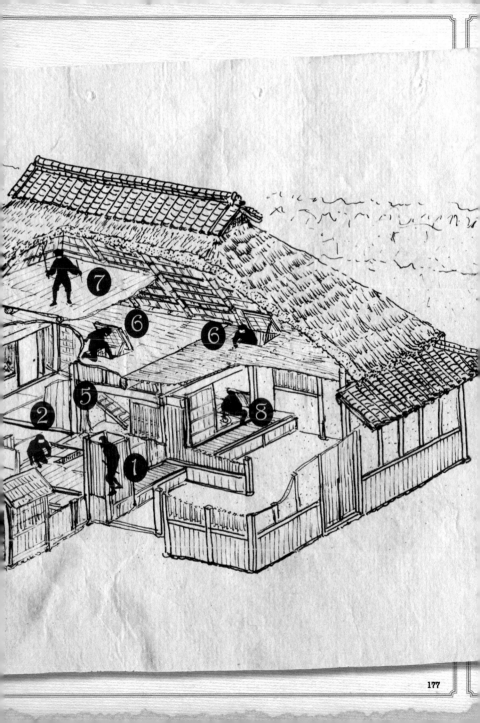

and by the end of the century many of these manors came to incorporate the wide variety of ingenious features that are now associated with ninja dwellings.

Superficially resembling contemporary country manors of the period, these buildings devilishly concealed a wide variety of ingenious features that allowed their inhabitants to quickly escape if needed—and just as quickly turn the tables on the invaders from behind the scenes. Perhaps most common were concealed doors called *donden* (1), which consisted of pivoting sections of wallboard that allowed access to hiding spaces or hidden hallways. Equally useful were *mono-kakushi* (2), spaces beneath false floorboards used to hide swords or other weapons—handy for close encounters. Artfully concealed hidden exits (3) sometimes connected to tunnels that opened in unexpected places, such as a nearby well (4).

Pull-down ladders or staircases (5), common in modern homes but unheard of at the time, offered access to the attic, where gimmicked flooring (6) could be lifted or removed to gain access to various rooms without having to return to the first floor. A hidden room (7) concealed in the space between the usual attic and the rafters was the perfect place for a conference away from prying eyes and ears, or as a safehouse for those who needed to keep their presence a secret for whatever reason. Other occasionally encountered modifications included well-concealed hiding places (8), unexpected grooves or height differences in flooring (not shown) to trip up invaders unfamiliar with the layout of the house, and deep pits concealed by trapdoors (spikes at bottom optional).

The vast majority of these ninja yashiki (also colloquially called *karakuri yashiki*, or "gimmicked mansions") were found in the Iga and Koga regions. The largest included those owned by Momochi Tanba, Fujibayashi Nagato, and the Hattori family, but many more are known to have existed as well. Even today, the remains of earlier fortifications (particularly high earth walls) can be occasionally seen on the property of homes in the countryside of these areas.

> "Ninja yashiki devilishly concealed ingenious features that allowed their inhabitants to quickly escape if needed"

The Illustrated Ninja
Weapons

Shinobi-gatana

Much controversy surrounds the exact form of the *shinobi-gatana*, the distinctive sword said to have been carried by ninja. Given that ninja, like all commoners, were forbidden to own weapons of any kind, it is likely that their swords were forged by countryside blacksmiths to individual specifications, lacking much of the finish and polish of their more well-known counterparts that were carried by samurai. In contrast to the often ornately worked blades carried by the aristocratic samurai, shinobi-gatana are generally known to have been pragmatic, utilitarian affairs. They had straight and fairly short blades, simple square guards, and were housed in a distinctive sheath with a pointed tip and a *sage-himo* cord wrapped around its circumference. The latter in particular allowed the sword to be used as a sort of "person detector" in conditions too dark to see. A ninja would proceed through a darkened hallway or other area with the sheath balanced half or more off the blade and the cord clenched in their teeth; the vibration of the sheath's contacting a soft body transmitted instantly through the tightened line, allowing the ninja to quickly draw back the blade from the sheath and plunge its razor-sharp tip into whatever unfortunate soul happened to be standing ahead.

The scabbard's pointed tip also allowed it to be planted in the ground, with the sword guard then becoming a makeshift footstool for climbing over obstacles. The cord then allowed the sword to be retrieved from the other side.

Shuriken

Is there any more iconic ninja weapon than the *shuriken*? They come in literally dozens of shapes, weights, and sizes, but are intended for a single purpose: impaling an enemy from a safe distance—and in utter silence. It is easy to understand their popularity among a certain rough-and-tumble set in an era before the advent of personal firearms, let alone silenced ones. Written with the characters 手裏剣 (literally, "a blade in the hand"),

senban

some are designed to be flung aerodynamically, while others nestle in a palm for discreet slashing and stabbing. In Japan, the stereotypical ninja slings them from a stack atop an outstretched palm-top, as though dealing cards; on the other hand, foreigners tend to fetishize them as invincible weapons of silent death and destruction.

The truth is that they were thrown in a variety of ways depending on shape, and that they likely served more as fairly close-range nuisance weapons intended to slow or stop an opponent rather than as a means of taking a life. The various schools of *ninjutsu* utilized individual shapes and sizes suited to their particular styles; the Togakure-ryu, one of the first to employ shuriken, derived theirs from a carpenter's nail-pulling tool. Their unique *senban* (as they were called) could be used, à la the Swiss Army knife, as makeshift shovels, rope-cutters, and of course nail-extractors as well as weapons, allowing them to be carried without arousing undue suspicion. A wide variety of designs of shuriken, from simple stars to metal darts, are known to exist.

Makibishi

A fiendishly simple and effective form of antipersonnel weapon: spiked objects of a variety of designs scattered along a pathway to lacerate the soles of unwary pursuers. Known as "caltrops" in the Western world, the first Japanese versions were very likely created by drying out the seed-pods of *Trapa japonica*, a.k.a. the water chestnut plant (which, not coincidentally, also happens to be known abroad as the "water caltrop").

The geometry of the seed pods is such that their naturally sharp points orient upwards even when tossed, making them extremely hazardous to tread upon in soft-soled footwear (such as the straw *zori* sandals favored in medieval Japan). Man-made *makibishi* were forged out of iron with the same principle in mind: four spikes oriented such that no matter how thrown, three form a stable base for the fourth, which points menacingly upward. Ninja enhancements included serrated tips, the better to hook in a wound, and, according to rumor, occasionally they were coated in poison.

Manriki-gusari

A distinctive weapon—perhaps "tool" would be a better term—consisting of a length of chain weighted on both ends. Generally kept coiled in a palm or shirt-sleeve, the weapon's weighted end can be hurled at lightning speed from concealment to startle, or even potentially disable, an opponent—and instantly retracted for another strike if necessary thanks to the chain.

Kusari-gama

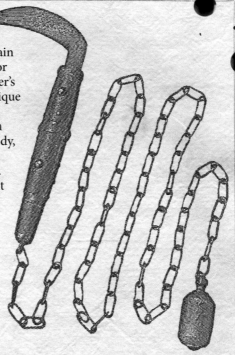

This distinctive weapon consists of a weighted chain attached to the pommel or blade of a modified farmer's sickle. The general technique is to swing the weighted chain so as to entangle an opponent's weapon or body, then finish them off with the wickedly sharp blade. Considered quite difficult to counter, their use was not limited to ninja. In fact, one of swordsman Miyamoto Musashi's most famous duels was against a kusari-gama master, whom he defeated by the expedient of flinging his short sword into the man's chest from a distance.

Kusari-katabira

The medieval equivalent of a modern Kevlar vest. Although in popular culture ninja are often portrayed as wearing chainmail shirts or hoods, the weight and noise made these useless for the average ninja mission, which relied on stealth and avoiding the enemy. Still, this isn't to say that ninja didn't keep chainmail in store for times when direct contact with enemy forces was inevitable.

Teko-kagi

Move over, "Wolverine." Modeled on the claws of bears or tigers, these gauntlets were forged from iron and slipped over the hands, allowing their wearer to both utilize the added weight and sharpened blades to disable (or, more likely, horribly maim) their enemies.

A similar weapon called the *shuko* features shorter claws on the palm instead of the backs of the hands, allowing the weapon to double as a climbing aid.

Neko-te

Literally, "cat's paws." A cute name for a dangerous implement: iron finger-caps terminating in claws, transforming a normal human hand into the equivalent of an animal's talons. The difficulty of keeping the caps on one's fingers means that *neko-te* are undoubtedly utilized mainly as one-off surprise weapons, their blades occasionally coated in poison for good measure, and quickly discarded once used.

Nigiri-teppo

Ninja began using—and improving—firearms almost from the moment they were introduced to the Japanese islands in the 1500s; they undoubtedly began attempts to miniaturize them from the very get-go. These pocket-sized firearms used fulminated mercury instead of a flint to simplify the mechanism. Its limited range and accuracy made it more suitable for shocking enemies (similar to modern-day "flash-bangs") than as an offensive weapon, though when pressed directly against a target it could potentially penetrate even thick samurai armor. (Best of luck getting that close to an armed samurai.)

Tekken

"Iron hands" of the sort used by brawlers since time immemorial, these metal knuckles let an already well-trained ninja pack even more of a punch. Remember: the emphasis isn't on fighting fair. It's on subduing an opponent quickly and hopefully silently, by any means necessary. Spiked and un-spiked versions exist, as do *kakute*, a similar weapon consisting of thick iron rings for individual fingers.

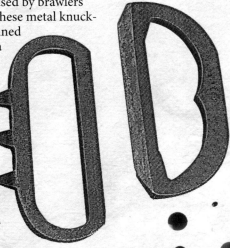

Ku-no-ichi: the femmes fatale

Female ninja—*ku-no-ichi*—have their own unique weapons. Many are modified everyday items, with techniques designed to use as-is: a spiral-patterned paper umbrella can distract opponents when spun, for example, and block their field of view. Or the wooden clogs known as geta can serve as makeshift bludgeons if wielded with a modicum of skill. As with many ninja tactics, these were largely intended to distract and aid escape rather than as offensive techniques. The bottom line: never judge a book by its cover, no matter how pretty.

Kanzashi

At first glance, seemingly normal traditional hair ornaments; upon closer inspection, they are made of metal instead of the usual lacquer, and feature razor-sharp edges and points, making them perfect hidden weapons. It is entirely likely that many a non-ninja female secreted gimmicked *kanzashi* in their coiffures as well, particularly when travelling or otherwise needing to go through questionable areas.

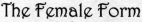

Hibashi

Even the humble chopstick can be deadly in the right hands. Similar to the kanzashi, these iron chopsticks, ostensibly used for turning coals in fires, can make ideal concealed weapons—especially if the ends are sharpened into points. The ultimate innocent-looking tool of death and destruction.

The Female Form

Centuries before Pat Benetar sang "Stop Using Sex as a Weapon," ku-no-ichi had elevated the technique to an art form. What better way to get information from a male target than via pillow talk, disguised as an average courtesan of the pleasure quarters?

The Illustrated Ninja
The Ninja Legacy

Ninja City: Tokyo

Japan is a nation founded upon the efforts of ninja. So it is only fitting that their footprints can still be found in the shadows of its capital city. Don't be mistaken: no fearsomely booby-trapped mansions occupy its back alleys, no subterranean training grounds lurk beneath its skyscrapers, no stray *shuriken* can be found in its streets. The signs are far subtler than that. But they are undeniably there. Though Tokyo is one of the world's largest and most forward-looking metropolises, many of its most basic features were first established by the ninja who once made their homes there, centuries ago.

To get the full story, you need to turn the clock back to 1590, when warlord Tokugawa Ieyasu inherited the Kanto region and began fortifying a fishing village named Edo into his new base of operations. It would be over a decade before it became the nation's de-facto capital, and two-and-a-half centuries before it would be known as Tokyo. But great change was afoot.

Ieyasu had been integrating ninja into his personal army as special forces units for years. When he moved to Edo, the ninja followed. These included fifty survivors from the fall of Negoro-ji Temple in 1585 and a mixed Iga-Koga corps of some two hundred ninja who had faithfully protected Ieyasu during his epic flight through the Iga homeland in 1582.

He garrisoned the majority of the ninja around the Koshu Kaido, a major commercial and strategic road leading west from his castle, and ensconced their commander Hattori Hanzo right outside the castle. (The gate nearest his residence became known as Hanzomon, or Hanzo's Gate [pictured], an appellation that remains as the name of the subway line that runs through the area today.)

Ieyasu then organized the Iga, Koga, and Negoro ninja into three *Hyakunin-gumi* (hundred-man platoons) armed with state-of-the-art flintlock rifles, stationing them in Yotsuya, Akasaka, Aoyama, Harajuku and Shinjuku. Rather than espionage, they were charged with defending the city and protecting the shogun—a sort of Department of Homeland Security and Secret Service rolled into one.

Those familiar with Tokyo may have noticed that the areas the ninja occupied encompass what is now some of the city's most sought-after real estate. Aoyama's swanky atmosphere today is due in no small part to the special status of the ninja who were first given residences there, establishing it as a place for warlords, high-ranking vassals, and other VIPs. The Harajuku district is an intricate maze of streets the ninja laid out there as a defensive measure to confuse potential invaders; centuries later in a time of peace, the deliberately convoluted street plan makes for an incredibly high density of potential storefront retail space. Now the Harajuku back streets teem with the shops of dozens upon dozens of indie fashion makers and retailers.

Meanwhile, over in the Okubo area near Shinjuku, the street blocks retain a distinctive elongated shape from a time when they were used as barracks and shooting ranges by the Negoro-gumi. In fact, the area around Shin-Okubo station is still known as Hyakunin-cho (hundred-man town).

There is a lack of hard information about where certain other ninja-related structures

once stood. Edo is and always has been a well-mapped city, even down to the names of people who lived on its individual plots. Yet no record remains of the exact location of Hattori Hanzo's mansion or the barracks and training grounds of his ninja. It could well be that this strategically sensitive information was deliberately kept off of maps in order to hinder potential invaders, like an Edo-era Area 51.

A NINJA TOUR OF TOKYO

Imperial Palace Grounds

The Hyakunin Bansho Guardhouse is located in the East Gardens of the Imperial Palace grounds, which is situated on the foundation of old Edo castle and is open to visitors. The guardhouse—which is completely original save for a new roof—served as the headquarters for the hyakunin-gumi teams that protected Edo.
Nearest station: Otemachi Station (Mita or Chiyoda subway lines)

Yotsuya

The former home of Hattori Hanzo, this otherwise unassuming section of downtown Tokyo is replete with ninja-related spots. The blocks currently known as Sanei-cho and Wakaba were known until the twentieth century as Kita Iga-cho (North Iga Town) and Mimami Iga-cho (South Iga Town), as this was where the majority of the Iga ninja in Ieyasu's service were garrisoned.

Hanzomon Gate
This was Hattori Hanzo's personal entrance onto castle grounds.
Address: Kojimachi 1, Chiyoda-ku
Nearest station: Hanzomon (Hanzomon subway line)

Sainenji Temple
This location houses both Hattori Hanzo's grave [left]
and spear.
Address: Wakaba 2, Shinjuku-ku
Nearest station: Yotsuya (Marunouchi subway line)

Chozenji (Sasadera) Temple
This temple was the site of the 1605 "ninja strike" (p. 98).
Address: Yotsuya 4, Shinjuku-ku
Nearest station: Yotsuya Sanchome (Marunouchi subway line)

Harajuku

Harajuku is, strictly speaking, only the name for the area north of Omotesando; the south side was called Onden—"hidden field"—its name a holdover from the time ninja lived there. The Onden Jinja shrine was erected to honor the Iga ninja who helped Tokugawa Ieyasu escape to safety in 1582.

Onden Jinja address: 5-26-6 Jingumae, Shibuya-ku Nearest station: Harajuku or Shibuya (JR Yamanote line); Meiji-Jingumae (Chiyoda subway line)

Shinjuku

Today, Hyakunin-cho, home of the Negoro-gumi, is now more famous as Tokyo's "Little Korea" than it is for ninja. But every fall, nearby Kaichu Inari Jinja shrine hosts a hyakunin-gumi festival in which a team of re-enactors dressed in period clothing stage a march and flintlock-firing exhibition in the area. There is also a large mural dedicated to the hyakunin-gumi directly underneath the railway trestle outside of the exit to Okubo Station.

Kaichu Inari Jinja address: 1-11-16 Hyakunin-cho, Shinjuku-ku Nearest station: Okubo (JR Sobu line), west gate or Shin-Okubo (JR Yamanote line)

Sendagaya

This now-quiet neighborhood is believed to be where Koga hyakunin-gumi units were once stationed, and is host to a shrine. The shrine can be found on the grounds of the Hatomori Hachiman Jingu.

Koga Inari Jinja address: 1-1-24 Sendagaya, Shibuya-ku Nearest station: Sendagaya (JR Sobu line)

REAL NINJA, REEL NINJA

How did a motley group of cloak-and-dagger mercenaries from medieval Japan come to symbolize sneaky behavior around the world? The answer lies artfully concealed in a handful of key works of fiction from the last two centuries.

During their heyday in the Sengoku Era (the Warring States period, 1467 - 1573) and for well over a century thereafter, "ninja" was synonymous with "trouble." Their role as the go-to guys for "plausibly deniable" solutions to sticky military and political problems made ninja the sort of thing one didn't discuss in polite company. The shroud of secrecy surrounding ninjutsu tactics and ninja activities fueled a popular image of them as essential villains.

That started to change during the Edo era, the period of stability and prosperity that followed Tokugawa Ieyasu's rise to power in 1603. Precisely as ninja were losing their raison d'etre in this period of relative peace, tales of their exploits inspired new generations of storytellers and consumers who had been raised in an environment blissfully untouched by the horrors of the previous century's civil war. Increasingly hungry for enter-

tainment, the citizens of Japan turned to the tales of a bygone era for excitement and adventure.

The very first ninja star (no pun intended) was Jiraiya, the fictional protagonist of an 1806 book by an author named Kanwatei Onitake. Jiraiya didn't resemble the stereotypical shadow-warrior fans love today. For one thing, the classic all-black outfit and mask hadn't entered the pop cultural vernacular yet. And for another, at this point the little-understood ninja were far more associated with the dark arts than the martial arts, portrayed as masters of hocus-pocus with a dangerous ability to cloud men's minds.

ぼくら科学文庫

秘伝 忍術の本

ぼくら3月号ふろく

He wasn't much for stealth, either. He strolled about in a resplendent kimono, dispatching opponents not with swords or shuriken but flashy magical incantations and giant phantom frogs. The book was popular enough, but when an illustrated version called *Jiraiya Goketsu Monogatari* ("Tales of the Hero Jiraiya") debuted three decades later in 1839, it sparked the world's very first ninja fad. It isn't known how many copies the volumes of this series sold altogether, but it must have been an even bigger hit than the original novel, since the publisher continued pumping out sequels for close to thirty years. Along the way it spawned legions of imitators, a popular 1852 kabuki play adaptation, and a 1921 theatrical version that is considered to be Japan's very first *tokusatsu* film—the forerunner of special-effects fare such as the Godzilla movies.

The concept of the perpetually black-clad ninja seems to have debuted about a decade after Jiraiya did. Some theories credit its creation—or more accurately, its association—to the woodblock print artist Katsushika Hokusai, famed for his sublime *Thirty-six Views of Mount Fuji*. A sketch of what appears to be a stereotypical black-clad ninja shimmying up a rope appears in his book *Hokusai Manga,* published in 1817. Near identically dressed stagehands called *kuroko* were (and remain) a common sight in kabuki, bunraku, and noh productions. In the theater, all-black outfits serve as a visual code to audiences to ignore stagehands as they go about their business of moving props, playing musical instruments, and otherwise supportting the actors onstage during performances. The question of whether Hokusai really was the first one to mash up the idea of the "invisible" *kuroko* and the stealthy ninja is up for debate, but he certainly seems to have been the first to actually put it down on paper. Even still, it would be decades before the the black costumes and the ninja themselves became inseperable in the public's mind.

The next ninja superstar leapt quite literally onto the scene in the pages of a 1914 novel called *Sarutobi Sasuke.* By modern standards, Sasuke leaned more towards the mystical than the mercenary; his powers are more of the superhero rather than martial arts variety, and contemporary imagery often portrays him clutching magical scrolls or casting spells. But the book breathed the first whiff of reality into the world of ninja fiction. It established the now-standard rivalry between the Iga and Koga ninja clans, and set Sasuke at the head of a special forces unit run by a real-life historical figure, the iconoclastic Seventeenth century warlord Sanada Yukimura. (Think of it as being like the "A-Team," Sengoku-style.) A near instant hit, *Sarutobi Sasuke* spawned dozens of sequels and homages, elevating its protagonist into one of the single most influential characters in ninja fiction. Even today, Sasuke remains the stereotypical name for a ninja in Japan.

Sasuke's exploits inspired a new generation of storytellers who came of age after World War II. In the late 1950s and early 1960s, ninja stories fueled a renaissance of Japanese fiction. Writer Yamada Futaro penned a series of bestselling historical fiction novels that introduced ninja as highly trained human beings rather than supermen, tricking opponents with camouflage and subterfuge rather than spells. (Unfortunately, none of these have ever been translated into the English language.) This in turn inspired manga artist Shirato Sanpei, whose beautifully illustrated and painstakingly researched ninja tales such as *Kamui* stoked more interest in the dark heroes.

Yamada and Shirato's works set off a new ninja fad in Japan that just so happened to coincide with a surge of foreign interest in the country. A chance viewing of the 1962 period-action flick *Shinobi no Mono* on a research trip to Japan inspired screenwriter (and *Charlie and the Chocolate Factory* author) Roald Dahl to incorporate ninja into a script he was writing based on Ian Fleming's James Bond novel *You Only Live Twice.* When it debuted in 1967, the film gave the West its first taste of black-clad assassins on the silver screen.

The success of Bruce Lee's *Enter the Dragon* in 1973 fueled interest in martial arts around the globe, and his untimely death created a vacuum that

was quickly filled by other "chop-socky" fare, including more than a few clumsily dubbed ninja action movies from Japan. The appearance of ninja in James Clavell's bestselling novel and 1979 TV miniseries *Shogun*, combined with the 1980s grindhouse hit *Shogun Assassin*, sealed the deal, kicking off the first international ninja fad— this time centered, somewhat incongruously, in the United States. Films such as *Enter the Ninja* (1981) and comic book series like *Teenage Mutant Ninja Turtles* (1984) ensured that ninja established their "beachhead" in the minds of foreign fans once and for all. Even after the boom faded, ninja remained a standard presence in Western action film fare, as seen most recently films like 2009's *G.I. Joe* and *Ninja Assassin*. And Japan has hardly forgotten its status as home of the ninja; the *Naruto* manga and anime series —which borrows heavily from *Jiraiya* and *Sarutobi Sasuke*—continues to enjoy popularity around the globe.

These books, shows, and films may not represent the van-

guard of accuracy when it comes to history, but they most definitely follow in the footsteps of equally fanciful fare from the home country of the ninja themselves. And before you get too worked up about the details, just remember. Fictional ninja have a job to do that's every bit as important as that of their real-life counterparts: entertaining us!

Ninja pop influences

JAPAN

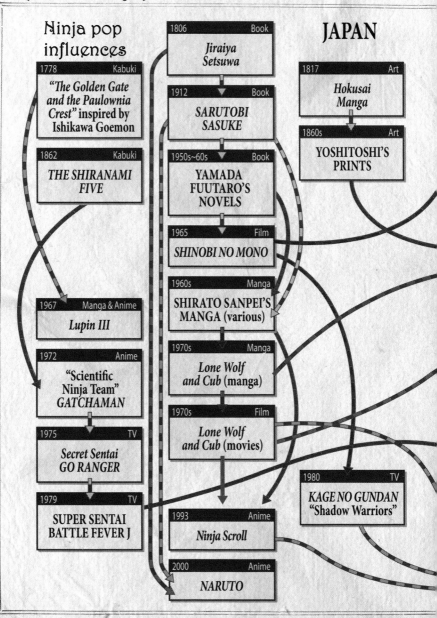

1806	Book
Jiraiya Setsuwa	

1778	Kabuki
"The Golden Gate and the Paulownia Crest" inspired by Ishikawa Goemon	

1817	Art
Hokusai Manga	

1912	Book
SARUTOBI SASUKE	

1862	Kabuki
THE SHIRANAMI FIVE	

1860s	Art
YOSHITOSHI'S PRINTS	

1950s~60s	Book
YAMADA FUUTARO'S NOVELS	

1965	Film
SHINOBI NO MONO	

1960s	Manga
SHIRATO SANPEI'S MANGA (various)	

1967	Manga & Anime
Lupin III	

1970s	Manga
Lone Wolf and Cub (manga)	

1972	Anime
"Scientific Ninja Team" GATCHAMAN	

1970s	Film
Lone Wolf and Cub (movies)	

1975	TV
Secret Sentai GO RANGER	

1980	TV
KAGE NO GUNDAN "Shadow Warriors"	

1979	TV
SUPER SENTAI BATTLE FEVER J	

1993	Anime
Ninja Scroll	

2000	Anime
NARUTO	

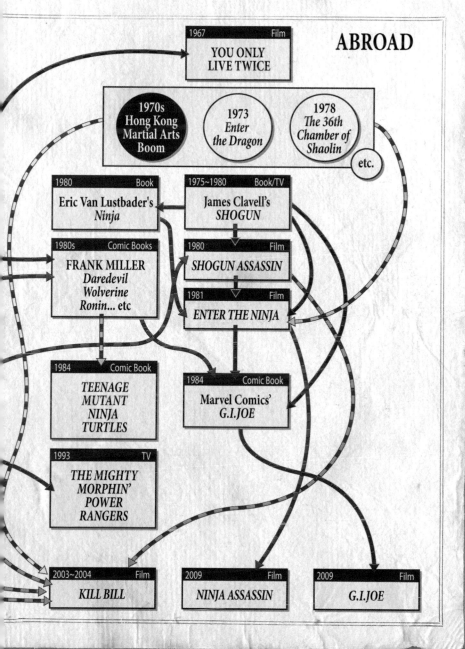

ABROAD

1967 | Film
YOU ONLY LIVE TWICE

1970s Hong Kong Martial Arts Boom

1973 Enter the Dragon

1978 The 36th Chamber of Shaolin

etc.

1980 | Book
Eric Van Lustbader's *Ninja*

1975~1980 | Book/TV
James Clavell's *SHOGUN*

1980s | Comic Books
FRANK MILLER *Daredevil Wolverine Ronin... etc*

1980 | Film
SHOGUN ASSASSIN

1981 | Film
ENTER THE NINJA

1984 | Comic Book
TEENAGE MUTANT NINJA TURTLES

1984 | Comic Book
Marvel Comics' *G.I.JOE*

1993 | TV
THE MIGHTY MORPHIN' POWER RANGERS

2003~2004 | Film
KILL BILL

2009 | Film
NINJA ASSASSIN

2009 | Film
G.I.JOE

REFERENCES

Sengoku Era "The Age of Warring States" (1493–1573)
Think of this as being like America's Civil War, only if every state was ruled by its own warlord intent on domination. A dog-eat-dog era, and the heyday of the ninja.

Azuchi-Momoyama Era (1568–1603)
Overlapping with the end of the previous era, this is the period in which the warlord Oda Nobunaga (p. 90) began to successfully impose order and bring an end to the Age of Warring States. The battle of Sekigahara in 1600 effectively ended this period and allowed Tokugawa Ieyasu (p. 104) to unify Japan once and for all, ushering in the . . .

Edo Era (1603–1868)
Named in honor of the transfer of the capital from Kyoto to Edo (now known as Tokyo). Popular culture flourished in this new era of relative peace and tranquility, but after centuries of civil war, many of the ninja and samurai found themselves adrift without specific roles to play in society. The Tokugawa Shogunate would reign for more than a quarter of a millennium, until the . . .

Meiji Era (1868–1912)
The appearance in Edo Bay of American Commodore Matthew Perry's steam-powered fleet of "black ships" proved enough of a shock to the crumbling Shogunate that the emperor of Japan was able to assert power and take over once again. It was a period of rapid industrialization with Japan playing catch-up with Western powers. The Meiji Era marks the official end of the ninja story; the last government-sanctioned use of ninja involved reconnoitering Perry's ships (see page 148).

GLOSSARY

(minor warlords). Daimyo as a social caste disappeared in the reforms following the Meiji Restoration of 1868.

genin
A ninja rank. A "ninja foot soldier" of the rank and file. The lowest rung of the ninja hierarchy. See also *chunin* and *jonin*.

Iga
Once a region of Japan, now a city located in modern-day Mie prefecture, Iga is one of the birthplaces of *ninjutsu*.

jonin
The highest rank of ninja in the Iga clan. A clan elder.

kakure-zato
"Hidden village." Also called *kakure-no-kuni* (hidden country). The peaks and valleys of the Iga and Koka regions in particular shielded inhabitants from much of the administrative reach of local rulers, giving rise to terms such as these to refer to villages and towns in the hard-to-reach areas. See also Iga and Koga.

katana
The longer of the two swords carried by a samurai. (The shorter was called *wakizashi*.)

Koga
One of the birthplaces of ninjutsu. Although actually pronounced "Koka," the ninja clans in the region referred to themselves as "Koga ninja." The city of Koka is located in modern-day Shiga prefecture.

Bushido
"The Way of the Warrior." A code that informed the lives of samurai, stressing loyalty, frugality, a mastery of the martial arts, and a death-before-dishonor mindset. It could be argued that the willingness of ninja to bend or break certain aspects of this code was part of what made them so effective.

busho
A generic term for a warlord. See also *daimyo*.

chunin
A ninja rank. Sometimes translated as "ninja commander," this represented a higher-ranking, more skilled ninja. In the Koga clan, *chunin* was the highest rank a ninja could attain. See also *genin* and *jonin*.

daimyo
A feudal lord, defined as one who amassed a certain amount of territory and wealth. Often quite influential both politically and militarily. Oda Nobunaga (p. 90) is an example of a powerful *daimyo*. Daimyo with smaller fiefdoms were sometimes called *sho-daimyo*

ku-no-ichi
A female ninja. See p.60.

ninja
See p. 20.

ninjutsu
The martial art of the ninja. By nature esoteric and difficult to define, in colloquial terms it could be expressed as the art of espionage and unconventional warfare.

ronin
A masterless samurai. See also *suronin*.

samurai
Literally "one who serves," this term refers to the aristocratic class of premodern Japan. But in actual practice the term is nearly synonymous with the warrior caste of feudal Japan. See also *Bushido*.

shogun
Literally "general," but more colloquially closer to "generalissimo," this was a formal title bestowed by the emperor upon the top military leader of Japan. The shogun effectively ruled the nation in the emperor's name. The administrative government of the shogun is called the shogunate.

Shugendo
An ascetic religion that is a fusion of native Japanese nature worship and Buddhism, inflected with Taoist and cosmological teachings from China. Practitioners are called *shugenja* or *yamabushi*. In times of old, the yama-

bushi (who were alpine survivalists and students of the martial arts) deeply influenced and in some cases directly mentored the ninja.

shuriken
"A blade concealed in the palm." A throwing weapon closely associated with the ninja. See p. 180.

suronin
Literally "just a ronin," these are the absolute bottom of the barrel of the warrior caste, often homeless wanderers. The lead character in Akira Kurosawa's film *Yojimbo* is a fictional example of a *suronin*.

tachi
A precursor of the katana sword, *tachi* were originally designed to be used on horseback and featured longer, more curved blades. Unlike katana, which were worn with their blades oriented upward, tachi were worn with their blades facing downward.

Tanegashima
The name of a small island off the coast of Kyushu in southern Japan, but colloquially the nickname for flintlock (arquebus) rifles of the sort used in feudal times. The first of these firearms to arrive in Japan came from Portuguese traders who made contact with Japan via Tanegashima.

yamabushi
A practitioner of Shugendo (see above). Often translated as "warrior monk."

BIBLIOGRAPHY

JAPANESE-LANGUAGE

Arai, Kunihiro. *Zusetsu Genpei Gassen Jinbutsuden* [An Illustrated Guide to the Individuals of the Genpei Wars]. Tokyo: Gakken, 2004.

Bungei Shunshu, ed. *Edo Kobore Banashi* [Edo Side Stories]. Tokyo: Bunshu Bunko, 1996.

Fujiwara, Kiyotaka, ed. *Tokugawa Shogunke no Nazo* [Mysteries of the Tokugawa Shogunate]. Tokyo: Takarajimasha, 1994.

Izumi, Hideki. *Tokugawa Yoshimune Otoko no Isshou* [Tokugawa Yoshimune: A Man's Life], Mikasa Shobo, 1984.

Kawaguchi, Sunao. *Suupaa Ninja Retsuden* [Legends of Super Ninja]. Tokyo: PHP Bunko, 2008. Kowada, Tetsuo. "Shin Zusetsu Nobunaga Ki" [A New Illustrated Guide to Nobunaga], *Rekishi Dokuhon: Oda Nobunaga*, April 20, 1978: 53 - 113.

Kuroi, Hiromitsu. *Ninja no Daijoushiki* [Common Sense About Ninja] Tokyo: Poplar, 2006.

Kuroi, Hiromitsu. *Ninja to Ninjutsu: Yami ni Hisonda Inousha no Kyo to Jitsu* [Ninja and Ninjutsu: Truth and

Myth About Talented Shadow Warriors]. Tokyo: Gakken, 2003

Kuroi, Hiromitsu. *Ninja Zukan* [An Illustrated Guide to Ninja]. Tokyo: Bronze Shinsha, 2008.

Miyazaki, Yoshitomo, ed. *Nihon Fushigi Kakuu Denshou Jinbutsu Dokuhon* [A Reader of Strange Fictional Japanese People]. Tokyo: Shinjunbutsu Ouraisha, 1994.

Miyazaki, Yoshitomo, ed. *Nihon Kengou Dokuhon* [A Reader of Japanese Swordsmen]. Tokyo: Shinjinbutsu Ouraisha, 1993.

Miyazaki Yoshitomo, ed. *Shinobi no Mono 132 Nin Datafile* [A Datafile of 132 Shinobi], Tokyo: Shinjinbutsu Ouraisha, 2001.

Okamoto, Yaeko, ed. *Senran no Nihonshi 16: Iga Ninja Kage no Tatakai* [Japanese History in the Chaos of War Vol. 16: Shadow Wars of Iga Ninja]. Shogakukan, 2008.

Shimizu, Torazo. *Togakushi no Ninja* [The Ninja of Togakushi]. Nagano: Ginga Shobo Shinsha, 2006.

Tanno, Akira. *Edo no Touzoku* [The Thieves of Edo]. Tokyo: Seishun Publishing, 2005.

Tsuru, Yoichi. Yoshitsune

Kassen Souran [An Overview of Yoshitsune's Battles]. *Bessatsu Rekishi Dokuhon: Yoshitsune no Subete* September 25, 1986: 75 -99.

Yamaguchi, Masayuki. *Ninja no Seikatsu* [The Lives of Ninja]. Tokyo: Yuzankaku, 1987.

"49 Stories of Iga Ninja." http:// www.pref.mie.jp/gkenmin/hp/ igabito/ninja_map/index.html (Indexed April 15, 2010)

ENGLISH-LANGUAGE

Adams, Andrew. *Ninja: The Invisible Assassins*. Santa Clarita: Ohara Publications, 1970.

Ashkenazi, Michael. *Handbook of Japanese Mythology*. United Kingdom: ABC-CLIO, 2003.

Aston, William George. *Nihongi: Chronicles of Japan from the Earliest Times to A. D. 697*. Vermont: Tuttle, 2005.

Basho, Matsuo. *Narrow Road to a Far Province*. 1702. Trans. Dorothy Britton. Tokyo: Kodansha International, 2002.

Bryant, Anthony J. *Sekigahara 1600: The Final Struggle for Power*. Oxford: Osprey Publishing, 1995.

Griffis, William Elliot. *The

Mikado's Empire. Berkeley: Stone Bridge Press, 2006.

Hatsumi, Massaki. *The Way of the Ninja*. Tokyo: Kodansha International, 2004.

Hayes, Stephen K. *The Mystic Arts of the Ninja*. New York: McGraw Hill, 1985.

Hearn, Lafcadio. *A Japanese Miscellany*. Boston: Little, Brown. 1905.

Mulhern, Chieko Irie. *Heroic With Grace: Legendary Women of Japan*. New York: M.E. Sharpe, 1997.

Musashi, Miyamoto. *The Book of Five Rings*. Trans: William Scott Wilson. Tokyo: Kodansha International, 2002.

Schrieber, Mark. *The Dark Side: Infamous Japanese Crimes and Criminals*. Tokyo: Kodansha International, 2001.

Ron, Roy. "Shoninki." http://www.ninpo.org/ historicalrecords/shnnkmkrk. htm (Indexed April 15, 2010)

Turnbull, Stephen R. *The Book of the Samurai*. London: Arms and Armour Press, 1982.

Turnbull, Stephen R. *Warriors of Medieval Japan*. Oxford: Osprey

Publishing, 2005.

Ueda, Makoto. *Matsuo Basho*. Japan, Tokyo: Kodansha International, 1982.

Wilson, William Scott. *The Lone Samurai*. Tokyo: Kodansha International, 2004.

GENERAL REFERENCE SITES

JAPANESE LANGUAGE

Iga-Ryu Ninja Museum
http://www.iganinja.jp/

Ninja Meister
http://www.2nja.com/

J-Texts
http://www.j-texts.com/

BILINGUAL/ENGLISH LANGUAGE

Iga Ninja 49 true Stories
http://www.pref.mie.jp/ GKENMIN/HP/igabito/ninja_ map/en/index.html

Genbukan's Translated Shoninki
http://www.ninpo.org/ historicalrecords/shnnkmkrk. htm

Genbukan's Translated Bansen Shukai
http://www.ninpo.org/ historicalrecords/bansenshukai. html

INDEX

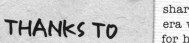

THANKS TO

Editor Greg Starr, for always having our backs. Designer Andrew Lee, for his ninja-like touch with the pages. Yoshiko Karasawa and Naoki Karasawa for sharing their ninja ephemera with us. Kenichi Yamaya for his awesome photo of Jiraiya at the Iwate-Ishidorya Festival. "Uncle" Warren Schwartz for the shot of the frog-ninja toy from his extraordinary collection. Andy "Ninjy" Szymanski for looking over early drafts of the text, not to mention endless beer-fueled ninja discussions. Alen Yen for shuriken-sharp art advice early in the project. Miki Yamaguchi and Chiharu Kouda of the Iga-Ryu Ninja Museum for patiently answering our many questions about ninja of old. Azby Brown, for coming through in a pinch with his great illustrations.

And of course, to all ninja, everywhere—real, fictional, and wannabe.